PENGUIN BOOKS

WHERE'S HANNAH?

Jane Hart, the mother of Hannah, is a native Kentuckian. She was graduated from the University of Miami and has a master's degree in public affairs from Kentucky State University. In her hometown of Lexington she helped organize the first class for the mentally retarded. She also helped establish the first public-school class in the state for the perceptually handicapped. As a volunteer director for a countywide recreational program for handicapped children, Jane Hart directed and moderated a series of weekly television programs. She is also the author of a book for children, *Let's Think about Time*. For the last eleven years she has worked for the Kentucky Department of Mental Health in the development of educational materials.

Beverly Jones received her bachelor's degree from Huron College, South Dakota, and her master's degree in speech pathology from Northwestern University. She also participated in two summer seminars at the University of Wisconsin under the direction of Dr. Ray H. Barsch and studied visual theory and training with Dr. Bruce H. Wolff for two years. After serving as speech pathologist in outpatient clinics and in a nursery for crippled children, Beverly Jones spent six years in Kentucky as speech pathologist and educational director for an affiliate of United Cerebral Palsy. It was here that she met Hannah. She then founded and was co-director of the California Foundation School in Los Altos for children with learning disabilities. Since 1969 she has been co-director of Leaf Center for Learning in Cincinnati, Ohio, a private school for children with learning problems, which she founded with Norma Harris.

Where's Hannah?

An Inspiring Story for Parents and Teachers of Learning-Disabled Children

by Jane Hart and Beverly Jones

PENGUIN BOOKS

Penguin Books, Ltd, Harmondsworth,
Middlesex, England
Penguin Books, 625 Madison Avenue,
New York, New York 10022, U.S.A.
Penguin Books Australia Ltd, Ringwood,
Victoria, Australia
Penguin Books Canada Limited, 2801 John Street,
Markham, Ontario, Canada L3R 1B4
Penguin Books (N.Z.) Ltd, 182–190 Wairau Road,
Auckland 10, New Zealand

First published in the United States of America
with the subtitle *A Handbook for Parents and Teachers
of Children with Learning Disorders* by
Hart Publishing Company, Inc., 1968
Published in Penguin Books 1980

Copyright © Jane Hart, 1968, 1980
All rights reserved

LIBRARY OF CONGRESS CATALOGING IN PUBLICATION DATA
Hart, Jane, 1922–
Where's Hannah?
Reprint of the 1968 ed. published by Hart Pub. Co.,
New York.
Bibliography: p. 243.
Includes index.
1. Brain-damaged children—Education. I. Jones,
Beverly, 1936–   joint author. II. Title.
[LC4580.H37 1980]   371.91'6   79-27936
ISBN 0 14 00.5454 5

Printed in the United States of America by
Offset Paperback Mfrs., Inc., Dallas, Pennsylvania
Set in Caledonia

Except in the United States of America,
this book is sold subject to the condition
that it shall not, by way of trade or otherwise,
be lent, re-sold, hired out, or otherwise circulated
without the publisher's prior consent in any form of
binding or cover other than that in which it is
published and without a similar condition
including this condition being imposed
on the subsequent purchaser

To Hannah

IN GRATITUDE TO:

Norma Harris, M.A. Whose love for Hannah and empathy for all Hannahs and their parents has never obstructed her objective viewpoint, either as a teacher of the deaf, a knowledgeable critic of this book, or as a friend.

Ray H. Barsch, Ph.D. For his theory of Movigenics, at once so profound and so superbly simple that each person who encounters its truth feels that he has always known it; for freely, graciously allowing us to publish his ideas for the first time outside of professional literature; and for his bolstering our faith in Hannah's abilities when we most needed support.

Bruce Wolff, O.D. For developing a viewpoint of visual functioning unique in its theoretical implications and unprecedented in its clinical results, who with his wife, Elaine, has yet to find an adult or child, including Hannah, whose functioning could not be improved.

G. N. Getman, O.D., and *Darrell Boyd Harmon, Ph.D., M.D.* For their contributions in the field of vision, of benefit to all children, including Hannah.

Ken, my husband, and Andy, my son. For their patience and tolerance of my writing efforts and for their forbearance of the time I have taken from them to devote to Hannah; and for the love and help they have given her.

JANE HART

Contents

Foreword by Ray H. Barsch, Ph.D.   1

Preface to the Penguin Edition by Beverly Jones   5

Preface to the Penguin Edition by Jane Hart   9

1. WHAT IS HANNAH?   13
2. WHO IS HANNAH?: The Developmental Process   17
3. WHO IS HANNAH?: What Learning Disorders Are Like   25
4. WHERE IS HANNAH?: Testing and Evaluation   67
5. HOW CAN HANNAH LEARN?: Teaching   91
6. HOW TO LIVE WITH HANNAH: Management   155
7. HOW HANNAH CAN LEARN TO LIVE WITH HERSELF: Building a Self-Concept   197
8. WHERE IS HANNAH GOING?   213
9. HANNAH AT ELEVEN by Beverly Jones   219

APPENDIX
  A. An Early History of Hannah   226
  B. Resources for Parents and Teachers   237
  C. Selected Bibliography   243

INDEX   **245**

Foreword

by RAY H. BARSCH, Ph.D.

The parent of a "special" child often finds himself caught up in a bewildering maze of diverse professional opinions, advice, and predictions. Day-to-day living is a series of trials, marked by progress and regression, hope and despair, and parental bewilderment. There are "moments of cohesion" when the child's behavior gives promise of what could be, but these moments are infrequent. They do give rise, however, to the persistent question, "Why can't something be done to make those moments endure?"

Jane and Ken Hart lived amid such bewilderment and such "moments of cohesion," and asked the same persistent question. Their "special" child is named Hannah. Hannah has probably been designated by every diagnostic label in vogue in this nation at one time or another.

Hannah is not the only one. There are thousands of children who are like her, and there are thousands of parents who have faced the same problems the Harts have faced.

It is important to recognize that the query "Where's Hannah?" is one that holds a dual meaning. It is not only an anxious question asked by parents seeking to locate the immediate whereabouts of their child; the question is of far greater significance because it is also posed to the child struggling for self-identification. "Who is Hannah?" and "Where is Hannah?" are questions of *self* that need to be answered with confidence and security by all children.

The spatially naïve child—who has trouble locating one foot in relation to the other when walking—obviously will have difficulty achieving security. In a very real sense, these children must locate themselves in a multi-stimulus world. They must acquire a position in space. Not only do parents pose the question, but the world of light and sound, heat and texture, force and energy continuously makes such inquiries of the child.

Hannah Hart is only a single representative of a large percentage of the nation's children who are lost in space. Diagnostic precision is unfortunately lacking to identify accurately the specific etiological factor in these cases. A host of labels are applied in general practice; but few, if any, are sufficiently precise to generate a well-defined program of action—to give the lost child an enduring and comfortable position in space. Children wander. Parents wander. Both search.

Where's Hannah is a very special kind of story. It tells how two profoundly concerned parents searched for ways to help their child organize her world. It is an exceptionally faithful report of a particular theory as applied in the setting of a particular family.

Theories are often intellectual exercises conducted as dialogues among scientists. Few theories reach the stage of practical application. Jane and Ken Hart both shared my deep conviction that Movigenic theory offered a social model for guiding parents in a child-rearing curriculum. The Harts willingly agreed to experiment in countless ways in the employment of behavioral techniques which, at times, seemed peculiar. In spite of the novelty of some of the concepts, the Harts faithfully adhered to the basic constructs of the theory, and even added many significant innovations along the way. Jane and Ken Hart took a professionally spun theory and breathed life into it, giving it a dynamic existence from Sunday to Saturday, day and night, all the days of the year.

With the able assistance of Miss Beverly Jones and Miss Norma Harris—two very astute, sensitive, and dedicated interpreters of Movigenic theory—the Hart parents, holding a deep faith in the inner resources of their little girl, set themselves the task of "finding" Hannah, and most important of all, helping Hannah to find herself, in what for her was the bewildering confusion of a multiplex world. "Where's Hannah?" was a question to be voiced with every possible form of emphasis and inflection. The question was laden with overtones of anxiety and, on all too many occasions, with panic and desperation.

Other parents who have been able to implement Movigenic

theory on a day-by-day basis in their own homes, must in a certain sense, be considered silent co-authors of this book. In the pages of this volume, Jane Hart has captured their experiences, as well as her own.

What Jane Hart has done is possible for other parents who find themselves in similar straits. This book, therefore, should be viewed as a model for parents for coping with the behavior of the disoriented child. The contents of these pages are systematically directed toward a single objective: improving the perceptual-motor competency of the child.

One might suspect that most parents would be unable to match the ingenuity of Jane and Ken Hart in devising unusual techniques, within the daily living situation, which would work systematically toward the inner organization of their child. Creative and dedicated parents like the Harts are not in abundant supply; yet there are thousands of parents who can approach the child-rearing task of their own Hannah with considerable innovative thought, provided someone were available who could guide their early efforts. This book will help such parents learn some of the things they can do.

It has long been my contention that the parent of the "special" child is the most neglected therapeutic resource on the rehabilitation scene. Only when the professional world comes to a full appreciation of the teaching potential of parents, and dedicates itself diligently to the task of helping them to fulfill this potential, will the full significance of any therapeutic orientation be achieved.

Jane and Ken Hart recognized their potential and acted upon that recognition. In doing so, they have set a pattern for others to follow. The parent of the "special" child need no longer be relegated to the therapeutic maze. Through their loving and diligent ingenuity, the Harts have found their daughter; and in the quiet of their own thoughts, they have found themselves.

But most exciting of all—Hannah has found Hannah. The question "Where's Hannah?" can now be asked as a simple query in the Hart household.

It has been a gratifying experience to me to have contributed to this discovery.

Preface to the Penguin Edition

by BEVERLY JONES

We've been increasingly able to answer the query "Where's Hannah?" during the twelve years since the first publication of this book in 1968. Since then we've met many parents of other "Hannahs," who have had to search, as did the Harts, for the potential in their disorganized child.

We've had the opportunity to know other "Hannahs," some younger, some older. Many of these children with severe learning problems were more fortunate than our Hannah—they found help at an earlier age. Many were less fortunate because the help that would truly have allowed them to change and learn has never been available. But we have not met many youngsters who were as spatially, visually disorganized as Hannah, or whose development lagged so far behind.

As Ray Barsch stated in his foreword, *Where's Hannah?* is a "report of a particular theory as applied in the setting of a particular family." We must now add: *in a particular time*.

Just as Hannah has not stood still physically, intellectually, or socially, just as her parents and former teachers have learned and grown, the body of knowledge focusing on children with learning problems has expanded considerably in the past twelve years.

Dr. Barsch's Movigenic theory certainly pointed the way for parents and professionals to begin to look at how children move, instead of how poorly they score on a test, as an explanation of why they have trouble learning. Since then we've come to understand that how a child moves determines how and what he will see. What and how he sees, how he attains one visual image from information available to two eyes, influences how he moves. All of this bears directly on what, how, and when he will learn anything . . . and everything.

Applying these principles of developmental vision in an

educational setting became the goal for me and Norma Harris. We started Leaf Center for Learning in Cincinnati, Ohio, eleven years ago. Because we had the benefit of Dr. Bruce Wolff's[1] thinking, and the children had the advantage of wearing lenses to enhance their visual efficiency, we began to see that children can profoundly alter their rate of learning regardless of the diagnostic label, regardless of the severity of the developmental lag, regardless of dire prognoses.

We have come to understand that it is because we *see* that we move *independently*, that because we see we know where we are, where we want to go, and how to get there. How we manage this ability to see determines how we coordinate our moving to where we want to go, whether it is across the room, around an obstacle, or through a math curriculum or a book.

When we are able to help a youngster with learning problems, regardless of their severity, learn to see efficiently and move independently, then he begins to know where he is, where he wants to go, and is able to find his own way of getting there.

Hannah is still finding her own way. She's had twelve years in which to continue the organization of her visual-spatial-movement-language abilities. She's had "up" times and "down" times, spurt times and lag times. Her development has never stalled.

Her parents have had to adjust to a teenaged Hannah, to Hannah as a young adult. Pushed by the developing needs of Hannah, her mother became involved in initiating and helping to maintain a social-educational group.

In twelve years Hannah has changed, her parents and teachers are wiser, and help for children with problems like Hannah's is more available. Yet *Where's Hannah?* fills a need that will always be current: the documentation of one child's and one family's struggle to survive intellectually, emotionally, and socially. Every parent of the "Hannahs" just born, and those yet to be, will face the same initial reactions and

---

[1] Dr. Bruce Wolff, of Cincinnati, Ohio, specializes in the visual problems associated with learning and learning disabilities. He is an authority in the Optometric Extension Program and serves as consultant to Leaf Center.

problems the Harts faced. They will want some kind of map to follow, some assurance that tomorrow does not have to be like today.

What might have been had Hannah had this training during her preschool and early childhood years we can only wistfully imagine. But because of what Hannah and the experience of helping her have taught me, I am hopeful that today's young "Hannahs" need not linger in the "wings" of childhood.

Preface to the Penguin Edition

by JANE HART

Life is movement and movement means change. Hannah is not where she used to be, and (thank heavens) neither are we.

Much of what we know about vision, development, and learning we've found out since *Where's Hannah?* was written . . . but our later knowledge is built upon what is stated here. Many magazines and books on learning problems have been published since our bibliography was printed . . . but the original list still contains a number of classics. There are new tests, of course . . . but those we mention remain in use. Information on what causes "brain damage" and other developmental disabilities is everywhere today—on the air, in newspapers, in pamphlets from the government and volunteer/advocacy agencies . . . but we realize now that such "causes" are irrelevant.

Learning disorder, learning disability, and *learning problem* are used interchangeably in this book, simply because we found these labels more helpful than "mentally retarded," "brain-injured," or "aphasic" (which have been replaced by "developmentally disabled," "hyperactive," and "dyslexic" in most of the recent literature).

Hannah is a beautiful young lady now, and I am older still and a good deal more frayed by the system. Once we paid for the services we got for her; now we struggle for what new laws say she and her friends are entitled to, the "privileges" the public is starting to protest against.

A lot has happened since this book was first published (see Appendix). In 1968 we moved back to Kentucky from Florida and Hannah went to her first public-school class, this one for the "trainable retarded" (the one for the "educable retarded" was teaching things she'd started to learn, but was much too large and demanding). By this time, though the inappropriate labels still rankled, I was willing to ignore words for services. But after the kind of teaching Hannah had already had, I could not ignore the fact that only one thing was being taught in that classroom: "Sit in your seat and be quiet." We withdrew her from school for a few months, until Beverly Jones and Norma Harris came back from California to open a new school in Cincinnati in 1969. This was a day school, so we found her a home to board in (three to be exact) and commuted from Frankfort to Cincinnati twice each weekend—to pick her up after school on Friday and bring her back late Sunday night. For eleven months a year, for four years, every weekend we made two grueling round trips of about two hundred miles each, which Hannah took, as she does many things, much more easily than we.

When she outgrew Leaf Center at seventeen we visited several residential places around the country. But none of us could face separation again so we opted for the new local sheltered workshop. It was a poor program, miserable for Hannah, whose poor motor skills placed her low on the totem pole. I tried to compensate for what she was missing with a good weekly socialization program, which a group of us started on June 1, 1973, and which has flourished and grown ever since—and with nighttime tutoring under an excellent private tutor, Sue Winans.

Where is Hannah in 1980? With her schedule, it's hard to keep up. Since Labor Day 1976 Hannah has worked as a teacher's aide in Sue's nursery school/kindergarten/day-care center, and taken exciting trips with her family to California, New York, and Florida. She goes to the women's fitness class at the "Y" three nights a week and to Wildcats (the recreational/socialization program) one night a week, bowls every other Saturday morning, swims almost daily in the summer. There are occasional movies with friends, three or four dances a year, a week of camp each spring. She celebrated her twenty-first birthday with a pajama party, and voted in the last four elections (on *issues,* not TV images). A friend has her own supervised apartment, and Han wants one too. She may get a chance in a year or so. As a result of all these experiences and opportunities, Han has made rather large developmental strides this year in vision, posture, vocabulary, and social behavior—the whole bag.

Hannah has strong ideas about what she wants to buy and to wear. Though she may bake a cake without following directions or use a cupful rather than a capful of shampoo now and then, she generally does her part around the house. She helps with cooking and serving food, washing and folding clothes, vacuuming and dusting, dishwashing and plant watering, and has taken care of her own room and clothes for years. After a long dry spell, when what she could read became too kiddish, she's become interested in books again, especially reference books and catalogues, which tell her things she wants to know.

But not everything has changed since *Where's Hannah?* was first printed. The idea that the most developmentally disabled child—that *all* people—can grow and change and learn and improve remains "revolutionary." Categorizing is a "bad word" today; yet people still use "moderately" or "severely retarded," "dyslexic" and "hyperactive" so "professionals can communicate" or so "we can get money from the feds." That "IQs are not important anymore" is proclaimed all over, yet programs and placements continued to be based entirely on the numbers game, the IQ scores that define levels of "functioning" (only retarded kids and wind-up toys, autistic people and racing cars "function").

Public Law 94-142 notwithstanding, some parents of young children still beg to get proper help for their kids in school. Until more people understand what Beverly Jones, Norma Harris, and Bruce Wolff know about learning, living, and developing, little problem kids will continue to have big, big problems.

Meanwhile, Hannah is here, living a full life, growing, changing, experiencing—and, more and more, taking her place in the world.

1

What Is Hannah?

Our eleven-year-old daughter is a slim, silky-haired charmer who looks like everyone else's little girl, except that she is prettier. Her name is Hannah Jill.

She is also called brain-injured, neurologically impaired, pseudo-retarded, brain-damaged, cerebral palsied, perceptually handicapped, interjacent, exogenous, an exceptional child, and a special child. She is said to suffer from neurophrenia, cerebral dysfunction, psychoneurological learning disorder, central nervous system impairment, developmental aphasia, learning and behavior problems. Children say she's naughty; strangers see a brat; friends have insisted she's "perfectly fine if you leave her alone."

It all started when Hannah was eleven months old. She was taken very ill with tracheal bronchitis. After she had been a week in an efficient hospital that rejected mother-love in favor of medication, inoculation, isolation, and sterilization, the doctors felt we would both be better off with her at home. Hannah would retain, for months, her fear of anyone in white clothing, but she was on the road to physical recovery. Before we left, we were told how to syringe her nose and swab her ears, and when to return for further treatment. We were also told that Hannah had cerebral palsy. I didn't——I couldn't——believe it!

"But she is so weak! She has had such a terrible time. She has been so sick...." I ventured. I didn't convince the doctor, but I half-convinced myself that her illness and her miserable hospital stay had colored his diagnosis.

Throughout the difficult months that followed, and despite the formidable evidence to the contrary, I refused to accept the idea that there was anything very terribly wrong with Hannah.

I refused to accept the idea that she was not normal, even though she was so placid an infant that I had to remind myself to attend to her needs. I wouldn't face the facts, even when she didn't coo or when she didn't learn how to play with her ball; and even when she didn't start to sit up, or creep, or crawl months later than children usually do these things; or even when her only entertainment was watching her fingers wiggle for hours at a stretch.

Nine months later, when Hannah got her first pair of eyeglasses and stood alone for the first time, I was convinced that her whole trouble was her visual problem. At least, I was finally admitting that there *was* a problem.

From this time, when I stopped lying to Hannah's baby book, until we found what her problem actually was, five years elapsed. Five priceless years when we could have been helping her—if we had known what to do, where to go, or whom to ask. And yet how foolish to regret. How much wiser to be grateful as my husband was, that Hannah wasn't born ten years earlier, for her condition was hardly defined until shortly before the Second World War, was recognized by only a handful of imaginative researchers for another decade, and even now is accepted as a treatable, distinctive phenomenon by a minority of pediatricians, neurologists, psychologists, and special educators.

Hannah, we learned, is not nearly so unique as our early failure to classify her had led us to believe. In 1954, Passamanick claimed neurological impairment in 10% of full-term births (not mentioning the predictably higher rate in premature births). In 1961, Beck thought that 60% of the educable mentally retarded children in a school population were probably neurologically impaired.[1]

Many families know that they have a child who has a learning disorder. Even more families merely suspect that a child of theirs has a learning disability, or they simply do not know what on earth is wrong with their child. Most parents are so hurried and harried, it might take a long time before they hit

[1] Estimated percentages from Charles R. Strother: *Discovering, Evaluating, Programming for the Neurologically Handicapped Child* (Chicago: National Society for Crippled Children and Adults, 1963). The late Arnold Gesell, pioneer and leader in the study of child development considered that from the developmental standpoint, all children suffer some degree of birth injury.

on the right people and the right books to find out exactly what *is* wrong.

Hannah's condition has been variously described and labeled by experts working with children with special, and theretofore unknown, problems.

A pioneer in the field was the German refugee Dr. Alfred A. Strauss,[2] who used the term BRAIN-INJURED to describe *a child from a normal family who has suffered an injury to the brain before, during, or after birth, who shows characteristic psychological deviations, and who can achieve educational improvement by methods and procedures based on these deviations, whether he tests normal or below normal in intelligence.*

Edgar A. Doll[3] considers the designations BRAIN INJURY or BRAIN DAMAGE too frightening and too inclusive, since these terms cover three separate classifications:

(1) Cerebral Palsy, in which the major symptom is severe neuromuscular impairment, with *motor handicap.*

(2) Mental Deficiency, of which the major aspect is incurable social inadequacy, with *intellectual impairment* primary, and social and other problems secondary.

(3) Neurophrenia (the term Doll prefers for Hannah's condition), in which there are over-all retardation and behavioral disturbances that can be improved, with over-all involvements primary, and specific disorders secondary.

Godfrey Stevens and Jack Birch[4] say the term BRAIN INJURY describes a cause, not a symptom. This term gives no clues for treatment. They prefer the term STRAUSS SYNDROME, in tribute to the man who devoted his life to the diagnosis and treatment of this condition.

---

[2] See Strauss's article, "Education of the Brain Injured," in James F. Magary and John R. Eichorn, *The Exceptional Child: A Book of Readings* (New York, Rinehart and Winston, 1960).

[3] See Doll's article, "Behavioral Syndromes of Central Nervous System Impairment." *Ibid.*

[4] In their article, "A Proposal for Classification of the Terminology Used to Describe Brain Injured Children." *Ibid.*

2

Who Is Hannah?

THE DEVELOPMENTAL PROCESS[1]

The Hannahs of the world are not quite like "normal" children, but they are not quite like each other either. They are the original funny, mixed-up kids—out of touch, gloomy, sensitive, babyish, wild or dull one week (or day or hour); interested, gay, imperturbable, curious, affectionate and relatively mature the next.

A child with learning disorders does not limp or drag a leg, but may look clumsy running. He is probably a dud at hopping, skipping, dancing, playing games, pushing, and pulling. Doors and chairs may attack him from all sides, keeping him constantly tattooed with bruises and scratches. He may be four feet tall and duck through a standard doorway, but stand up straight when entering a car that is three inches lower than his head. He may underreach, overreach, step too high or not high enough, move his hands in the wrong direction or not move them at all to catch a ball.

If sent to Daddy's room to get a red sweater out of the bottom drawer, he might: (a) go to the dining room; (b) go to the bedroom but open the closet instead of the chest; (c) find the chest, but open the wrong drawer or all of them; (d) open the right drawer but bring back a handkerchief instead of the sweater; (e) get the sweater, but take it to the kitchen instead of back to Daddy; (f) put it on himself or decide to wash it in the bathroom; or (g) manage the whole deal but trip over a stool on the way back.

He may be way behind other children his age in what he knows, how much he can do, and how he handles himself with

[1] This entire perspective for viewing the developmental process, and the formulation of the ideas of stress factors and degrees of freedom, are based on the theories and clinical work of Ray H. Barsch, Ph.D.

other people. Actually, he is retarded, but only in his rate of development. He is not mentally deficient, in the usual sense of that phrase.

He may not know a rectangle from a circle. Or, like Hannah, he may recognize forms at an early age, but have a terrible time reproducing them.

He may talk too much or too little, too loudly or too softly, without expression, or not at all. He may be hard to understand, or he may speak clearly, but he may have trouble finding the right words.

He is famous for his hyperactivity, which Barsch calls "purposeless action, inability to sustain a performance." Less generous people call it maddening; no one calls it endearing. A hyperactive child simply keeps moving, constantly touching and getting into things, unable to behave or sit still. He does little a normal child might not do—for instance, leaving his blocks to run to the window when he hears a car—but he does such things more often and when such actions are more out of place, and he continues to do these things after he is much older. Getting an impulse, off he goes, headed for another place or no place, headed for something interesting or headed for near disaster.

He is almost equally notorious for his perseveration. This is the habit of repeating words or actions over and over again, long after the original reason for them has passed. For example, he will take every object out of a cabinet after he originally took out one bottle that interested him.

A child with learning disorders is generally distractible; he is unable to sustain attention. Such a child is also notably lacking in rhythm.

Everyone who has had anything to do with such a child—whether he is called brain-injured, neurologically-impaired, or perceptually-handicapped—is familiar with one or more of these characteristics. Such behavior is a trial to the child's family and a shock to the public—a public who see only the outward behavior.

But a child is more than a sum total of his faults. Hannah, for instance, is, or was, hyperactive, perseverative, retarded in her intellectual and social development, moody, excitable, distractible, distracting, and destructive to an unusual degree. Yet, when her brother came back from the hospital with both ankles taped up after a trampoline accident, Hannah's reactions were more than adequately mature for any eight-year-old. They were typical of the humor, sympathy, and empathy which she often revealed beyond her chronological age. She first relieved the strain by making us all laugh at her imitation of his limping walk. Then, realizing his discomfort, she put her arm around him for support and told him to "Lean on me." She helped settle him on the couch, adjusted his covers, then hurried off for pills, water, and a thermometer. With her usual good grace, she accepted the fact that her remedies were not used, then sat down by her brother to feel his forehead, pat his arm, and tell him a story.

If Hannah was capable of such high-level understanding, why then did Hannah behave so erratically?

NORMAL DEVELOPMENT

Regardless of race, creed, or color, every child faces the same task in life: to become acquainted with the world; to orient himself against gravity; to gradually gain more and more control over himself so that as an independent adult he will be able to gain some mastery over his world.

These familiar milestones in a baby's life are points on the continuum of development: a simple skill provides the base for the learning of a more complex skill, which in turn becomes the base for an act of even greater complexity. Thus any given accomplishment, whether it be sitting without support or solving a problem in calculus, is merely the result of previous learning; it does not come like a flash out of the blue. Through development, a child is ever adapting to more and more complex tasks, ever expanding his world.

His development occurs in the constant presence of *gravity*, which he learns to overcome; his development occurs within *space*, in which he learns to orient himself so that he will have a place to begin from and a place to return to; his development occurs sequentially in *time*, which, always progressing, requires another orientation so that he can distinguish between *now* and *before,* and *yet to be.* Continuous development of his basic equipment is the vital business of childhood.

A child's earliest development revolves around his mouth; this is the *gustatory* stage. He starts with the simplest skills —sucking, teething, blowing bubbles—which prepare him for finer skills, such as chewing and precise articulation in speech.

All aspects of *olfaction,* sensations in the nose, are closely tied up with gustation, and are present early in a child's life.

In his *tactual* stage, the child organizes the use of his hands and also learns to use his entire skin surface to recognize differences in temperature, texture, shape, and the pressure of objects.

When he enters the *kinesthetic* stage, the child begins to develop the automatic muscular activity involved in normal coordination. For example, he comes to walk down the street without thinking about what his legs are doing.

While a child is learning to get around on his own and develop some idea of how to cope with space and gravity, he also begins to organize his world through *sound.* He identifies sounds, localizes them, and soon begins to imitate the noises that come from the giants who serve him. As this concentration on hearing continues, he finds that sounds can be used to refer to the gustatory, olfactory, tactual, and motor experiences he has had. With this great discovery, he becomes a human being who can exchange ideas with other human beings by using LANGUAGE.

Of course, *vision* is associated with all these learning experiences and has been developed in conjunction with all the other ways of functioning. But vision—*to know through seeing* —is the highest and most complex ability of all. Since it is a way of knowing something without having to touch, taste, smell, hear, or move it, a child must have tasted, smelled, heard, and moved many things and must have organized his previous experiences before he can understand the world by merely seeing it. If he has already found out that balls are round and bouncy and rolly, and that they can be hard or soft, big or small, red or white or blue, etc., then a ball on a shelf can be all these things to him. If he has not had experiences with a ball and has not organized his experiences, the ball on the shelf is only a blob.

If development occurs in the proper sequence, if a child has an organized foundation, he will learn to read meaningfully and to survive in school. He will use his visual system to receive ideas from people removed from him in time and space. He will expand his world by adding to it the past and the future and cultures other than his own. Thus, a child's development should proceed GOTKAV (gustation - olfaction - tactuality - kinesthesia - audition - vision). That is, a simpler means of comprehending the outside world is followed by a more complex one, which, in turn, is followed by one still higher and more complex, and so forth in the order nature has prepared for the human organism. If all goes as it should, the child's major method for future learning will be VAKT (that is, vision will be his principal method, followed by audition, then kinesthesia, and finally tactuality), with the other abilities lending support and flexibility.[2]

But life being imperfect, it would be a rare phenomenon indeed if adults could structure childhood experiences to match a child's developmental stages to perfection. As a result, most of the time an ability will develop that is out of phase or disorganized.

OUT-OF-PHASE DEVELOPMENT

A child's development from one stage to the next may be interfered with because of inadequacies in his environmental experiences, or because of inadequacies in his own physiological make-up.

A child might grow up in a musical, or in a quarreling, or in a talkative family and be dominated by sound. He might be forced or encouraged to stand or walk before he has mastered

[2]Note that the ideal learning organization for human beings (VAKT) utilizes the highest developmental ability, *vision*, most; the second-highest, *audition*, next in frequency, etc. The higher the ability, the more developmental foundation it needs and the later it properly dominates a growing organism. Also, the higher the ability, the more valuable it is for successful, independent survival in contemporary society.

crawling. He might be taught to read and write before he has been fully prepared for the visual stage.

A child might receive inadequate gustatory training because the nipple on his bottle is too hard or too easy to suck, or because he is deprived of his bottle too early, or because his thumb is always pulled out of his mouth. Or because whenever he starts to examine something with his mouth, someone always squeals, "Ooooh, spit it out! It's dirty!"

He might get inadequate tactual practice because his hand is slapped every time he reaches for something, or because he has little opportunity to squish and squeeze, cuddle and wallow, and stroke and touch all sorts of wonderful everyday objects.

He might spend most of his time confined to a carriage, crib, playpen, or high chair, with no chance to experiment by moving his body around when ready for kinesthetic practice. He may have a very loving, efficient mother who is not very talkative and who doesn't provide him with enough words and sounds to hear. He may not be given an opportunity to see all sorts of colors and shapes on a shopping trip or in books.

Some individuals learn by ATKV (audition-tactuality-kinesthesia-vision): they learn best through listening, next best through touching, less well by moving, and rather poorly through vision. Such individuals will have reading problems.

Other individuals, who are organized KVAT, are "movers," individuals who prefer to do things themselves and must *move in order to know*. They tend to underline the text when they are studying, and they move some part of their bodies when they are required to listen or to look.

When a child's (or an adult's) learning organization matches the requirements of the task he must perform, he will be successful with little effort. Otherwise he can succeed only by exerting more energy than the task should require.

A little task like putting pegs in a pegboard was a monumental challenge for Hannah at six or seven. Her poor tactuality made it hard to find the small peg with her fingers, which was not helped by her poor vision. Her poor kinesthesia made it difficult to pick up a small peg. In fact, one peg was too fine a task; she made the more gross movement of picking up a number of pegs and trying to drop all but one. Then she had the VK job of getting the peg in a particular hole. Copying a pattern without a chalk or cardboard guideline on the pegboard was impossible for her visually. No task is simple when one does not have the learning organization to match it.

SPATIAL ORGANIZATION

A child's development takes place in space as well as in time. How is he organized in space?

His first developmental experiences—gustatory, olfactory, tactual—take place within the radius of his arms, in *near space*. Almost everything that happens to him occurs within his home.

As he develops, his spatial world expands. He begins to move about, and gains direct experience beyond the length of his arms by orienting himself visually as he moves toward his target. Now he is experiencing *mid space*. He moves on all spatial planes—forward and backward, up and down, in order to perform tasks that occur on different planes.

He is always the center of *his* spatial organization. Up, down, in, out, over, under—these only have meaning as he relates them to himself. *Up* is toward *my* head; *down* is toward *my* feet; *in* is toward *my* midline; *out* is away from *my* midline, etc.

Once such a child has oriented *himself* in space, he can use this same scheme to orient other objects in the world. The cup is behind the book because in relation to him, the cup is farther away than the book.

After he has organized himself in relation to the experiences closest to him, the child is ready for the world beyond his reach, and eventually, the world out of sight. Each step contributes to and is dependent upon the other. His world expands from *near* to *mid* to *far*, and then to *remote* space. As each area becomes organized, the child improves in handling a growing number of tasks in all areas.

Each individual should be effective in all spatial areas, but most people are much more comfortable and effective in one spatial area than in another. Some prefer the reading, sewing, and desk work of *near* space; others, the games, sports, and social contacts of *mid* space; still others, the daring schemes and romantic trips of *far* space.

THE DEVELOPMENTAL GOAL

A child is a dynamic being, preparing for independent survival by interacting with his environment in such a way that all his learning abilities (GOTKAV) will progressively help him gain more information about the world. He is always living and dealing with the world in a given spatial area. With the help of parents and teachers, his goal is to learn to function efficiently in all spatial areas, combining all ways of learning—*to survive*, in other words, as an independent, organized, thinking being.

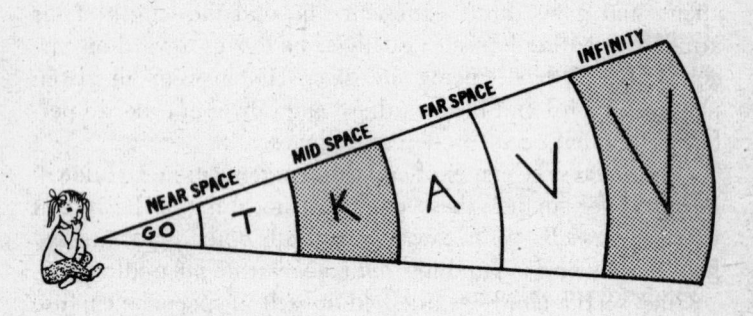

IDEAL DEVELOPMENT   In the normal sequence of development, a child starts by exploring the world closest to his own body (near space) through his gustatory, olfactory and tactual senses. He then reaches out a little further, exploring midspace through kinesthesia. Finally, he is ready to organize far space through audition and vision. Ultimately, his world expands to include past and future and infinite space. A sound foundation at one stage is necessary for success at the next stage.

3

Who Is Hannah?

WHAT LEARNING DISORDERS ARE LIKE

INEFFICIENT DEVELOPMENTAL PROCESSES

For orderly, expanding development toward the goal of independent survival, a child must have appropriate stimulating experiences which he can organize by himself in all spatial areas. If his experiences are not appropriate or his systems of learning (GOTKAV) are impaired, he will not develop proper functioning.

If a child is deaf, blind, missing a leg, or otherwise deformed, he begins his development with a minus factor. If he starts with all systems in good working order but is brought up in an environment that does not give him a chance to move, or to touch, or to learn language, he is being deprived in another way. Born with sensory organs intact but with a lesion in the brain, he may suffer from faulty feedback.

Feedback means responding to both present stimuli and past experience. If the developmental lags of a brain-injured child are severe enough to be detected by his parents at an early age, that child is considered "handicapped." If these lags are present but are not severe enough to be apparent at an early age, his later learning and social problems will tend to be less well understood.

Whether he has a label or not, his learning tasks are the same as every other child's: to orient and perform in space, gravity, and time. He will be successful at any task—learning to walk or passing solid geometry—if he has the capabilities to meet it. If he does not, he will fail—or he will succeed by using inefficient methods which expend needless energy.

An axiom in physiology is: Stress alters function; function alters structure. Any kind of stress placed upon a growing child will change the way in which he does what is required, and eventually, such stress will change *him*.

All of us bear the marks of this principle, some more than others. Few of us have had optimum learning conditions. Chairs were too short or too tall; work tables too high or too low; lighting that made it difficult to use both eyes at once was the rule rather than the exception. Over a lifetime, thousands of conditions have combined to force us into imperfect postures.

We have come to accept as a way of life asymmetrical appearances, back and shoulder pains, headaches—conditions that arose from our efforts to meet the abnormal demands of our environment. Now that our children are growing, adaptable organisms as *we* once were, they are showing the same warps in their postural alignment, in their visual skills,[1] and in their general behavior.

Children with learning disorders whose development is inadequate, out of phase, and—as a result—uneven (a six-year-old may have movement skills appropriate to a five-year-old, may function visually like a three-year-old, and may have the auditory proficiency of a two-year-old)—such children are constantly faced with tasks they are not prepared to handle. They try to meet these tasks the best way they can, constantly suffering the stress and exerting the surplus energy this takes (stress alters function), constantly magnifying and multiplying the warps (function alters structure) that inevitably follow.

INEFFICIENT ORGANIZATION

The key to understanding children with learning disabilities is not only to remember that these youngsters differ from children whose development is adequate for the tasks demanded at a given age level. It is of utmost importance to bear in mind that each child with learning disabilities differs from all other children with learning disorders in the *uniqueness of his organization*. Let us look at examples of inefficient organization for each system, for each perceptual mode.

[1] Darrell Boyd Harmon, *Notes on a Dynamic Theory of Vision* (Austin, Texas, published by the author, 1958).

GUSTATION. Children with poorly organized gustatory systems will probably be poor eaters, disliking solid foods or foods with texture changes. Inefficient at chewing, they will not care much for meat. They may suck and swallow poorly. Although voluntary tongue movements may be poor, their speech can range from unintelligible to quite adequate. If such a child is asked to move the tip of his tongue from side to side in rhythm, he may move it in jerks, have poorer movement on one side, jerk it in the middle, revert to an in-and-out movement. If asked to lift the tip of his tongue or place it at a certain spot inside or outside his mouth, or to imitate lip movements, he may find it impossible. He may have little awareness of sensation in or around his mouth.

The most surprising thing is that a child may chew adequately, talk well, and appear to have no problem, yet perform these tasks badly when *asked* to do them. When he *tries,* he can't get started on the right pattern, often looks as if he were "shifting gears" until, by trial and error, he finds the right movement.

If his gustatory stage is not well organized, he is not ready to leave it for another. He may continue putting things into his mouth well past the acceptable age for such behavior. At nine, Hannah was still sucking her thumb when tired, relaxed, or bewildered. The lady who drove her home from school at noon teased and scolded Hannah for thumb-sucking because she was concerned about what she considered undesirable behavior. When I found out, I begged her not to. A child sucks his thumb —or twirls his hair, or chews his pencil, or bites his lips or the inside of his mouth, or grows up to more expensive habits, such as chain-smoking, because he needs to—because he is not yet ready to give up his oral needs and must regress, under stress, to less mature behavior. As Hannah's speech, chewing, tongue control, and oral sensation improved, her sucking decreased; at ten, it vanished altogether.

OLFACTION. A child with learning disorders often seems to have no "sense of smell." He may not respond appropriately to the smell of smoke, sweets, pleasant or unpleasant odors, and may show little reaction or be unable to localize them. If TKV (tactuality-kinesthesia-vision) is very poorly developed, he may pay too much attention to smell, since it is his more efficient way of knowing about something. He will examine everything with his nose, being easily distracted by odors.

Although small children are humored when they do not want the smell washed away from a favorite toy, actually, this mode is not encouraged in our culture. It is suppressed. Even our language uses *taste* words, such as *sweet* or *sour*, to describe odors.

TACTUALITY Young children touch and poke at everything—ash trays, water, walls, knicknacks, people, tables—just about anything they can manipulate. Young children like to squish things through their toes as well as their fingers, to roll on a hard floor as well as on the soft grass. If tactuality has developed in phase, they show good reactions to skin stimulation and can localize pressures anywhere on their skins, with equal ability on both sides of their bodies. Older children can identify forms, letters, or numbers they know when they are "drawn" on their skin.

If tactuality is inadequately developed, a child may appear quite insensitive to stimulation, react in varying degrees to stimulation on different body parts, be unable to recognize objects and marked textural differences through touch alone. If his VAK (vision-audition-kinesthesia) development is not adequate for the task, he may be unable to stop touching.

Poorly organized tactuality would seem to be the basis of the typical hyperactivity often found in children with learning disorders. A child with an inadequate system for know-by-touch is further impaired because he is probably poorly organized in his visual and auditory systems as well. If he cannot "know" about something by looking at it as most children his age are able to, he must touch the object. In order to touch it, he must go to it. If his VAK development is even less well organized than his tactuality, he is likely to be unaware that many of his specific actions are socially unacceptable. He will not realize that his hyperactivity is both appalling to others and exhausting to his mother and father.

Like most very small children, Hannah was first an "opener." She opened doors, drawers, boxes, letters; took out clothes, cards, toys, books, cans, puzzle pieces, medicines; threw away money, eyeglasses, groceries, anything loose in a car (from trash to her good pair of shoes).

At five or six, she became a "closer." She closed doors and drawers, turned out lights, locked the car, put away her clean clothes and her dirty clothes in their proper places. Unfortunately, she also felt compelled to fill other containers—the sink drain, the garbage can, a storage chest, drawers, or any handy hole indoors or out—with chalk, crayons, jewelry, credit cards, her eyeglasses or any of the wonderful creams, oils, lotions, or pastes she could find in the bathroom or kitchen.

A hyperactive child finds it impossible to stay in any one place for longer than a moment, because he must examine everything that moves or is movable. He also collects more dirt than other children. Hannah, for instance, used to walk on city streets dragging her hand and brushing her body against any wall, storefront, or car she passed, arriving at her destination in an unbelievably filthy coat or dress. It was hard to accept this situation graciously even when I came to realize that touching was her only means of orienting herself in strange surroundings.

KINESTHESIA. Human mobility, like all development, proceeds from the head to the feet, from the middle out, from gross to specific. Like all development, each advance is based on the one before and forms the basis for the next. Obviously, then, a child should crawl before he walks, organize his big, full movements before he tries to write.

A child cannot sit or stand until he has developed enough *muscular strength*. Some children move inefficiently or very little because they are not strong enough. If body strength is uneven—one side stronger, top or bottom weaker—they must learn to compensate in order to move, for muscular strength provides *support*. This, too, is on a continuum, a graduated scale: *no* one has *no* muscular strength, although a child with muscular dystrophy may have very little; *no* one has the *ultimate* muscular strength, although a weight lifter has much more strength than most people.

If a child can stand up, he has attained some relationship between the two sides of his body, some *dynamic balance*. His posture gives clues as to how good a balance he can maintain between the two sides. His head may tilt to one side; one shoulder or one hip may be higher or more forward than the other; his feet may not be parallel—one foot may be turned in or out, one may be behind the other or in front. Since none of us has had an ideal developmental organization, you may recognize these characteristics in yourself or someone you know.

Perhaps the child cannot maintain his balance. He may have to spread his feet wide apart or may have to constantly shuffle them, so that he is actually moving when he should be standing still. Often he has to lean against a wall, a table, a person, or whatever support is handy. Such leaning for support is another common trait of children with learning disorders.

Awareness of the body parts is essential for efficient movement. It is hard to keep legs and arms moving in rhythm if a child does not know "where my legs are." He can only find out by internally *feeling* them; so body awareness is a development of tactuality, as well as a basis for good movement. With good body awareness, Hannah's best school friend, Ralph, would not have tried to lift a table by keeping his arms rigid and leaning backward when he could have managed so much more efficiently by simply bending his arms. Good body awareness means that a child (or an adult) can automatically line himself up properly for a task. He knows his body is there, so he can use it, without having to stop and think, "What am I doing? What must I do next? What did I do wrong before?"

At nine, Hannah was no more aware of someone's stepping on her toe than of her stepping on theirs. She did not know which arm or leg to move when it was pointed to. We did not know whether to be glad or worried because she still seemed to feel no pain and could rarely account for her bruises and scratches. We suspected that her reactions to extreme heat or cold were a pretense.

When we complained to Dr. Barsch that all our efforts to teach Hannah not to manhandle her small dog had come to nothing, he said: "How can she understand how *his* legs and ears and tail are attached and which way *they* are supposed to move, when she doesn't even know where her own body is or how it is put together and how it works?"

Operating from the neck up, with very poor tactuality and kinesthesia, especially in her legs and feet, she would start from her seat at *A* to get to her goal *C*. Her feet would not "know" that the drop *B* was in between, so she would trip and fall at *B*.

POOR BODY AWARENESS

Once a child has found out "who I am," he has a reference for learning "where I am" and "where I am going." We call this *spatial awareness*. His body follows his head, and his head follows his eyes. If his eyes cannot find a target and stay on that target, the rest of him will move inefficiently toward that target, or he may not get to the target at all.

Hannah had always been like Alice's friend, the Cheshire cat, a head afloat with no connection to the ground. One of our biggest problems was her "running away," which she did at every possible time and place, regardless of obstacles or hazards (which, of course, she could not "see"). She did not know where her feet were in the first place. And, once she started, her body awareness was so poor that she could not stop until somebody or something stopped her.

At five, she vanished in the middle of West Virginia when we stopped for gas. On the same vacation, while supposedly safely napping in a chain-locked motel room next to ours, she crossed a highway bristling with trailer trucks and, fully clothed, walked into the deep end of a motel pool. At six, she was missing for an hour one day before a patrolman found her and brought her home. At seven, her brother's new tree house had to be junked because it gave her a start up a 60-foot tree from which a fireman was called to rescue her. At eight, she dropped from a second-story window one night to romp with her dog, whom she'd heard barking.

In between these more dramatic escapes, Hannah practiced running away four or five times a day, whenever my back was necessarily turned. When she was given her special bifocal lenses[2], she suddenly stopped having to run away because she could deal more efficiently with what was near her. She didn't constantly need to get "out there," but her body awareness was still so poor that she still did not know where she was, where she was going, or how to get there.

If a child's image of himself (his body awareness) is not fully developed, his impression of the world (his spatial awareness) is bound to be confused as well. He cannot point to the top of a picture if he doesn't know that his own feet are below his head. He cannot turn in the right direction or distinguish the word *was* from the word *saw*, if he does not feel the difference between his right side and his left side.

Hannah used to get furious because she could not fit into the clothes of a six-inch doll, or fit the doll neatly into my sweater. She would try vainly to crawl under a dresser or footstool that was three inches off the floor, and hit her poor head hard every time she hid under the dining-room table for hide-and-seek because she did not know how low to duck. If a paper airplane or a ball hit her from behind, she was astounded; since she had not seen it before, it did not exist before. One little girl in her school had to have her mother remain at the school for the whole session, for when mother could not be "located" she did not exist, and the child was devastated.

To walk well, a child must be able to go directly to any target he chooses. He must be able to overcome small steps, objects

---

[2] By Dr. Gerald Getman, a founder and leader in the Optometric Extension Program, a group of specially trained, dedicated men who are getting very wonderful behavioral, academic, and postural results by their successful efforts to correct visual problems.

in his path, cracks in the sidewalk, or any other simple obstacles without interrupting his walking pattern—and without having to give his full attention to overcoming the obstacles and not tripping over or bumping into them. He must be able to walk backwards pretty well, with his target in mind to guide him, stopping before he bumps into the wall or falls off a step.

With poor kinesthetic organization, a child does not walk well; nor will he read well, or even crawl well.

In rolling, if the top half does most of the work, a child will roll in a circle with his feet at the center; if the bottom half does the work, he will roll in a circle with his head at the center.

Good crawling takes equal thrusting and counterthrusting between top and bottom halves, right and left sides. As with trotting horses, the right arm and left leg thrust together, the left arm and right leg work in a team. The hands should be flat on the floor, with the fingers pointing forward. The head should be up, so as to visually guide the movement in the right direction. But the body should remain level as the limbs are moving forward.

A child with poor kinesthetic development will either employ the wrong arm-leg combination, display little rhythm in his thrusting, lack proper visual direction, or rock from left to right instead of moving his body directly forward. Some children display various combinations of these defects in crawling.

Gross movement (as with the arms and legs) develops before finer movements (hands and feet and, finally, fingers and toes). A child might do all right with the big movements, but not be able to tap his toes on the floor or perform small dance patterns, play finger or thumb games, or handle pencil and chalk well. If a child cannot copy, draw, or write, there is obviously a deficiency in grosser, lower-level movement development.

With poor kinesthetic development, a child may have either very tight or very loose muscles. He will not be flexible or know how to adapt his movements to the situation without effort. He may use both hands simultaneously, or one hand to the exclusion of the other, when he should be doing the opposite. Only when he has achieved control of both sides of his body is he ready to decide whether he should use his right hand or his left hand, or both. As he grows older, the child with poor K will have trouble in comprehending the meaning of time and in learning how to sequence, read, write, and do arithmetic. He will have even greater difficulties in learning how to think things out and how to plan, as well as in taking part in activities such as sports which demand good physical and mental coordination.

- *Learning About Time*: A child begins to understand what time in the sense of duration means when he first discovers that it takes longer to get from Point A to Point B, than it does to get from Point A to Point C. Once he grasps the elements of sequencing as well, he will be able to understand the other, more complex aspects of time.

- *Learning About Sequences:* On the most elementary level, a child learns how to carry out his actions or how to arrange objects and ideas in a systematic order or sequence in the following way. First, he moves his body from Point A to Point B.

Next, he repeats this movement a number of times, until the sequence A-B has been assimilated by his body and his mind. He then applies the knowledge derived from this simple sequence to objects and ideas outside himself.

Gradually, he also expands the original sequence of movement from A via B to C, then to D, and so forth. He also is experimenting with and assimilating new and increasingly complex sequences. Depending on the number, scope, and complexity of sequences he has mastered, a child will ultimately be able to arrange objects by size, shape, color, etc. He will get to know the order of the days of the week and the months of the year. He will also increase his ability to understand *time* in terms of *yesterday* and *tomorrow, last week* and *next week, three years ago* and *ten years from now*, and so forth. When he has learned to read, and depending on his reading proficiency, he will be able to find information in catalogues, files, encyclopedias, telephone directories, and similar source books in which the subject matter is arranged in an identifiable sequence.

- *Learning to Do Arithmetic:* Put simply, all mathematics (as well as other forms of abstraction) is nothing more than grouping and organizing certain concepts in one's mind and in space. The child, by first relating a single object, and gradually a growing number of objects and ideas, to himself, discovers that objects and ideas that are similar in certain respects belong to a *group* or *set*. In learning to carry out the operations of arithmetic, the child must apply his experience in sequencing; and he must develop skill in manipulating two or more numbers and groups of numbers, according to prescribed rules.

- *Learning to Read:* On the most elementary level, reading involves the ability to perceive written words in an orderly sequence, instead of seeing a meaningless jumble of letters, and then to relate an object or an idea to the word symbol.

  Normally, the child will learn how to read a word by grouping the letters according to certain recognizable patterns, and by associating certain sounds with certain printed symbols. One of the major problems in learning how to read is the visual confusion created by similar-looking letters and sequences of letters or numbers, for example, *b* and *d*, *p* and *q*, *6* and *9*, or *411* and *114*.

  Before the child is able to distinguish visually and mentally between such confusingly similar symbols, he must have mastered *space, shape,* and *direction*. He must be able to discriminate between the *left* and the *right*, the *top* and the *bottom*, and the *back* and the *front* of his own body. Then he will be able to move his eyes from left to right over a page, and from line to line.

- *Learning to Write:* Physically, writing requires both the ability to execute fine hand and finger movements and their coordination with eye movements and visual perception. The prerequisite for these accomplishments is sound development of the grosser kinesthetic organization.

AUDITION Every child comes equipped with two ears, the indispensable external equipment of the *auditory system* that conducts sound to the brain. This system gives the child contact with the world from a distance, and alerts him to what is about to happen. Audition is the primary means for learning how to communicate with other human beings through spoken *language*.

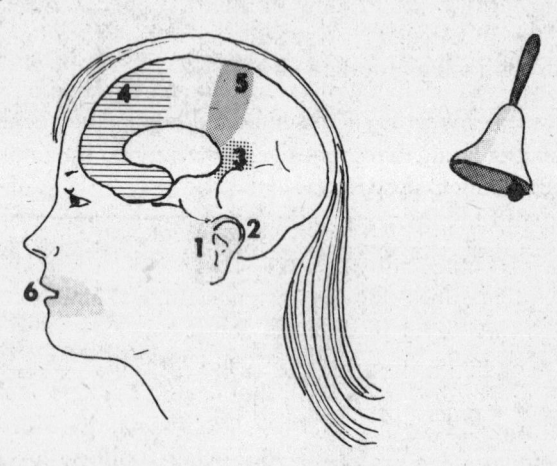

PLACING THE DEFECT   *The sound of the bell may not be responded to if a person suffers from any of these defects:*
1. *Damage to outer, middle, or inner ear causing deafness.*
2. *Damage to auditory nerve causing deafness.*
3. *Inability of brain to organize auditory stimuli effectively—receptive aphasia.*
4. *Memory for verbal symbols is impaired; or there is difficulty in organizing motor patterns to produce speech—expressive aphasia.*
5. *Developmental, physical or emotional problems causing poor speech.*
6. *Malformations of speech organs.*

The following disorders interfere with proper auditory functioning:

Being Deaf or Hard of Hearing   (1) The structure of the ear itself (outer, middle, or inner) may be faulty, or (2) there may be damage to the nerve, preventing sound completely or partially from reaching the brain.

Receptive Aphasia   This condition is a pseudo-hearing problem. Although a child's hearing equipment may be perfectly normal, he *appears deaf or hard of hearing*, because his auditory organization is poor. The mere physical ability to hear a sound carries little significance. In order to make a meaningful response, the child must learn how to be alerted by sound, how to localize sound, how to identify and interpret sound, and how to associate a specific sound or a combination of sounds with an appropriate idea.

Expressive Aphasia This child will probably understand speech but be unable to recall or produce the speech symbols he needs, much like an adult who has suffered a stroke, or he may remember the symbols but be unable to organize his motor patterns well enough to respond. It is too easy for testers and educators, as well as parents, to assume that a child cannot understand language because he does not successfully carry out verbal requests, does not answer, or may show no sign of having heard—fairly significant handicaps for Hannah and others like her on a standard psychological test.

Other expressive problems After the child begins to speak, he may misuse and leave out pronouns, verbs, adjectives, prepositions, articles, and conjunctions (Hannah at seven: "I'm help you." Translation: "Will you help me?" Hannah at ten: "That's where we went . . . Mrs. Smith had a baby." Translation: "That's where I want to go . . . Mrs. Smith is going to have a baby."), which is bound to confuse his listeners. We often assumed that Hannah had misjudged a situation because she could not describe it grammatically.

Speech Problems May be due to (1) developmental physical causes (e.g., cerebral palsy), (2) physical defects in the organs of speech themselves (tongue, palate, teeth, lips), or (3) emotional causes.

Such speech problems should be distinguished from expressive aphasia.

LANGUAGE AND SPEECH It is useful to distinguish between language and speech. *Language is a system of symbols* providing us with (1) the means of communicating with others and (2) the basis of logical thinking. *Speech is the correct articulation of words.* It is possible for a child to have a language problem but no speech problem, having difficulty comprehending the symbols he receives or trouble finding the words and producing them, but pronouncing them correctly if he can get them out. A child can have a speech problem but no language problem, being able to say whatever he wants but pronouncing words in such a way that he is difficult to understand or unpleasant to hear. And a child can, of course, have both problems. A child can have a hearing problem with either a language or speech problem, or both, since he cannot learn from the speech of others.

How Language Develops The child's progress in comprehending and using speech and language skills is dependent on his general level of development. Before his audition can be adequate, he must have organized GOT and K (gustation, olfaction, tactuality and kinesthesia). In fact, the words he uses indicate his developmental organization. If the child's K is not well developed, he will tend to use tactual words rather than words describing how things are used. For example, to him a ball will be hard, or rough, or round rather than something to throw or to roll.

If he is confined to a little low chair whenever he is in the kitchen, "kitchen" to him is a patterned floor, mother's legs moving around, disembodied smells and noises. If he is, on the other hand, allowed to crawl and climb, explore, play with pots and pans, sit in something high to watch mother bake and clean up, and sometimes help her, then "kitchen" is a whole lot more. He has found out how things in the kitchen feel, what makes which noises and which smells. He has an idea what must happen before food is ready to eat, before dishes and utensils are clean. Only by experiencing directly can he form a foundation for the space world he must build for himself. Then, with the development of language, he can compare the particular way in which he has organized his space world with what others—his family, his friends, and finally, strangers—tell him about his and their space worlds.

But he can only understand from his past experience. To talk about a bowl of flowers on the mantel without lifting a four-year-old up to where the bowl is, so that he can touch and smell and see it from all angles, especially if he has never previously pulled a flower apart and examined it himself, is ridiculous. In the same way, speaking to a child on an adult level rather than his own, viewing things from what you have learned about them and from where you see them rather than from what he knows and how he sees them, leads only to misunderstanding, confusion, and arguments.

The Significance of Language With the development of language, a child advances beyond the stage of mere survival at which, after all, animals often surpass him. He has the means to communicate and tools with which to think. He can form concepts from groups of symbols, which allows him to learn to think abstractly and, perhaps one day, in metaphors.

Hannah's Language She did not coo when she was little. She hardly made a sound at all until she was three, or appeared to hear what we said. Even when she started producing single words, she did not seem to know what they meant nor to use them to represent a whole idea, such as "out" for "I want to go outside" as very young children do. She knew the primary colors and all the animals in her books by four, but could pronounce few of them by five. By six, she could use the essential words (milk, eat, teetee, etc.), and at the times she could not get them out, she could let us know when we hit the right word. By seven, she was putting two words together quite often and sometimes three. By eight, she was just beginning to tackle tenses and plurals, and suddenly brought in pronouns at nine.

When, at nine, Hannah reached for Andy's big turtle and offered him hers, saying, "I take your turtle my school;

you take my turtle yours," her brother was so pleased that he let her. When she looked down at the full half-gallon bottle of milk she had accidentally smashed on the floor and said, "I drop bottle floor. It spill," I happily helped her clean it up.

At ten, her worst problem (which she has not completely overcome) was imitating the useful clichés we all use for opening, closing, and carrying on simple conversations. If she cannot find the words she wants, she uses fillers to play for time or to substitute: "Uhhh, just one more thing . . . uhhh, I got to tell you somethin'. . . . uhhhh, you come back some more?"

VISION Good binocular vision, the ability to gain additional meaning by fusing the information that we receive through both eyes, is the highest, most economical way of learning— the goal of development. Since good vision depends on all our other learning systems, deficiencies in them show up in inefficient visual functioning. And, since few of us have developed all our systems to their highest potential, most of us have some resulting visual inadequacies.

A child can see that "a rose is a rose is a rose" only if he has previously tasted it, smelled it, felt it, pulled it, torn it up, and scattered it. When he learns to read, what he sees on a page will make sense rather than appear as meaningless squiggles only because of his previous experiences.

Binocular vision is the teaming of *both* eyes to maintain *one* image, a true representation of reality. A child must have first developed a good bilateral motor system before he can have good bilateral (binocular) vision. You might say he needs "to have his head on straight"—so that his two eyes are equidistant from the object of gaze—in order to see things as they are. He cannot get a true, clear picture of a tree unless both lenses of his eyes receive the light from the tree equally. For such ideal eye balance, his head must be balanced properly; for a well-balanced head, the body that supports it must be aligned vertically for optimum dynamic balance: head over shoulders, shoulders over trunk, trunk over hips, hips over feet.

Any imperfection in the process of development previous to the visual demands of school affects the alignment of the body and, consequently, the ideal balance of the two eyes. Any conditions in school or at home that later are not ideal for study and reading cause the body to contort and distort itself in order to get the job done (stress alters function). If these conditions continue, they will cause warps in the body that were not there before. These warps make proper balance of the head and eyes more difficult, and may cause the body to make further adjustments (function alters structure).

No wonder that by the end of the first grade a child who entered school with quite adequate balance and alignment will usually show the beginnings of the lopsidedness which he will exaggerate and carry through life. By the end of the third grade, children begin to turn up with "far-sightedness," "near-sightedness," "alternating eyes," "astigmatism," etc., with which they were not born, but which they have developed to survive in school. Unfortunately, their visual impediments are *rarely* discovered, and they go about innocently assuming that they have 20/20 vision. Hence it is not surprising that their teachers and parents diagnose their inadequate balance, poor reading skills, bad study habits, school work well below their abilities, and behavior problems variously as sheer laziness, stubbornness, disinterest, or the influence of undesirable companions.

A child who has not developed good binocular vision may use only one eye most of the time, and may have to rotate or tilt his head or turn his eye to do so. He may not be able to follow a moving target unless he moves his head as well as his eyes, or may be able to do so in some directions and not in others. He may not be able to look at anything long enough to get the job done. He may not be able to tell the difference between a round pie and a round watch, whether a tree is small and near or large but far away. He may be extremely friendly, waving to and greeting every passerby or crawling into a visitor's lap because he cannot "see" whether he knows someone or not.[3]

[3] All very young children exhibit these characteristics, since it takes learning to develop good binocular vision.

HOW TO BEHAVE WITH PEOPLE *The fact that strangers, acquaintances, and relatives require different responses has given Hannah a great deal of difficulty.*

Hannah has had a terrible struggle trying to learn the difference between strangers to whom you do *not* speak, acquaintances and friends to whom you *should* speak, and relatives and friends whom you *may* hug and kiss. As her vision gradually improves, she is more and more successful in these distinctions.

To tell a child with a poorly organized visual system "Look before you leap" is pointless. He does not know how. The worst aspect of Hannah's "running away" was her night prowling. Awakening at night to go to the bathroom, she would simply take off in the direction of any light she saw outside, with no thought of how she would get to that light or how she would return. She was no more deterred by locked doors and our eternal vigilance than she was by fear of heights, traffic, or inclement weather.

The incident that finally inspired a solution took place one Sunday morning at 7 o'clock when I answered the doorbell to find a neighbor returning a filthy, tangle-haired waif, covered only with deep scratches and a boy's jacket. The solution was a buzzer on Hannah's door that rang as soon as she opened it, allowing me to steer her back to bed. By the time we moved to another house when she was ten and a half, she no longer needed the buzzer.

"HIGHER" LEARNING

Once a child gets vision and all his other systems organized at a *perceptual* level, he has a basis for learning on a higher, or *symbolic,* level at which he can comprehend signs, gestures, and words that mean or represent the things that he has already found out about. Finally—and this is the goal of our society—he must learn to use everything he has learned through his basic physical equipment and through the recognition and use of symbols as a basis for logical thinking.

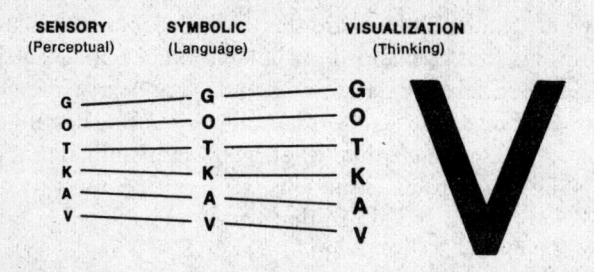

SENSORY (Perceptual)	SYMBOLIC (Language)	VISUALIZATION (Thinking)
G	G	G
O	O	O
T	T	T
K	K	K
A	A	A
V	V	V

DEVELOPMENT OF LEARNING   Given the proper sensory experiences, the child can go on to organize his world perceptually. Ultimately, he will form concepts at the highest symbolic levels.

For instance, let us take the kinesthetic approach to the world. At the sensory or *perceptual* level of K, we learn to move ourselves, then to move around in space, then to repeat our movements, increasingly integrating this modality with the others. At the symbolic level, we learn symbols for movement: lift, open, stretch, run, yawn, pinch, skip, squeeze, push. At the *visualization* or abstract level, we use all these symbols with all the symbols based on other types of perceptual training so as to visualize, think, reason, and plan. Anyone whose K is well organized can juggle ideas in his head, move them around in various positions and try them in various combinations in his mind, until he arrives at different, more satisfactory ideas. In this way, he can anticipate results and solve problems *before* they occur, not *after*, when it may be much less profitable.

Many children with learning disabilities are arrested at the perceptual level. As a result, they typically tend to think in concrete terms and are unable to think in abstract terms. For example, Hannah's handsome, quite articulate, beautifully mannered friend, Ralph, got very angry in school one day when another boy was asked, "How was the weather yesterday, Hal? Rainy? Sunny? Cloudy?" Ralph leaped out of his seat, yelling, "Hal doesn't know about the weather! He wasn't even in school yesterday!" For Ralph, the weather was where *he* was, nowhere else.

On the *concrete* level, a picture of a cow is exactly what it is, with no past, no future, and no connection with anything else. A child might even turn the page to see the cow from the back (many very young children do this). On the *conceptual* level, "cow" means that cow and the whole group of female cattle—here and there, already slaughtered and yet to be, real or make-believe—as long as they conform to the varieties he has already encountered. On the *abstract* level, a cow is an animal that can be imagined in various situations, that can be used to help understand what a buffalo is, that can be considered in terms of how it helps us, how we should feel toward it, and even how *it* may feel. On an *abstract* level, a child reads ideas.

Hannah reads ideas. A concept is a grouping of objects or qualities. Only on the abstract level, using concepts, can a child relate one thing with another or know what does not fit in with something else. When all the experts were still insisting that Hannah was a trainable retardee or worse, according to her test scores, I consoled myself with "How could she have such a wonderful sense of humor if she didn't have any sense?" *I knew she was bright,* although then I could not say how I knew this. Eventually I realized that a sense of humor implies a grasp of concepts. The essence of what is "funny" is that it is *not* appropriate, that it does *not* fit into the normal scheme or order of things, that it is *unexpected* because it is not in a certain group or category. To know that it does *not* fit means that one knows what *does* fit.

Daddy played a game with her, pretending to have a tiny imaginary bug (sometimes it was a tiny little man) which he watched fly, caught, put in his pocket, took from her mouth or ear. She caught on to the game right away, at six, while Ralph today, at ten, would probably completely refuse to accept the premise. She even gave "the bug" a name, took it herself, and played with it, then gave it back.

She began her impersonations when she was still at the single-word stage, pointing to members of her household and giving them other people's names (e.g., pointing to Daddy, saying "Mommy"; to Andy, saying "Hannah"; to herself, saying "Daddy"), then acting out her role and obviously expecting others to act their parts. Later, she said, "You, Hannah. Me, Andy." And, by six or seven, she was doing sharply accurate and usually hilarious thumbnail impersonations of anyone she knew, normally in pantomime. When we had family shows, her daddy would introduce her. Without wasting any time, Hannah would imitate what (to her) seemed everyone's outstanding characteristics. For example, for her uncle, an incurably hungry man, she picked a huge jar of pretzels while entering the room and started stuffing them into her mouth. For her aunt, a lady extremely concerned with her appearance and always looking just right, Hannah came in prissing, stopping at each step to pose and pat her hair, saying, "Honey, dear, don't I look pretty?" When asked to represent a teacher, Hannah sat down, sternly shook her finger in someone's face and sent "Hannah" from the room. As her grandma, Hannah bent over and held her back.

Although she still is not ready to handle all the visual requirements of everyday life, she knows what is expected of her because it has been explained to her. She realizes that she is not competent to cross a busy street without help, even though she resents it, knowing that smaller children are allowed to do it. She realizes that she must not accost strangers, and so she seeks help in identifying them by asking, "Is she a stranger? . . . he is a stranger? I do not talk to him. Only friends."

When cattle were discussed in school when she was nine, she had to bring up and find out all about branding irons, which she had discovered on TV. When we climbed a steep rock formation on a family outing, Hannah wanted to know if we would each have a stick and a rope between us and walk in single file, even decided the order in which we should go, another TV carryover. After a crossing-the-street lesson, she would notice how other people crossed, whether or not they stopped, looked, and listened, as they should. In other words, she could apply what she had learned in one situation to another situation. This was an accomplishment most of her friends with learning disorders could not match, even though they seemed superficially brighter, because they had less trouble with language. In short, although Hannah could not compete with these other children on the symbolic level, she was far beyond them on the higher, conceptual level.

SPATIAL ORIENTATION[4]

All the abilities we have been talking about take place in space. Whatever he does, a child must relate himself spatially to his task.

- *Near space.* Very young children perform best when what they must do is right in front of them, in *near space*. The farther away they are from what they must watch and listen to the more distracted they will be. They are most comfortable in near space, often curling up under a table or in a packing box, seeking physical contact with somebody or something when they find themselves in a wide-open area. Their first jobs, like eating and dressing, are in near space. Their first play, with rattles, blocks, and stuffed toys, is in near space. They don't care much about anyone but themselves and the "giants" who meet their needs.

- *Mid space.* When children hit the kinesthetic or movement stage, they are ready to tackle *mid space*. They slide, swing, ride trucks, play ball, tag, ring-round-the-rosie, and hide-and-seek. If they are lucky, they are no longer confined to a crib, playpen, or even a small room, but are allowed to crawl and climb in, on, and under all kinds of fascinating things and find out what the world is really like from every

---

[4] The following ideas on spatial orientation are also part of Dr. Ray H. Barsch's unique interpretation of development.

angle. Their interests have spread to their playmates, Grandma and Grandpa, and perhaps a few other relatives.

- *Far space.* Finally, when a child is physiologically ready to do most of his learning auditorially and then visually, he gets around to organizing *far space* (20 feet from his middle and beyond). He can learn from sounds that mother is vacuuming the next room, that a car is going by the house; and through language, he can learn of things much farther away. He can see to the horizon and, eventually, as he masters the art of reading, he can look back through the ages and to the other side of the world.

DISTRACTIBILITY A certain amount of distractibility in children is normal and is definitely not confined to children with learning disorders. Being distracted is merely the result of the inevitable confusion that overwhelms us when we are being bombarded by conflicting perceptual stimuli from near space, mid space, and far space. For example, can you yourself carry on an important telephone conversation while somebody keeps talking to you at your end? Can you balance your checkbook or finish a chapter in a book in front of an exciting TV mystery? A child whose learning disorders have prevented him from organizing even his near space is actually oblivious to the distractions of stimuli from mid space and far space. Nevertheless, he is worse off because this understimulation prevents him from developing good spatial organization.

Because she was poorly organized in all systems in all spatial areas, Hannah found it hard to focus her attention on anything for very long. Hannah was *highly distractible*. She could not carry on a conversation in the car over the sounds of the motor, the horns of other cars, the sirens, and the twittering of birds. She was also distracted by the sight of other cars, trucks, people, and buildings. Even the feel of her clothes distracted her; also the touch of the car seat, and the feel of the wind. Nor could she eat in a restaurant or visit a circus or fair except on her "best" days. She could not maintain her near space, poorly organized as it was, in the presence of all the activity going on in mid space. Things that she could do for herself—bathing, dressing, working a jigsaw puzzle—when someone was near her (structuring her near space for her, closing out mid and far space, enclosing an area in which she was able to function), she could not do as well or at all when left alone. She seemed to be taking advantage when a back was turned, but it was another matter altogether. As she improved in organizing each task as well as all her systems in each of the spatial areas, she could handle tasks at an ever increasing distance from whoever was supervising her. At the age of ten, Hannah could be relied on to take her suitcase into her room, unpack it, put her clothes away in the drawers and closet, close the bag, carry it to the garage, wash her hands, then return to the family ready for dinner. By ten and a half her spatial organization had so improved that she is now much less distracted by sounds than either her father or I. (Audition has been her strong point for some time now.)

SPATIAL PLANES   A child moves in all directions, one or more at a time. He organizes *vertical* movements, up and down, which he learns from the balance between both sides and the proper alignment of his own body in his fight against gravity. He organizes his movements on the *depth* plane, back and forth, which he learns from the equal thrust and counterthrust of his own body. His *lateral* plane, left to right and right to left (across), is organized when he has a good balance between the two sides of his body.

If he learns from his experiences in these various planes and combinations of planes, he learns to move efficiently; if he cannot organize his experiences, he will not move efficiently. The behavioral problems which usually accompany learning disabilities can largely be accounted for by the distortion or inadequacy of a child's spatial organization.

He may stubbornly refuse to participate in any physical activity, including games, simply because he is terrified. He has a right to be terrified when he is so poorly organized that he doesn't know where he is, whether or not his feet are on the floor, whether he is upside-down or downside-up, let alone when he doesn't know how to move himself forward or backward, up or down. A five-year-old boy we know is so completely without orientation in the spatial world, that when once moving fast across a room, he bumped into a dining-room table and went sailing across the table with the impetus of his forward motion. Yet he continued to work his legs as if he had no idea that he was no longer walking on the floor.

A five-year-old little girl at the same school might appear a nasty little brat to outsiders, for she continually finds herself in situations in which she stands helplessly and wails, "Help me!" —situations like trying to put on her coat, or standing in an alleyway with a truck coming toward her at a great distance. But this obviously bright little girl is not seeking attention for its own sake. She simply knows that she does not know how to move, and asks for help because she desperately needs it.

To a child who has only near space fairly well organized, far space situations are a threat. Sitting at a desk and facing near space schoolwork is just as threatening to a child who needs physical contact with the world and cannot maintain near space visual tasks—the child that Hannah once was.

We have already mentioned that a child who does not know how to move himself about in space has no frame of reference for understanding time, literally has no possible way of visualizing past and future. No matter how much he is told, he cannot really "know" what will happen *next*, and so he is grief-stricken when what he is doing *now* is interrupted. At the mercy of fluctuating circumstances, he cannot bear change, and will try to maintain his stability by resisting change however he can. He has no base—literally—for movement in the world, no basis from which to judge and choose.

Although the behavior of a spatially disorganized child is disturbing to us, we need only look at the world from his point of view to see that he is merely fighting to survive.

DEGREES OF FREEDOM

To move through life freely, we need to have many and varied responses on tap. If we can respond efficiently with only one perceptual technique, in only one particular spatial area, we have little freedom of movement. We can survive inde-

NORMAL MATURATIONAL SEQUENCE

pendently *only* if we can behave in a fluid way in many situations. Such a high degree of freedom depends on certain characteristics: bilaterality, rhythm, flexibility, and motor planning. Since these characteristics develop from movement experiences, children with learning disorders are likely to have inadequate degrees of freedom.

BILATERALITY   Both sides of the body must learn to move independently, yet together as a unit, in a dynamic, reciprocal relationship.

The first expert who prescribed for Hannah recommended that we tie her left arm to her body under her clothes for 18 months, from the time she was two and a half until she was four. A leading advocate of the importance of one side of the brain taking over control for efficiency of speech, movement, etc., he was concerned that her right side was not sufficiently dominant. So off with her left arm! (She was so slim that the bound arm under her dress actually appeared to be missing.) His technique was similar to the splinting of arms and legs or the patching of eyes that aim for extra practice for the unhampered side.

But nature's aim, the developmental goal, is *bilaterality*. When both sides have learned to work alone, and then together, the next step is a reciprocal relationship, which requires dominance of one side to initiate movement. Hannah learned to put on her shoes, take down her panties, and ride her tricycle with *one* arm. But she is still making up the time lost in bilateral practice; a reciprocal job like washing her hands is a mighty task for her.

I know personally of a little girl whose right eye was patched when she was two years old. In order to keep her from snatching off the patch (her own drive for survival was strong), both her arms were put in splints. Imagine the marvelous learning that took place for all those months, while she was physically prevented from developing visually or kinesthetically!

Speaking of eyes, visual fusion, or convergence, the highest developmental goal, is based on all a child's previous bilateral practice. Any flaw in "basic training" will necessarily result in less-than-perfect vision. So many children have not yet learned to use their eyes together, and "get rid of" one eye so that they will not have to look at two images. An eye may turn up, out, or in. Oho! Patch it! If that doesn't work, a surgeon cuts a little muscle. If the eye goes off again in a few years, cut that old muscle again. A more sensible solution: let the child learn to use both eyes together, so that one eye will not have to turn away. And then one day the two eyes will converge, fusion will take place, the child will be operating on a high visual level and, consequently, functioning as a whole at his best level.

More subtle children, who are disturbed by two images when using both eyes, are often congratulated on their 20/20 vision in each eye and win blue ribbons in health examinations. Yet a target-following test would show them (and most adults) up as notorious one-eye users. No one can explain their reading problems, learning problems, and social problems. Or perhaps they have no special problems, but are merely missing the richer, fuller life that visual fusion and flexibility would give them.

Hannah's struggle to reach bilaterality of movement is still going on, for she had a harder struggle than most of us. Naturally, hers is a more serious visual problem than the average. It is not surprising that she cannot yet safely cross the street on her own, cannot entirely discard touch and audition in all her visual tasks. Her symbolic, higher-level abilities are far advanced, but she reads on an early third-grade level because her visual difficulties require fewer words, larger type, plainer print, and less clutter to a page.

RHYTHM Rhythm is a regulated, consistent relationship in time: equal thrust and counterthrust, equal action and reaction. Rhythm is also matching one's own consistent relationship in time to external changes (the changing tempo of clapping or marching as music or teacher changes; following a male dancing partner, matching the rhythm of the band). Rhythm is the tempo of nature that allows the tides, the moon, the sun, the earth, and all the energies that surround us in space to move in order instead of chaos. Rhythm is essential for efficient sawing, sewing, swimming, running, writing, typing, playing a piano, brushing teeth, elimination habits, sleep behavior, walking, talking, and chewing.

Perhaps the inner rhythms that regulate our lives are even more important than the outer rhythms which are so apparent. Besides circulation and breathing, there is a temperature cycle which rises and falls in a rhythmical pattern during the day for most people. When our temperature is higher we have the energy, ambition, and ability to move and to act; when our temperature is lower, our bodies are prepared for the rest and sleep that refresh us.

A child is not born with such a rhythmical pattern, but gradually develops it, as we can see by observing his sleep-wake pattern. Probably connected with this temperature cycle in some way, either as cause or effect, is the chemical cycle within us which provides the basis for our moods. With poor internal rhythm, a child is not likely to have regular, smooth chemical changes operating inside, which may account for the unpredictable, unreasonable *mood swings* with which children with learning disorders are fairly universally identified.

By the time she was three or four, we realized that Hannah definitely had "good" days and "bad" days; by then she was having enough "good" days to demonstrate the difference. Later, we noticed that she could have good hours and bad, good moments and bad, and we stopped racking our brains for the cause of every radical mood change. The more organized she becomes in all areas, the more her good days outnumber the bad. And not only are her good days better, but her bad days are not nearly as bad.

"Good" days at nine meant that she talked more and said it better, walked more gracefully and descended the stairs one foot to a step, enjoyed our lesson, and handled each task better than ever before. She also ate comparatively well and behaved reasonably at the dinner table, slept only nine or ten hours and was full of vitality, and played alone well inside or out. On good days, Hannah hugged and wrestled gently with her saintly collie more than she pulled his ears and tail, and she did not go to pieces if the dog could not get inside a big brass kettle we have, or could not climb the ladder we keep in the garage. She was friendly to everyone, and she started to use new words and expressions, new and better ways of doing things. She kept her eyes in focus most of the time and refused to be upset by teasing, disappointments, or excitement.

"Bad" days meant that Hannah hardly spoke and had trouble finding the right words when she tried, that she came downstairs with two feet to a step, that she refused to cooperate during her lessons, and that she could not perform the tasks she had found simple the previous day. She ate almost nothing, spending her time at the table throwing forks, tipping over chairs, or seasoning the water glasses with pepper and catsup. She slept 11 or 12 hours but seemed exhausted, could find nothing to amuse her, tormented the dog, and was furious at him when he could not do the impossible. She used only one eye, with the left one turned up, and regressed in her over-all behavior to such an extent that she might run away or tear up books. Her "look" was foggy and glassy-eyed.

There were, of course, degrees in between. By ten, Hannah's "bad" days had virtually disappeared. Their only trace was the rare day or hour in which she seemed a little tired, a little foggy, and could not converse as freely. There were even rarer *moments* when, in the middle of enjoying a meal or a bedtime story or a game, big tears would suddenly roll down her cheeks and she would feel very sad, without knowing why; or when, in the middle of a bright, gay conversation, she would suddenly become quiet and dreamy. This is probably not too atypical of a child who is approaching puberty.

The epitome of a mood swing into a negative direction is the *catastrophic condition,* too often mistaken for a temper tantrum, and too blithely explained by whatever immediately triggers it—excitement, frustration, shock, disappointment, personal failure. It can vary from the much-less-frequent withdrawal into a shell to what may appear to be a violent seizure. Actually, it is more akin to a seizure than a temper tantrum because it is involuntary; the difference lies in the fact that the child is, to some degree at least, conscious. He can remember the incident afterward with guilt and the insecurity of knowing that he was helpless to prevent it himself.

At four or five, Hannah would warn us with a period of giggling followed by crying. Before we learned to recognize the signs and to do something about it, she would proceed to the real thing: throwing herself on the floor, pounding her head against the floor or wall, biting her fingers, and kicking out at anything or nothing. Later, we knew that something had to be done to prevent a catastrophic condition when her voice got higher in pitch, as she grew more and more negative and cranky. Still later, we learned to avoid even this manifestation by recognizing "bad" days and relieving her of every possible stress we could. Usually this approach worked, but not always.

Long before I had heard of the term "catastrophic condition" or "catastrophic reaction," it was clear to me from living with Hannah that she was not having what superficially appeared to be temper tantrums. I assumed this would be equally clear to the experts who saw her, but I was proved wrong.

There was the speech therapist who bore with fortitude her shrieks and fierce struggles to escape his office, but refused to open the door when I explained that Hannah was terrified of all closed doors since her electroencephalogram six months earlier. Neither of us could hear the other, and neither changed his mind.

When she was two and a half, Hannah and I took a train to Baltimore during an airline strike. We lined up early for the dining car, but when Hannah had spilled the water, overturned the chairs, crumbled all the crackers, and thrown all the silver against the window before the waiter even took our order, we dined on a box of cold cereal in our roomette. We retired before sunset, but spent the night trying to adjust both of us comfortably into a single berth. We had to use the sink as a toilet, since we could not get to the commode.

In the morning we amused ourselves with a "game" called "get out the clothes," in which I tried to find our clothes by "feel" in the suitcase crammed under the berth. (I could not pull the bag out by closing the berth; this meant letting Hannah down on the floor, whence she could escape, and I did not care to risk having to chase her up and down the train in my pajamas.) Hannah tried to jump on the berth to smash it down every time I lifted it. She was winning all the points, for both my wrists felt as though they were broken, when I won the game by plopping her down hard to have another go at my lifting. This was so funny, she threw her head back and cracked it on the sharp metal window ledge. It bled copiously and required six stitches, followed by a series of treatments for infection when we returned home.

After a memorable hour in the jammed Washington terminal and a short hop in a plane (during which I was actively ill), we taxied to our hotel. That night Hannah spent wetting the bed and getting lost in the halls every time I dozed off, four times each as I recall. We arrived at the doctor's office battered, bruised, hungry, and sleepless. The doctor offered Hannah a sucker, and she exploded. To his credit, this doctor could see that this was no tantrum. However, it was so much like a seizure that he insisted on a second electroencephalogram and prescribed anticonvulsive medication.

Three years later, we consulted experts in St. Louis, following an all-day car ride and another sleepless night at a hotel. This "temper tantrum" almost lost her the opportunity that they were to give her to develop her language. On her next trip, they were amazed at how fast I had improved in managing my child; I was no longer "wound around her finger." They did not consider that the place, the people, and the situation were no longer strange and overwhelming to Hannah and that she was better able to withstand stress.

Hannah's teacher and I had tried to trace her mood swings to illness, loss of sleep, too much excitement or strain, sudden weather changes (especially from sunny to cloudy), and high pollen count. All of them seemed to be a factor, especially the last two, for Hannah and for many of the children in her class.

Unfortunately, her allergic reactions (manifested early in croup and later in asthma) extended to whatever medication we tried for behavior control. Our first breakthrough came when she was nine and a half and suffered a series of violent catastrophic conditions, sometimes three or four a day, over a period of two months in the late fall. These were the first such reactions (which I had always called collapses) in two years.

This time, each incident was preceded, accompanied, or followed by an asthma attack. Regular medication to prevent asthma controlled her behavior as well.

This seemed to prove the link between dysrhythmia and mood swings. Hannah's breathing apparatus was apparently so poorly organized that it could not cope with temperature changes or the different demands of strenuous exercise or sustained laughter, which therefore brought on asthma attacks. This added stress to her system lowered her resistance to other irritations. Possibly, too, the same biological conditions which cause the membrane of her bronchial tubes to swell cause her brain tissues to swell also. Her allergist had mentioned that behavior problems of "normal" children often disappeared with allergy medications.

FLEXIBILITY The ability to choose quickly and easily, from among a number of possible responses, the right one to match the demands of a particular situation is *flexibility*, a third degree of freedom. If he is to apply such flexibility, the child must have developed (1) a number of responses from which to choose and (2) the capacity to select the necessary *speed*.

If he is not flexible, because he is not well organized, he still has three choices:

(a) *He can escape.* Hannah's auditory mode was once so poorly organized and she had so little flexibility that her only response to too much noise was to run away physically, to escape to her room and to close the door. Later, she learned to cover her ears with her hands, or simply to withdraw into herself when playing children or a houseful of adult guests were too noisy for her. Now she is so much better organized that she can tolerate much more and much louder noise, and can maintain her near space in the presence of auditory distractions better than many of us.

(b) *He can stay there and fail.* When Hannah was asked to draw a square at seven, she was fairly sure that she could not. But she tried, she failed, and she suffered the disappointment of personal failure.

(c) *He can offer the best response he has on hand,* even if it does not fit. The response he is most likely to have at hand is the one he has just used. In other words, he behaves or answers in a way that was appropriate a moment ago but now has no connection with the situation—he *perseverates.* For instance, he has been asked "Are you a bad boy?" No. "Are you 30 years old?" No. "Is it cold in the summer?" No. Now, when he is asked, "Would you like some candy?" or "Is your name John Brown?" the answer is still "No." Most small children do this before they develop more flexibility; but they seldom do it to the same extent as a child with learning disability, who is typically *perseverative.*

Hannah loved looking at books when she was very young. She would spend a peaceful half hour enjoying the pictures. Then she might see a tiny rip on a page. She would try to make it stay together. She could not fix it but she could not stop trying, until she ripped it more. Then she could not stop ripping, until she tore out the whole page, then another and another, and perhaps all the pages from every book on her shelf.

She played in cycles, perseverating in the same activity week after week or month after month. "Cooking" was a favorite (before the buzzer) in the wee morning hours while others slept. One daybreak found her afloat in a sea of batter. Without doubt she had started in all good faith to make a cake, using perhaps one egg (then two or three), one pat of butter, one spoonful of bacon grease, flour, sugar, and coffee. But then she got going. She used a dozen eggs (with shells); a whole pound of butter; the entire contents of the canisters containing grease, flour, sugar, and coffee; a dash of water; and a half gallon of milk—all in a six-inch frying pan on a burner she herself had lighted.

Once, on a hair-cutting binge, Hannah found scissors we did not even know we had hidden in that hiding place. She loathed the bald spots and unnatural cowlick she had given herself as much as we did, but found herself quite unable to stop.

She imitated a TV mirror test for hair spray—with hair spray, deodorant, bug killer, throat antiseptic, and (but for providential intervention) gold paint. If left brushing her teeth, she might be found scrubbing the floor, the dog, or the toilet with her toothbrush. She might start by washing her hands or getting ready for her bath—and end by pouring out all the cleansers, medicines, shoe polish, mouth wash, bubble bath, and soap flakes into the tub.

One sad day she realized that Daddy used tonic on his hair. She tried hair tonic too—also hair cream, hair lotion, hair spray, toothpaste, hand cream, liquid makeup, backrub, athletes'-foot balm and Vaseline. Finally, she applied—also to her hair— a much-advertised preparation for curing hemorrhoids. We tried vinegar, alcohol, and every other kind of treatment recommended for removing the hemorrhoid cure. Her hair fell out in chunks, but the goo remained for nearly six months.

Hannah's increasing flexibility and slow conquering of perseveration are obvious. She no longer must sit in the left rear seat of a car, watch TV from the right end of a certain couch, squeeze the catsup bottle or spoon cocoa into her milk until they are all gone or someone stops her.

MOTOR PLANNING Once a child is aware of his ability to move, knows where he is, and is able to move from one place to another, he has to learn the *best way of moving and acting* if he is to be able to be where he would *like* to be, to do what he would *like* to do, and to learn what he would *like* to learn.

He must learn to move automatically in the most efficient way, eliminating wasteful movements and choosing proper movements without even having to be aware that he is doing so. If his movements are not well organized, he not only moves inefficiently but must devote all his attention to what he is doing. In the first instance he is using motor planning; in the second, operating virtually without motor planning.

Hannah by no means always stepped into puddles because she found them irresistible; she simply did not know how to get around them, even when she wanted to. Chatting, we cut up our meat at meals with little thought of how we are handling knife and fork. Cutting meat was a major project for ten-year-old Hannah. It took all her concentration to hold the fork in the down position with enough pressure to keep the food from jumping off her plate while she had to saw her knife back and forth with the other hand, making sure the cutting side was down. She knew by then that outside conversation was impossible, so she structured the situation as well as she could for herself verbally: "Do you mind? . . . Will you please be quiet? . . . How would you like if I talk? . . . Be quiet, please . . ." and, by the hardest means, performed this "simple" operation.

Motor planning, which allows us to do a job efficiently without having to think about how we are doing it, is an essential part of our lives—for packing a suitcase, opening a door with an armload of packages, balancing a plate at a tea party, unloading a truckload of furniture, condensing a business letter into one page, or leaving on the canvas enough room for the head when painting a portrait. On a higher level, motor planning is essential to any planning ahead, from the simple task of planning our day in such a way that we shall be left with some leisure, to solving financial, moral, and other weighty problems.

Poor kinesthetic control makes motor planning even harder for a child with learning disorders. He may have too little control, which forces him to move constantly. Or he may have too much control, which makes him sluggish and withdrawn.[5]

STRESS FACTORS

Regardless whether a child has developed sufficient degrees of freedom to move through life pleasantly and without complications, he still has to move. *Life is movement.* The law of life is the struggle to survive. A child *acts* because he *must*. But if he is acting under stress, his efforts will be excessive and wasteful, the result being anxiety.

Stress confronts all of us every moment of our waking lives. Usually it presents us with a challenge to get things done, and done well. Stress factors (multiplicity, language complexity, time, space, and the level of a task) overwhelm a child who has

---

[5] His mixed-up "control" is a possible explanation of why the stimulating drugs, amphetamines, subdue his hyperactivity (maybe by stimulating his control or inhibitions), while the barbiturates, which generally sedate, increase hyperactivity (perhaps by repressing his control or inhibitions).

not been able to learn how to cope with them. The older he gets, the more society expects of him; the more society expects of him, the more stress weighs him down.

He faces tasks all day long, some of which he cannot do at all and some of which he could do easily under ideal conditions. Without the necessary degrees of freedom to handle the stress factors, he continually fails.

If a child's abilities are equal to the demands of the task, he experiences success. If, however, the task demands far exceed his abilities, he suffers severe stress. In a stress situation, the child experiences intolerable tension, which is reflected in a pattern of anxious behavior. Periodically, he will release his anxiety by letting off steam through catastrophic reactions.

TIME Daddy says, "Hurry up or you'll be late!" Mother says, "Get dressed quickly or you'll miss the party!" Brother says, "You better get moving or you won't have time for breakfast." A horn blows or a doorbell rings impatiently.

Just enough pressure and we stop "fooling around" and get the job done. Too much pressure and we can't do anything. A child with learning disabilities is not really "fooling around." He may be dawdling by our standards because he moves slowly and keeps getting sidetracked, but he is using all the organization that he has. With the stress of time piled onto what he is already giving his "all" to accomplish, his inadequate organization falls apart. He uses lower control systems or he explodes.

Time is involved with learning problems in another way— the additional time it may take a child with learning disorders to respond. Often, given the usual time, he fails and is considered incapable of performing a certain task. Because he cannot come through in the expected time, he does not get a chance to perform at all, perhaps, and does not then get the experience and practice he needs, nor the success he deserves. If the delay is in responding verbally, other people either do not wait, so that he does not have the opportunity to participate in conversation, or take so long to quiet down to await the response (as when directed by the teacher) that he forgets what he meant to say, feels it is not worth all the commotion, or responds with a thought that is by now no longer timely.

A typical eight-year-old-Hannah delay occurred when she showed her drawing to another teacher as she left her own class one day. Asked what it was, she went into her "It's a . . . hmmm . . . It's a . . . wait a minute . . . uhhh . . . don't talk . . . it's a . . ." routine, until the teacher was no longer listening. Five minutes later, Hannah was driving past the teacher in the parking lot and leaned out the window to call, "It's a tunnel. It's a tunnel!" The teacher had no idea what she was talking about, but Hannah had found the word.

If Hannah is singing, she will stop when someone joins in. Not that she is acting the prima donna; she simply can't get the words out fast enough for the normal tempo. She has learned not to attempt it, except with her parents, who always adjust to her speed.

MULTIPLICITY All learning goes from the simple to the complex. We must first learn to deal with one toy, one voice, one figure in a picture before we can handle two, then many. A child must learn to handle the sights, sounds, smells and textures of his quiet, stripped-down room before he can handle all the stimuli of a party, a restaurant, or a busy street.

A child with learning disorders may be able to sit quietly and eat his meal when faced with only one plate, one fork, one food item, and one familiar person; but not when he must deal with three people and all their equipment, plus the ringing, clicking, chewing, and talking sounds. He may be able to point out many objects, one at a time, but identify none when they are offered in a group. He may read on a third-grade level from one or two lines in large print, but on the first-grade level from a more cluttered page. He can "go to the bedroom" then "turn on the light," then "open the bottom drawer," then "take out a scarf," then "bring it to mother" when given one assignment at a time. Given the whole job at once, he will leave something out, do everything wrong, or simply wash his hands of the whole business.

At nine, on a "bad" day, Hannah visited a small grocery store. Her behavior might have been expected on such a day, but I could not think of what else to do with her. She began by studying the pictures and names on the cereal boxes that she recognized from TV, a purposeful task except that it rearranged four shelves. When we had straightened things up, she was asked to push the cart. While I pondered over the meat, she went down the entire next aisle, placing samples from every section on both sides in her cart. While I replaced the merchandise, she was left with a friendly checker. By the time I got back to her she had punched the cash register and tried to fill a stamp pad with a bottle of indelible ink which had sprinkled all over a new tile floor. My own stress took its toll. I put Hannah in the car so that I could check out and leave, but forgot to remove the keys. She promptly dropped them inside the car door. We took a taxi home.

At nine and a half, Hannah was so much better organized and so much better able to handle multiplicity that she accompanied me to the beauty salon, where she observed but did not bother the open storage closet filled with jars, spray cans, boxes, and linens or the many mirrors and hairdressing implements. She simply watched me get my hair cut, commenting and admiring, never touching even a towel or a magazine.

CONQUERING MULTIPLICITY   Hannah had finally progressed from being able to handle only one *stimulus at a time, to being able to* integrate *several stimuli, and, finally, to being able to withstand and successfully organize many stimuli.*

LANGUAGE COMPLEXITY   More often a *multiplicity* of words, rather than unfamiliar words or sentence structure, is complex for a child: "Come on Hannah it's time to go we'll come back another time I promised Daddy we would be home soon and it's nearly time for dinner anyway and besides Andy is supposed to go to the barbershop for a haircut now come on put that book down I told you we'd have to leave soon come on that's a good girl we've got to go," instead of: "Come."

This language complexity factor applies to all young children —not to mention older children and adults as well. Parents, teachers, and job supervisors might find that they were getting their point across a lot better if they stuck to the meat of the matter instead of tacking on justifications and explanations that are not only unnecessary and sometimes annoying, but extremely distracting from the point. A half-hour lecture on children's duties to their parents and themselves, the value of beautiful landscaping, and the wages of sin is not only less effective but less clear cut than, "No, Robert. You can't go to the movies. You didn't cut the grass."

SPACE   We have already covered space in our discussion of development. One cannot operate well in near space unless one is sufficiently well organized in that dimension of space to maintain a certain competence in mid space and far space. For example, one cannot very well play ball, or even watch others play ball, if one's mid space is not well organized. Nor will one be able to pay attention to a football game down on the field while sitting on the stands if one is essentially not organized for far space. If one is not well organized in any of the three spatial areas, one will not be able to attend to any task for long.

LEVEL OF THE TASK   If a child is asked to learn something that is harder than what he has learned before, he will probably be eager to tackle it. Basically, all of us want to learn all we can. But if one asks a ten-year-old to understand philosophy, an adult of average education to deal with problems in nuclear physics, or a child with learning disorders to tackle problems that are appropriate for his chronological age peers, but not for himself, he will not learn, he will not be eager to try, and he will not know how to start or what to do next.

A task is easy if we are developmentally prepared for it, difficult or impossible if we are not.

THE GOAL OF DEVELOPMENT

A human being is always moving, constantly struggling to keep his balance and to survive. In the process he learns better and better ways of dealing with the forces that surround him so as to achieve growing competence in personal survival until—step by step by step—he reaches the intellectual, the *visualization* level that is his goal and that will allow him to use *all* his systems in a more organized, profitable way.

If, for one reason or another, a child is unable to organize himself adequately, or in the proper sequence, he will not function at his best in one or more of the perceptual abilities or in one or more of the spatial areas. He will always do his best—everyone does the best he can at a given moment—but his best will not be good enough. Thus, in addition to his other troubles, he faces social stress: children mock, neighbors shun, parents scold, strangers glare—and all the while he is doing his darndest. Under perpetual stress, his endocrine glands are constantly throwing his system out of balance, disturbing his physiological equilibrium, he is *anxious*. *Anxiety,* this visible sign of an inner imbalance that threatens his survival, is often noted in children with learning disorders.

If, on the other hand, a child has developed step by step, organizing economical and efficient ways to overcome stress and maintain balance, he is adaptable. His body and his experiences are fused to such a degree that he can benefit from the past and plan for the future. He has an integrated ego. He should have no major problems in school or in society. He is a very lucky fellow.

4

Where Is Hannah?

TESTING AND EVALUATION

It is easy to pin a label on a child: IQ below 75—mentally retarded; IQ between 70 and 100—slow learner; IQ above 100, but functioning poorly or making bad grades—emotionally disturbed; electroencephalogram reveals lesion on the brain—brain injured.

But parents aren't interested in what label is pinned on their child. If something is wrong with him, they want to know what the cause is and what they can do about it. Our story in this regard is pretty typical of the experience of other parents whose children have learning disorders.

Hannah's first pediatrician soothed our doubts with, "She's a fine, healthy baby."

When she was 11 months old, a supposedly more sophisticated physician diagnosed Hannah's condition as cerebral palsy. He maintained that he could tell that her brain was not functioning normally because of abnormal tightening in her muscles. He advised us to wait until Hannah was two years old before consulting a neurologist.[1]

---

[1]Although he is the one who is consulted most frequently in matters of learning disorders, the neurologist is only one of a number of specialists to whom either the family physician or the pediatrician will refer a child with learning disorders. These other specialists are:

Orthopedist—specialist in treating disorders of the muscular-skeletal system, often involved in diagnosing and treating cerebral palsy (a neuromuscular disease); treatments given include bracing, physical therapy, surgery.

Otolaryngologist—specialist for ears, throat, etc., usually consulted when hearing loss is suspected, since some hearing losses (in the middle and outer ear) are treatable medically and surgically. The diagnosis of hearing loss rather than aphasia is usually made in conjunction with an:

Audiologist—trained in testing hearing ability, but not a medical doctor. Uses special testing equipment (audiometers) and requires much training and experience in making the fine distinctions essential in testing these children. Does the child respond to sound? How loud must the sound be for response?

The neurologist we eventually visited seemed charming enough while he interviewed us and tested Hannah in his consulting room.[2] However, he refused to let me stay with her while the EEG[3] was being taken, despite my plea that, as an

Does the child recognize the sounds to which he responds (an aphasic child might not)?

Ophthalmologist—medical specialist trained in diagnosing and treating diseases of the eyes. As we have seen, a young child may appear to have difficulty "seeing," but have no specific eye problem—just as a child might appear to have difficulty "hearing," with no significant hearing loss. Since more than the eyes are involved in seeing, children with learning disabilities often are given the "all clear" sign by the ophthalmologist when they have visual problems not detectable in the eyes alone.

Optometrist—a specialist in fitting lenses for problems in seeing. An increasing number of optometrists who are members of the Optometric Extension Program (a post-graduate education foundation) are specifically trained in developmental vision and techniques of visual training.

Speech Pathologist—a non-medical specialist trained to diagnose and treat problems in speech, language, and hearing. Not all speech therapists or correctionists are speech pathologists. Specific language training is also done by teachers of the deaf (e.g., with receptive aphasic children).

Allergist—medical specialist in discovering and treating allergies in patients, when specific allergic causes for the child's condition are suspected.

In most cases, the child with learning disorders shows no visible signs of disease or malformation, and the specialist in question will report that the child's eyes, ears, muscles, or nervous system are normal. Sometimes, if the EEG is abnormal, medication is prescribed; or, if a child does not pay attention to objects in the distance or to those close by, he may get a prescription for glasses; or, if he has an odd gait, he may be measured for special shoes. But on the whole, the problem of the child with learning disorders is not considered medical, and the various specialists one consults rarely offer suggestions for future training.

[2] A neurologist tests a child's reflexes, sensation, and abnormal movements, comparing them with those seen in "average" children and adults. In addition to the electroencephalogram, which he usually takes, he may also make a pneumoencephalogram, which involves injecting air into the ventricles (the spaces usually filled with fluid) of the brain so that these spaces can be viewed by X ray. Any unusual displacement of the brain will change the shape of the spaces. Since neurology has traditionally been concerned with adults, most neurologists will agree that they are on the frontier regarding neurological testing of young children.

[3] Electroencephalogram. Small electrodes are attached to the scalp so that the electrical energy present in the brain can be "scanned." The pattern of this energy is traced on a graph by a floating pen controlled by the electrodes. The neurologist compares the pattern to the "brain wave" patterns of "normal" children, and may assume that unusual patterns come from injured brains.

I have frequently been told that having an EEG taken is not as frightening as it looks. But it is still a scary experience, even when you know what to expect. Although I had no way of preparing Hannah for what was about to happen, she was not allowed my familiar presence for reassurance. Instead, four strange giants strapped her to a table, fastened strange contraptions to her head, and stuck pins in her body. She screamed for minutes, whimpered for experienced nurse's aid, I had comforted hundreds of children during the same ordeal. When he finally brought her back to the office, the neurologist, patting Hannah's curly head, said with less than delicacy: "Let's face it, folks, you've got a bad deal. Enjoy her while you can, until the time you will have to put her away."[4]

All right. We had learned that Hannah had a problem and finally knew what that problem was: she couldn't learn as *fast* as the average child, although this did not mean that she couldn't learn most things *eventually*. But none of this knowledge helped us much in planning her future. All the books I had ever read on child development had stressed that the *early* years were the most crucial ones in a child's life. Yet here was Hannah—learning nothing, as far as I could tell. Nobody seemed to have any sound suggestions to offer, and nobody seemed to have just the place that would suit Hannah's needs. As a result, we were forced to try in turn the following facilities that might speed her learning:

Cerebral palsy school—until we took pity on the teacher who, having more than enough on her hands in trying to teach her palsied children how to sit up and how to swallow, could hardly cope with the extra burden of Hannah, who was whirling from room to room, hurling about books and breaking toys, or racing up and down the ramps.

Three normal nursery schools—until she was kicked out after a brief stay of from two weeks to four months.

Speech therapy—for which she was refused because she couldn't talk!

hours, and carried a bad case of claustrophobia with her for a year after this experience.

[4] It is interesting how many special education programs as well as neurologists exhibit such faith in the EEG. Experts seem to agree that this device is quite unreliable in very young children. An abnormal EEG is no proof of actual brain injury, and a normal EEG is no guarantee of a perfectly functioning brain. I did not doubt that Hannah had a brain injury. What puzzled me, however, was how abnormal brain waves could be considered diagnostic of irremedial failure in a child.

An audiology clinic—where she did learn to sit still for five or ten minutes, although she romped about in between.

The famous specialist—who had bound her arm to her body for a year and a half.

A second EEG—requested by the neurologist, this time while Hannah was in a sleeping state. Our previous neurologist, so as to find a satisfactory level of sedation for her, had prescribed barbiturates in ever larger doses.[5] Despite a week of extreme anti-barbiturate reactions (anorexia, insomnia, muscular weakness, and restlessness requiring forcible restraint), the neurologist insisted on her EEG. On the 60-mile drive down, we stopped the car about every ten miles, so that her daddy and I could relieve each other from the physical effort of restraining her. The doctor greeted us with a syringe full of barbiturate, laughingly described as "big enough to kill a horse," and Hannah finally "relaxed." On the drive home, we stopped every ten miles or so because her color was so bad and her breathing was so shallow, that we could not detect it while the car was moving. That memorable week of Hannah's without food or rest was followed by four months of virus infections, which in their turn were succeeded by four years of eating problems.

By the time she was five and a half, it began to look as though someone might be able to do something for Hannah. I found some books about children who sounded like Hannah. A clinic for aphasic children in St. Louis accepted her warily, but luckily without an IQ test, and was as amazed as we that Hannah learned to put two words together almost at once, and made marvelous progress in reading and language in three visits within the next year.

When she was six and a half, the head of the university psychology department who tested her for a local group starting a program for children with learning disorders advised the group not to accept her: "She is too retarded." She could not do things

---

[5] Barbiturates being notorious for working in a reverse way on the majority of brain injured children, I am baffled that he did not try other sedatives.

that two-and-a-half-and three-year-olds could do. None of her test scores indicated better abilities in any area. He suggested that Hannah be enrolled in a program for the trainable mentally retarded. I was crushed by what he said, the figures he showed me—but I didn't believe him. He had the facts, and my feelings made no sense at all, but it seemed to me that testing her at tasks that she couldn't do because she had not learned how made less sense. And, even more unreasonably, I could not see Hannah as a retarded six-year-old; she was more like a bright two-year-old.

The educational director of this new program was even more unreasonable—she accepted Hannah. She assumed that Hannah *came* to the standardized psychological tests with learning problems and would therefore function unlike a child her age. With her serious expressive language problem and poor organization in other areas, no final judgments could be made. Hannah was taken on trial, to see if she *would* function better in a specialized environment. She was not going to be denied the opportunity to learn *now* just because she had not been able to learn certain things in the past.

Given the opportunity of a learning environment with which she could cope, Hannah began to learn—rapidly in some areas, slowly in others, but often faster than either the teacher or I dared expect. During her three years in this program, Hannah *did* perform well on many tests (she was not given intelligence tests per se). At last we had palpable evidence of her ability.

During this same period I was being taught why Hannah learned differently from other children, and how to apply the same principles that were successful in school to managing her at home. Knowing her IQ had been no help, knowing the level on which Hannah was functioning in each area—receptive language, expressive language, coordination, vision, etc.—helped us both. With everyday tasks tailored to her abilities, she enjoyed success after success. The more she could do, the less helpless I felt.

EVALUATING A CHILD

You are a parent. You already know a lot of general things

about your child. The trick is to look at him objectively and see what you can recognize specifically.

He lives in this world of gravity, space, time, sound, light, textures, temperatures, etc., that we have been talking about. Like Hannah, he is coping with these energies with only part of his coping equipment in good working order. Because he is alive and moving, he has organized these factors (energies) the best way he can; he is functioning with the least amount of stress that he can manage.

How is he organized? *How* is he functioning? *How* does he handle stress? Let us see how Hannah, at ten, had learned to cope with the factors in the world. This may make your own job of analysis a little clearer.

HOW WE EVALUATED HANNAH   After ten years of attempting to cope despite underdeveloped coping equipment, Hannah found ways which were successful for her, although they may have appeared immature, reckless, destructive, or aggressive to others. Our evaluation of her learning organization, based on Dr. Barsch's unique approach in evaluating all children, helped us to help Hannah learn more satisfactory ways of coping with the world. This has finally helped others besides one teacher and one mother to see that Hannah really is going somewhere.

Hannah, in ten years, had found that her most successful way of learning was through her ears. They have been her "radar," helping to guide her around the world when her system of visual perception failed her. While moving about, she would jabber, talk, hum, sing, or yell, so as to compensate for the techniques that for her had proved unreliable. Because her visual system is more mature now, she relies less on audition and more on vision to move. She has always resorted to auditory clowning to help her through a stressful situation: "Don't say a word . . . just a minute . . . if I do, what might happen?" A wily youngster with a cute phrase can often distract an adult from the task at hand.

At ten, Hannah was still a toucher, but infinitely less than a year or two earlier, when "Look" sent her hand reaching into a drawer or a box. At ten, "Look" meant looking with her eyes.

Only when faced with too many words on a page, too many people or things in a large room (the epitome of which was a seemingly interminable airport, crowded with people), did she resort to touching to find her way. Along with audition, tactuality has long been a strong area. No wonder her fingers took over when knife and fork grew unwieldy. No wonder she always responded to patting and rubbing when she was upset or excited.

Her receptive auditory abilities are better than mine. She can follow our conversation closely, hear and answer a question from another part of the room, and know what is being said on the television set—all at the same time. I can hardly carry on a conversation in the presence of other sounds, and miss a lot that I hear under the best conditions.

The inconsistencies of the English language still present an expressive problem for Hannah. But, if minimum responses are accepted as language, she has "discussed" such topics as menstruation, brain injury, and ethics. This is hardly the accomplishment of a child half as smart as a ten-year-old. When Hannah can indicate her comprehension with a yes, a no, or a short phrase, she scores at her age level on standardized tests.

Hannah's visual and movement skills have improved tremendously and she uses all she has, although, compared with children her age, she is still an inefficient "looker" and "mover." She reverts to touching when she is excited or must contend with increased multiplicity; numbers are still at a tactual level, for she must manipulate materials in order to know "how many." She knows left and right in herself and other objects, and can direct her movements and the movements of others from verbal commands. At nine, on a trip downtown or to the movies, catastrophe was avoided with whispered stage directions, one sequence at a time, so that she could move "independently" without physical contact. Under most conditions at ten, Hannah needed no verbal instructions.

As all these abilities (TKAV, tactuality, kinesthesia, audition, vision) got organized, she was able to sustain near-space tasks for longer periods of time, was not distracted from completing a task, needed fewer reminders, and could do more than one thing at a time (talk while moving, look while talking, etc.). At nine, Hannah's learning organization was ATKV. At ten, it was AKVT—pretty remarkable considering that movement and visual skills were almost at an infant level a short time before.

Hannah's proficiency in spatial areas is becoming more flexible; she can operate in near, mid, and far space. Near space is not the most stressful now, and shifting from one spatial area to another does not "set her off" as it once did.

The *goal* is still to help her increase her movement and visual proficiency, to integrate all abilities for greater flexibility, and to give her opportunities to practice her new organization. Her academic successes and almost normal (though younger than her age) social behavior are, and will be, the evidence that the goals we had set for her are being met.

EVALUATING YOUR CHILD Now, how can you estimate *your* child's learning organization and spatial proficiencies?

The younger the child, the easier it is, since he will still be relying on early developmental modalities: GOT, perhaps K and A.

What does your child do when given something new or unfamiliar to him? Does he shake, poke, roll, or throw it first (K)? Does he smell it or put it in his mouth (GO)? Does he pick at it with his fingers, manipulate it with his hands (T)? If he is a little older, he may ask you what it is, may be most interested in the noises it makes or that he can make with it (A). (Hannah's favorite animals at the zoo were the "screaming" monkey, the "smelly" wild dog that sounded like a "whimpering" baby, the "noisiest" birds, the "laughing" hyena, and the "trumpeting" elephant.) Your child's investigation of things in the way that is most meaningful to *him* enables *you* to observe the ability or abilities he relies on most.

How does your child describe an object—if he can talk and understand some language, that is? Give him a block, a ball, a pencil. Ask him to tell you about it. You may have to get him started with "What is it?" or "What does it do?" or "How does it feel?" But once he understands that he is supposed to tell about the object, give him another one without asking him about it, and write down everything he says. He'll probably say two or three, rarely more than six, different things about it. After he describes a number of objects, analyze his responses. Are there more K words ("it rolls," "you can throw it"); more tactual words (hard, rough, soft, etc.)? Visual words (square, yellow, big, etc.) are not likely to dominate. You can be sure that he will be consistent in the kinds of words he uses most. It's up to you to "break the code."

It is as important to know which abilities do *not* help your child as it is to know which ones he *does use* to become a viable person. His general movement patterns may be so poorly organized, that just moving from room to room amounts to a major achievement, or cannot be accomplished without falls and much bumping into walls, doors, and furniture. In that case, while he is preoccupied with the problem of moving *himself* about, he will be unable either to reply to any questions you may be asking him, or to fetch you anything you may want him to bring you.

If your child's movements are pretty good, but he is poor in audition, he might still be a bad risk for an errand—but for a different reason. In this case, he could carry something as he moved, but he might not remember what you told him, or he might remember the words but not know exactly what they meant.

If your child has little near-space organization, he might be able to move easily to get his coat, knowing that he is supposed to get his coat, but fail to come back with it. When you go to see what has happened you may find him playing with a penny he has spotted on the floor. Ask him what he is supposed to be doing, and he will probably answer, "Getting my coat," and proceed to get it. Without your extra help, he failed. Why? Getting his coat when you told him "Go get your coat" was an AK task. His audition is poor, and so he failed.

When he fails, try to analyze what the task required, and why he did not succeed. Be a detective. Ask yourself such questions as: (1) Exactly what must be done to succeed at this task? (2) How many separate parts are there to this task? (3) Which body parts and which perceptual abilities are involved in this task and which are not? (4) How much previous experience does he need to succeed? Let's try this on a few specific tasks.

Putting on a coat. A child must recognize (visually) that there are different parts to the coat and that those parts match his body (top, bottom, sleeves for arms, buttons in the front, etc.). Once he finds the place to start, he must get his hand in the proper sleeve hole, pull the sleeve up over his arm with the other hand, find the other side of the coat in back of him, and repeat the arm-in-the-hole process. (This is essentially a kinesthetic-visual task, requiring bilateral arm organization and some organization of back space. Simple? Yes, unless a child has poor kinesthetic or movement organization, has underdeveloped bilaterality, and has hardly begun to organize his back space.)

Going to greet daddy when he comes home. Young children do this without being told. First, a child must have learned through repeated associations that the sound he hears (daddy's car) is a car. He must recognize this sound among any other sounds that are occurring at the time. He must know that this car is daddy's car, which means that daddy will soon appear. In order to get to the door to meet daddy, the child must know both *where* the door is relative to his *own* position, and *how* he can get there. (This is essentially an auditory-visual-kinesthetic task requiring a great deal of mid- and far-space organization.)

Playing detective makes it clearer that your child needs not only *organization* of perceptual systems if he is to succeed at anything, but that he must be able to *use* these systems in certain spatial areas. This adds one more question to our list: *Where* does the task occur? He will be fairly consistent as to the spatial areas in which he will succeed and those in which he will fail. You must observe to find his pattern. (In Hannah's case, near space was very poorly organized. So I structured her near space for her by sitting close to her so that she could finish her lunch or get dressed faster and better.) If your child cannot sustain looking at a book, playing with puzzles, or finishing a meal in the presence of normal family distractions, he does not have sufficient near-space organization. Yelling at him from across the room gets no results, so you have probably learned to go over to get his attention, or even to touch him, as I often had to do with Hannah.

On the other hand, he may be able to play for hours with one thing, but he will not hear you when you walk up to him or will be completely surprised if someone shouts at him. If he relies too much on near space and the perceptions operating in it (GOT), he will be thoroughly upset by attempts to change his world. He will avoid mid- and far-space activities, because he cannot attend to whatever is "way out there."

While the world of the "far-space child" needs to be contracted for building his perceptual organization for use in near space, the world of the "near-space child" must be expanded to enable him to function perceptually at ever greater distances from himself.

Now you can estimate your child's learning organization:

1. He relies most on .... to learn and get along. (For Hannah, *now* A and V.)
2. If the task is too difficult for the systems he now prefers .... (Hannah's A and V), he will "regress" to the lower ability .... (Hannah uses T to enhance A and V.)
3. He is deficient in .... (Hannah's greatest problem is K; V is difficult.)
4. The spatial area he prefers is .... (Hannah's once was *far*, but now *far, mid,* and *near* are very nearly balanced.)
5. Under stress, he will prefer .... space. (Hannah prefers *far* under stress, and may start "wandering.")

You can analyze a task:

1. To *begin* the task successfully, one must .... (look, listen and comprehend, feel, move?)

2. To *perform* the task, one must then .... (look, answer with words, move oneself, move part of oneself, feel?) *All* successful performance involves movements, but which systems must be moved? Most successful performances involve vision.

3. To *complete* the task, one must ....

4. Therefore, this task requires this sequence of abilities: ....

5. The task and the abilities necessary to perform it must be carried out in which spatial area or sequences of spatial areas? .... (near, mid, far?) on which spatial meridians? .... (lateral, vertical, depth?)

The whole point of these endeavors on your part is to find tasks, or to adjust tasks, to *your* child's learning organization.

ANALYZING EACH MODALITY You can guess which tasks your child *is* capable of mastering now, and *how* he manages to do so; which tasks he *is not* capable of mastering yet, and *why* he cannot do so. To some degree, you can accomplish this by learning which perceptive techniques and spatial areas he prefers. But this is only part of your evaluation. Although very likely he is not even proficient in those techniques on which he relies most, your child probably has some degree of capability even in those most poorly organized.

Your next step is to attempt to find out *how* well each system is organized in your child. A youngster with learning disabilities will not be proficient in all aspects of a given approach to learning, even when his life almost depends on the mastery of it. Here is a checklist for each perceptive system. Add to it whatever additional aspects come to your mind:

- *Gustation*—chews, sucks, swallows (both food and saliva), blows, inhales and exhales voluntarily, blows his nose, talks intelligently, imitates tongue and lip movements.

- *Olfaction*—becomes aware of, actively smells, identifies, localizes, differentiates, and associates various odors with their sources.

- *Tactuality*—localizes a place where he is touched, identifies textures, matches similar textures, names textures and degrees of heat (hot, warm, cool, cold, etc.), recognizes the source of pain and relates objects with the source of touch (matches burn, knives cut, fur is soft and feels good, etc.).

- *Kinesthesia*—moves from place to place; hops on his feet; rolls reasonably straight; crawls forward or backward; performs two-handed tasks (beading, unscrewing jar lids, removing box lids, etc.); uses fingers separately (especially thumb and forefinger); catches an object and aims it at a target with either hand; maneuvers under, around, and over objects without knocking them over or bumping himself; skips; rides a two-wheeled bike; does a forward or backward somersault in a straight direction, landing on his feet; draws and writes appropriately for his age.

- *Audition*—localizes sound, identifies voices and sounds, understands language and follows commands, imitates sounds and words accurately, remembers a series of numbers, sounds, or words (2, 9, 7 or do-mi-la), hears likenesses and differences in sounds and words and can rhyme words; *expressive:* talks in words, sentences; uses pronouns, adjectives, and prepositions accurately; answers questions with appropriate response. His expressive language will mirror his general learning organization.

- *Vision*—reaches and grasps accurately with either hand; locates items he drops; knows proper places for items in the house (his clothes, toys, food); recognizes and points to pictures; recognizes visual similarities and differences in objects and pictures; locates with his *eyes* objects near and far; sustains looking at something for more than a few seconds; follows with his *eyes* a moving target (at first near him, then farther away); keeps a task in front of him at his midline with his head straight; *both eyes* remain "on target" when a small, bright object is moved closer to him (up to three to six inches from his nose); in general *looks at* what he is doing and where he is going (eyes lead movements).

You might summarize a child's performance in each modality as follows:
1. The child moves easily through the majority of tasks involving this modality.
2. He performs some, but not the majority, of tasks using this modality.
3. He performs few, or none, of the tasks well, involving this modality.

In this way, you'll have some gauge for judging "How good is his Audition, his Tactuality, his Kinesthesia, his Vision? How much can he use his A, his T, his K, his V, or his GO?"

You won't know everything. It would take an optometrist trained in childhood vision to evaluate fully your child's visual-movement skills; a speech pathologist trained in language development to evaluate fully his receptive and expressive language and speech. But you will be able to begin seeing the "peaks and valleys," his better and poorer abilities, which are so familiar to professional personnel. You will understand how he can read his sister's first-grade book but cannot tie his shoes, and many of his other seeming inconsistencies.

Although Hannah consistently used tactuality as a primary method for learning about the world, her tactual abilities were quite deficient in some areas. I have mentioned her poor awareness of the lower part of her body, her apparent insensitivity to pain. Poor tactuality probably explains why she was so interested in all kinds of injury and wanted to explore their possibilities: "If I do, what might happen?" She wanted to touch a lighted match, to put her finger between scissor blades, to hear about jumping off high places, and she speculated on trying all these things. Mere explanations could not satisfy Hannah's curiosity about dangerous situations, for, without the *experience,* Hannah had no conception of what "hurt" meant. Over the years, we have had quite a few lessons in which we let her experience the nature of small "hurts," so as to enable her to remember "what might happen" and thereby quell her desire to court danger at every opportunity.

Once you know as much as you can about how your child learns, you will profit a lot more from his next psychological or educational evaluation. You will have a key to why he made a poor score. By changing difficult tasks into achievable tasks, by adapting the world to your child's levels of performance, you will allow him to succeed more often. Where he previously failed, he will learn, beginning a positive new cycle. He will be a better-organized, more self-sufficient, happier child. Like Hannah, he will change "I can't how!" into "I did it myself!"

PSYCHOLOGICAL TESTING

Hannah had been tested and found "too severely retarded" for the program into which she was nevertheless accepted. But, after three and a half years, her class was beyond the age limit for this program.

They all had to be tested with standard psychological tests as candidates for the year-old public school perceptually handicapped class. Once again, Hannah's difficulty with expressive language and movement skills hampered her performance to such an extent that she was on the bottom of the list of 30 children under consideration for the seven openings.

She was again classified as mentally retarded, which popularly means a reduced capacity for learning regardless of the training she might be given. Since she had been advancing at the rate of two or three years in one year's time, in one area after another, this label did not stick with her teacher or her parents. Of course, her behavior and performance were not up to the level of other children her age; she had learning problems that they had never had to face. She could not learn as they did yet. But if she *could* learn standing on her head, lying on the floor, or hanging from the light fixture—whatever environment it was determined that she needed—then she did have the capacity. Maybe she *was* functioning like a four-year-old in her sixth year, but she had jumped from two-year-old to four-year-old in less than one year when given the opportunity.

She has continued to "make up time," increasingly closing the gap between her chronological age and her developmental age. A mentally retarded child cannot learn *one* year's work in one year; Hannah has learned two and three years' work in the same time. Hannah had striking variations in her various abilities; a mentally retarded child may function at a lower level than a normal child; but, like a normal child, his visual, auditory, and movement skills will all be at about the same developmental level.

THE PRINCIPLES OF TESTING A psychologist's job is to find out how much your child, or my child, has learned in comparison with other children his age. The tools used for this comparison are various psychological tests. The amount a child has learned, combined with his ability to apply his knowledge and experience, constitutes his "intelligence."

The forbidding term IQ (or intelligence quotient) means that for practical purposes a number is attached to the comparison between children. If a certain test is given to a thousand seven-year-olds the majority of whom pass all the items in that test, then that test is considered to determine what is average for seven-year-olds, and the number 100 is assigned to it. An average seven-year-old, then, has an IQ of 100. A child who passes not only all the seven-year-old items but many tasks that average eight- and nine-year-olds pass would be above average and have an IQ above 100. If he does not pass all the items the average seven-year-olds pass, his IQ is below 100. This would seem a reasonable way to compare children, and has been the best way available for over 50 years.

The assumption in this kind of testing, however, is that most seven-year-old children have had equal opportunities for development, that they have organized their learning equipment at about the same rate, function equally in most spatial areas, etc. Each test item requires some combination of processing abilities, usually VAKT, which means that a child must have his abilities sufficiently organized to succeed at that task. If children with learning disabilities do not have the organizations for learning that they should, they do not have an equal chance for success on any kind of test item.

But how can a test prove that because Hannah cannot fold

a piece of paper into a triangle as well as other children her age and younger, she will never learn to do this, nor learn to read and write? All this really shows is that she has such difficulty in performing this visual-kinesthetic task that, at six, she operated more like a three-year-old than a six-year-old.

SPECIFIC TESTS Here are a few of the tests most commonly used for children with learning disabilities, and what can be learned from them:

- *Stanford-Binet.* One of the most widely used intelligence tests, it is largely a verbal test. The child is asked most of the questions, and is expected to indicate what he knows through talking. This assumes that a child can use language to represent his past experiences and to indicate his abilities in problem-solving, etc. Obviously, a child with speech and/or language difficulties would do poorly on this kind of test.

- *Wechsler Intelligence Scale for Children (WISC).* The WISC, the other widely used intelligence test, is used more often for children with learning problems because it attempts to test language and performance separately. Verbal tests include vocabulary, language comprehension, arithmetic, memory. The five performance tests, which do not require talking responses, include block designs, putting picture stories in the proper sequence, assembling cut-up objects. Although we end up with one score for the verbal tests, another score for the performance tests, and a general score combining the results of the two, each task must be analyzed separately if we wish to know what is really required for passing each test item. The reason for this is that some of the verbal tests—arithmetic, for example —are not purely verbal, and that some of the performance tests go beyond performance, inasmuch as the child has to be able to understand and follow the directions for doing the test.

- *Illinois Test for Psycholinguistic Abilities (I.T.P.A.).* The

I.T.P.A., available for about six years, gives a more accurate learning profile. Both visual and auditory abilities are divided as to comprehension, expression, and association (thinking). On the Stanford-Binet, Hannah's IQ was 49. On the I.T.P.A., which revealed her strengths as well as her weaknesses, she scored within normal limits in auditory comprehension and association at seven years old. After two years of training, more and more areas appeared within the normal limits on this test, while she still made a "mentally retarded" score on the WISC.

- *Bender-Gestalt Test.* The child is required to copy several cards with drawings of forms and patterns on them. This test involves visual-kinesthetic and spatial organizations performed nearby. It taps only one spatial area of function; therefore it cannot be a definitive diagnostic tool. Unless the child is observed in *how* he does the task, the score alone reveals little information useful for specific training. Since most children with learning disorders are notoriously bad at copying tasks, they could be expected to score poorly.

- *Frostig Test of Visual Perception.* A test for visual-kinesthetic organizations, a comparison with "normal" children on drawing of lines, recognizing and copying shapes, recognizing directionality, etc., which determines the age level on which the child is operating in each area.

- *Peabody Picture Vocabulary Test* and *Ammons Picture Test.* Both tests offer the child a series of pictures together with a spoken word. He is to find the picture which most accurately matches the meaning of the word. Often IQ's are derived from these tests, which are primarily auditory-visual tasks and chiefly indicate the child's receptive vocabulary skills and ability at interpreting pictures, certainly not his over-all abilities.

HANNAH AND THE TESTS There are hundreds of other tests which assess certain modalities of a child and compare his performance with that of other test subjects. The score, that is, an index of what the child knows and can do, permits one to form certain expectations of a child's intellectual and manipulative capabilities. The average score per age group is 100. Hannah's IQ score was 49. Usually, children with IQ's below 50 are classified as "trainable mentally retarded." "Educable mentally retarded," meaning that they will eventually learn to read and write, fall between 50 and 75 or 80. Children who score nearer normal, 75 to 100, are called slow learners or "children with learning disabilities." Children like Hannah, who do poorly on a static test, are often denied the opportunity to learn simply because their learning problems have kept them from learning in the past, under "normal" conditions.

And, on this basis, three well-known residential schools for "brain-injured children" turned her down. They were all kind, sympathetic, and helpful, recommending various institutions for trainable retarded children around the country. Apparently, one had to know Hannah to love her, or to have any idea of what her capabilities actually were.

I had always been sure she was bright, regardless of the documentary evidence to the contrary. But, under the pressure of rejection after rejection and fear that if she *were* finally admitted to the local public school program it would be an inferior situation, I tried to analyze my faith in her real capabilities.

There was of course her ability to see the humor in many situations and to create humor even before she could express herself verbally. For example, her "If I do, what might happen?" meant she understood cause and effect and was interested in learning more. It made for real comedy if she managed to intimate, even though she could not express it in so many words, "If I do put this onion in the chocolate-cake batter, what will happen?"

There was also Hannah's ability to perform a difficult task if she understood "why." Young children learn proper behavior and correct speech largely by imitation, a method Hannah found difficult to follow. But once she understood why you don't talk to strangers and why you usually kiss only relatives, she could try to act on this knowledge. If the mad intricacies of the English language were explained to her—you go *to* your house, but you are now *at* your house—she would try to use the words in the right place.

Perhaps, most of all, there was her fantastic drive to learn, in spite of her tremendous problems. She struggled to learn to tie her shoe, because one expert had said that she could and told me how I could teach her, step by step, when it was a task, even now four and a half years later, way beyond her developmental level—but she learned it. When she needs to be "alone" she manages the situation for herself, once by going to her room, now merely by turning away or asking others not to talk to her. Frustrated but undaunted by the many things she still cannot do, she continually returns to the tasks that have beaten her to try again, like riding a two-wheeled bike, which has challenged her for years. She often speaks of "when I grow up" or "when I'm big" in regard to the things she is not yet allowed to do, as "I'll cross the street by myself" or "I'll walk to school" or "I'll drive the car when I learn how." When her teacher explained that she could not yet cross a busy street alone because "sometimes your eyes forget to tell your brain," and that that was the reason why Hannah had to do the visual-training tasks, Hannah worked harder at them than ever before.

All right, her teacher and I knew we had a smart little girl on our hands, but the rest of the world seemed to have an opposite opinion. Either the world was wrong and we were right, or we were wrong and the world was right.

At nine and a half, she was taken to Dr. Ray H. Barsch for an evaluation. Dr. Barsch had become widely known for his research in Movigenic theory, which is the relationship between movement and learning efficiency. And so, given the nature of Hannah's problem, we were eager to see what he had to say.

For the first time, in front of my eyes, someone was finding out everything I knew that she could and couldn't do, and many things that she could and could not do that I had never discovered. I was thrilled, but fearful of his prognosis. He told us that there was no question but that Hannah had a very high potential. We must decide where to go from here. If we sent her to a residential school, she would surely come out organized and controlled, with a probable IQ of 85 (quite a jump beyond 49), for the low points of her irregular learning organization would be brought up, while the high points would be brought down.

If we could keep her at home and provide her with some sort of school situation to provide her with a substitute for the social experience she was missing, while continuing her movigenics training by means of her teacher's tutoring and my home "lessons," we had a good chance of raising her IQ to 125.[6]

There was no question in my husband's mind or my own that we had no choice. We had to gamble for the 125 IQ, for we could, if need be, fall back on the set-up for an IQ of 85.

HANNAH'S SCHOOL EXPERIENCES

So we tried keeping Hannah at home. With the daily tutoring by her teacher and my home lessons, her learning proceeded by leaps and bounds. After she had been out of school six months, we arranged for her to sit in at a regular first-grade class of a nearby school for an hour each afternoon. Soon after this arrangement began, the perceptually handicapped class finally accepted her. Hannah was blooming, nourished by movigenics training and renewed social experiences with other children.

Then the fine teacher of the "normal" first-grade class had to retire because of pregnancy, and a student teacher who replaced her was "afraid" of Hannah. Soon Hannah's behavior regressed so markedly that we looked for further reasons—and found them in the teacher of the perceptually handicapped class; she was without training, experience, or inclination for teaching children with learning disorders. We had to withdraw Hannah from both classes, since she was not welcome in the former and was being harmed by the latter.

And once again Hannah was asking her brother each morning, as she handed him his books, "You go school today?" Once

---

[6] According to the Stanford-Binet scale, an IQ of 125 places a child in the highest 10% of the intellectual scale. Yet, with her developmental lags that remained at nine and a half, Hannah still could not perform many of the six-year-old level tasks on the Stanford-Binet test.

again, watching the "big" children boarding a school bus or the "little" children (smaller than she) cutting through our yard to their school, she asked me, "When I grow up, I go to school?"

She became bored and rebellious during our lessons, began to have foggy days again. Clearly, a little girl who loved children so much and who had had such rewarding school experiences could not go another year without children or school. When she was ten and a half we enrolled her in a residential "school for children with emotional disorders," which was willing to have Hannah just *because* she had problems. Giving her up for we knew not how long was hard on us. Yet Hannah was more than ready to be with children. It was high time for her to find her "place" in the world beyond our four walls and her immediate family.

As soon as her father could get situated in a new business, we sold our house and moved close enough to the new school so that Hannah could come home for a weekend each month. In only six months, the clouds lifted. We found a tiny but excellent school in our new home town. The school rearranged itself in order to admit Hannah. Hannah had already organized herself well enough to be admitted. The school's director was a revelation. Except for Hannah's one great teacher who had worked with her now for four years, "educators" had looked upon Hannah as (1) uneducable; (2) incorrigible; (3) the shocking product of gross mismanagement by her parents; or (4) a sort of monster, from whom anything might be expected. This educator saw only a child when she looked at Hannah, a child with gifts and a child with gaps in her education.

WHAT YOU CAN DO FOR YOUR CHILD

Your child may not be called mentally retarded. You may be told that he is just slow and will grow out of it. It is true that you can create problems by comparing children too closely. It is also true that parents who have been anxious about their children have received no help—only reassurances—until their children were rejected for, or failed in, the first grade. For five or six years, when they needed it most, they had no help in learning to live with their child and his problems, nor in learning how to help him develop more efficiently.

If your child is classified as mentally retarded, or if your fears for his "slowness" are called groundless, don't give up if you are not satisfied with the evaluation. If he is called brain injured, perceptually handicapped, or neurologically impaired, don't give up. There are people and places and ways to help you and your child.

Ten years have passed since Hannah was diagnosed. You may not be in the discouraging situation that we found ourselves in when Hannah was three, four, and five, and again when she was nine, and there were no programs available for her. You may not have to send your child away for a suitable education. You may not have to move your whole family to a community that offers him what your present community does not. Look first in your own city. If your child is younger than school age, help may be waiting at a local speech and hearing clinic, a nursery school for handicapped children, a branch of the Society for Crippled Children, or a United Cerebral Palsy program. If there is a college or a university nearby, find out whether it has a department of special education or one of speech and hearing which needs certain children in training its specialists.

When your child reaches school age—or preferably before—visit the head of your local school district. This is the first place to start seeking help. You, as well as the medical doctor who may have given you the bad news, might be surprised at what you can find right in your own backyard. Your United Community Fund, if your town has one, may also be able to advise you which local agencies are set up to meet needs such as yours.

Just don't give up. And don't wait. Six is not the magical age we have long considered it. A child's preparation for academic and social survival starts long before kindergarten and first grade.

The best answer lies in your own community. If there are no classes for your child yet, parent groups usually start the ball rolling for public or private classes. You'll be surprised to find that you are not alone, that there are plenty of other parents with similar problems who are as concerned for their children as you are for yours.[7]

If all else fails and a residential school does seem to be the best solution for your child and his family, there are a few excellent ones. However, because of the necessity for very small classes, individualized teaching, and heavily supervised living arrangements, the cost is higher than for the ordinary private residential school.

Your child's behavior will tell you what he needs if you learn to observe him carefully. For example, try to determine what holds your child's interest the longest when he is looking at a book. Is it acting out the pictures, pretending to eat the pictures of food (G and K)? Is it pointing to the picture asking you to supply the names (T), or naming and talking himself (A)?

It is not likely that merely looking at the book, getting all the meaning available through his eyes alone (V), will hold his interest. What helps him to pay attention while he looks at the book? Does he wiggle his foot, his arm, or himself (K)? Does he jabber or vocalize constantly (A), twist and untwist his hair or clothing (T), or chew on his fingers, hair, shirt, or tongue (G)?

As you learn to evaluate your own child and to understand his learning organization, you will be better able to decide what situations would be detrimental and which educational techniques or special classes would be most helpful to him. You will listen respectfully and with an open mind to professionals as they explain your child to you, but you will temper their verdicts with what you know yourself. They may not be 100% right, but you are probably not either. You may even be able to accept for your child a mediocre program (in order to keep the whole family in your present community) because you can bolster his development with what you understand about him, and supplement his training with some of the ideas presented in the next two chapters.

[7]There are a number of national organizations which exist in order to advance the status of handicapped children. They will send literature on progress in their special fields, available training programs, parent groups, etc. See Appendix B for names and addresses of some of these organizations.

5

How Can Hannah Learn?

TEACHING

She cannot learn much in an ordinary environment, so we have to change the environment. She cannot learn easily in the ordinary way, so we have to teach her in the ways she can learn best.[1]

ENVIRONMENT

Poorly organized spatially and perceptually, Hannah needs more than the stripped-down classroom and bedroom we have read about. She needs *all* the stress factors reduced in order to operate more efficiently.

SPACE Like most young children, she cannot maintain much near-space organization of her own. We must build this organization for her physically: keep her close to us when we want her to pay attention, even touch her if she is more in need of our support. When Hannah outgrew sitting on my lap, or when I read to another child at the same time, I learned to read upside down, so that she could see the story right side up, and so that she could touch the pictures (tactual-visual experience precedes visual experience alone) when I gave her permission to do so.

For desk work (coloring, tracing, dots, drawing, etc.) I faced her table or desk to a blank wall. I put my arm on the back of her chair when her task was hard for her, for the nearer I was the better she could do. I held her interest by focusing on her work area, delimiting the space with a colored placemat, a colored tape outline, or a frame drawn with a marking pen, and

---

[1] According to the principles of Dr. Ray H. Barsch's proven theories of development and how it can be enhanced.

with a spotlight or some other marked lighting contrast. I had to remind myself to keep near-space activities short, even when she was doing well; to break them up with less stressful activities. No one learns anything under too much stress.

For moving around, I had to learn to spell out every move. "We're going out" was almost sure to draw a blank. I learned instead to say, "We're going to the park. First we will get our coats. Let's see, where are our coats?" We found them. "Now, let's put our coats on," and I stayed with her until she got hers on. Now, if my coat was not already on or I had forgotten to get my keys and purse first, "Stand by this chair and wait." If I had to leave the room or be gone more than a minute, I reminded her to wait another time or two, "I will tell you when we are ready!" Ready. Okay, "We are going out the back door." (Earlier, or in a strange place, I would have said "We're going that way" and pointed. I may have had to lead her physically.) "Stop at the door. Wait. Now, open the door." In case she took off for the driveway, bypassing the car, "Stop!" "Come." When she came, "Wait until I open the door . . . Get in . . . Can you close the door? Try. Good. Lock it. Now I will get in, and we will go to the park."—and we were still in the garage!

A lot of words, but never many at once, the bare minimum to get the job done. I had been told by her teacher that Hannah must never wander, that she must move meaningfully. Left to her own devices, she would wander, so I had to direct her movements. Directing the movements of a child as disorganized and hyperactive as Hannah once was often meant forming a circle around her with my arms. When we went to a movie, the zoo, or downtown, I could not expect her to go in the right direction or stay with me. With her poor kinesthesia, she could not have walked in a straight line even if she had known then what "straight" meant. She could not stay with me on her own because she could not keep track of where I was; she was having enough trouble just moving. I held her hand as we went down an aisle or a street.

TIME   An extremely important yet often-neglected factor in a child's success is *time*. Everyone has a built-in rhythm. A child's is usually faster than an adult's. But some children with learning problems have exceptionally slow rhythms. Whatever your child's rhythm, you must accommodate to it if he is to succeed. Time, like space, is a constant factor in every task and every performance.

Hannah "got lost" in the middle of any activity, so I would often need to remind her during tooth-brushing, for instance, always keeping just a tiny bit ahead of what she did, to squeeze just a little toothpaste as she was unscrewing the cap, to put the cap back on just before she finished squeezing, to put the tube away just before she finished getting the cap on, etc. Since she also tended to get lost *between* activities, I would prepare her for target-throwing just a fraction of a second *before* she finished tracing, suggest riding her tricycle just a fraction *before* she finished her breakfast.

A child with expressive language or kinesthetic problems needs extra time to come up with a response. With Hannah, who had both, we had to reduce the stimuli as much as possible and wait for a response, as long as 30 seconds or more. Any new stimulus, any kind of visual, auditory, or tactual interruption, would distract her and she could not respond. If we asked, "What do you think is in that box?" then took a bite out of an apple, and next suggested she change her seat or move her table closer to her, she lost the sense of all these disparate questions and statements. Since it took her so long to get herself moving, we could not ask her to "pick out the longest stick" and then interrupt the request and still expect her to perform, for we had distracted her.

Most mothers take a long *time* to realize that a child who does not answer or act as quickly as most children may nevertheless know how to answer or act, if he is just given enough time. Many teachers and evaluators who give timed psychological tests to children with learning disorders have also failed to discover this.

Several short lessons are much more effective than one long one for any child with learning problems. Three 3- to 5-minute target-throwing sessions get better results than one 15-minute session. He may get worse the longer and harder he tries. And he will probably gain a lot more by stopping as soon as he has achieved one successful hit than he would by trying to duplicate his feat drill fashion.

If he is like most children with learning disorders, there is no time like "the present" for him, because for him there is no time *but* the present. "Before," "after a while," or "not yet" mean nothing to him. He doesn't remember when something is going to happen, because he never understood in the first place when it would happen. Obviously, since he can't know what to expect, *any* change might upset him, even a fairly regular one in the normal order of his day. Imagine his suffering when there is actually a variation in his routine! That is why I helped Hannah to structure her time, told her what would happen next, and what had happened before "now" so that she could finally understand it, and be reassured.

A calendar alone is not enough, but it helps, with its static, visual clues to the past and future. Daily, weekly, and monthly calendars all help. On a weekly or monthly calendar, I (later, Hannah) would see what happened yesterday, talk about its being "finished," "all gone," X it out. We could look back and see what else had gone before. We talked about what the calendar said would happen today, how the weather was today, and where we would go and what we would do first, next, and next, and next, sometimes referring to it several times in a day. We talked about what would happen tomorrow, and what would happen the next day and next week (seven days or "seven sleeps"), and even next month. We rarely had more than a monthly calendar, except to discuss holidays, birthdays, the sequence of months, or the seasons, which were not personal calendars for daily reference. But a boy in Hannah's school, who was violently disturbed by any variation in his routine or even any change from what he was doing at the moment, needed a yearly calendar, which he thumbed through and looked at 20 times a day.

Don't worry if your child cannot read yet; he can still get the idea, especially if you draw any kind of crude picture illustrating the activity or event. He can still mark out (or "help" you mark out) what is already gone, learn to understand where "today" is and that tomorrow will come next, and may very well get a big boost in his reading by examining the words and numbers from his calendar. "Tomorrow" may make no sense to him, but he will begin to understand "wait" or "one sleep." "Next week" becomes something he can grasp when it is "wait, wait, wait, wait, wait, wait, wait," always as you are pointing, of course, with his hand or finger until he can do the pointing himself.

Parents must develop a great deal of flexibility and learn to pace their conversations with their child and to adjust the tempo of his lessons and activities. But this effort is worthwhile, because of the tremendous effect time has on the child's stress threshold, and hence on the level of his performance.

LANGUAGE Parents have to adjust their language to fit their child's comprehension, even if it means talking in "shorthand." When "It's time to play with the blocks now, Hannah. Get your blocks and bring them over here by the window. You can sit next to this chest. Put your blocks on the floor" floated right over Hannah's head, "Hannah, blocks on floor" got the job done.

Hannah learned best through audition, so I used audition in all new tasks so she could succeed. I would structure a visual-kinesthetic-tactual task for her auditorially: "Pick up the red block. What is it?" If she answered correctly, we continued. If incorrectly or not at all, I gave her more structuring: "Is it a triangle? When is it a square?" If she still could not answer, but I assumed that she knew it but could not initiate it, "It is a ...." Then, "Where does it go? Put it there."

Gradually, as she became more familiar with a task, auditory structuring became less definite and more "decisions" were left up to her. Soon I had only to say, "Pick up a block. Put it where it goes." The goal for each task—sorting blocks or whatever—was to perform with *no* auditory clues.

If a child uses audition least efficiently of all his systems, tasks may include some auditory aspects, combined with his better-organized areas. If he can manipulate (VK), add some audition to his visual-kinesthetic tasks. Have him fit a piece to a jigsaw puzzle or throw a beanbag at a target only when he *hears* a signal (bell, word, noise). When the main idea of a task is to teach him all you can about movement and space, by playing Musical Chairs for instance, you wouldn't use music as a signal and thereby make things tougher for him. Instead, you might use a flashing light as a guide.

Some children have trouble organizing auditory space. They may ignore commands from across the room which they obey from nearby. They may "hear" directions better when they are whispered, or "hear" them better when they are almost shouted.

Watch your phrasing. Think positively for positive results. "Don't move that chair" verbalizes the very thing you want him to stop. "Put down the chair and come" tells him what to do. Don't reinforce an incorrect response by restating his error. If he is four and answers "Five" to "How old are you?" don't say "No, you are not five. How old are you?" A simple "No. How old are you?" is much better. You may have to help him a bit more by saying, "You are . . . ."

If your child gains little information auditorially, use gestures (V) and physical contact (T) to get an idea across. The purpose of language is, after all, to communicate. If he is young and disorganized but can "listen" to some extent, talk to him in concrete terms, about the immediate, in language on his level.

MULTIPLICITY Your child, like Hannah and the Signal Corps, may be able to "do the impossible" if the task is broken down for him into its component parts, and if you present each part, in order, as he is ready for it. This is another way of finding out, too, which parts of a task are the hardest for him.

"Hannah, wash your hands" once meant failure or chaos. Breaking down the multiplicity and complexity of "washing your hands" into one part at a time got her to wash her own hands:

1. Find the faucet (VT).

2. Turn it that way *or* turn it on *or* turn it to the right (K).

3. That's enough. Stop turning.

4. Find the soap (VT).

5. Pick up the soap (K).

6. Rub the soap on your hands (a bilateral task).

7. Put the soap back where you got it (visual memory as well as K).

8. Rub the soap all over your hands. No. Keep rubbing until the dirt is gone.

9. That's enough. Stop rubbing.

10. Put your hands under the water.

11. Rinse off all the soap.

12. Find the faucet again. No, that's the wrong one. Yes, that one.

13. Turn it off. Turn it that way *or* in the opposite direction *or* to the left.

14. Stop turning. It's off now.

Note that she has not even started to dry her hands. But it is surprising how many self-help and household tasks a child can perform with this kind of breaking-down into parts.

A child will succeed at a task that is appropriate for him: too easy—he balks, whines, wiggles, or fools around; too hard (because it is too complex)—he will probably try. He may become so frustrated with a jigsaw puzzle with too many pieces on hand that he will have to cry, or throw the pieces, or explode in some other way. Hand him one piece at a time and he may work the same puzzle in short order. The secret of your child's success lies in your knowing how much "extra" he can tolerate and still be able to perform, so that you can limit the multiplicity factor for all tasks he has to accomplish. When in doubt, choose too few parts, never too many.

LEVEL   Does a task fit a child's abilities? Yes? He will succeed. But if none of his spatial or perceptual areas are as well organized as they could be, remember that you must find out how well *each* is organized. Just because a child can do *one* thing on a certain level does not mean that he can do *everything* on that level. As far as learning goes, none of us is on a perfectly even keel, much less a child with learning problems.

This fools many people. Take the case of Hannah-and-the-hanger. When Hannah sat in on the first-grade class, for the first time in her life she was required to hang her coat on a hanger. She had had hooks in school and at home. The excellent (but inexperienced in special education) first-grade teacher assumed from this and other things that Hannah could not do that she was simply functioning on a very low general level. To save Hannah embarrassment and promote kindness in the smaller children, she had them hang up the coat for Hannah.

When Hannah started in the perceptually handicapped class a few weeks later, she was again faced with a hanger. This teacher had found out how well Hannah could read. She assumed that Hannah could do everything on the relatively high level of her reading, but was deliberately making an issue of it. Being a very poor teacher as well as inexperienced in special education, she insisted that Hannah hang up her coat. She gave her no verbal help (merely urging her to "hurry" so that the stress factor of time was added) nor spatial help (standing across the room as Hannah struggled to comply).

When her teacher of three and a half years, now her tutor, learned what was happening, she taught Hannah over one weekend to hang her coat on a hanger, using illustrations and words for each single step of the operation, one at a time. When Hannah returned to the first-grade class with her new skill, the teacher there was delighted, and Hannah's status was now raised in the eyes of all the children, including Hannah's. It did not help with the other teacher, who still did not give her the time or the understanding that such a difficult task required.

Today, Hannah can climb a tree like a 12-year-old, but her expressive language is at a six-year level. Her reading comprehension is excellent, her arithmetic regrettable. Her grasp of concepts is astounding, but she still has a terrible time printing her name.

SCHEDULE   *This* then is *structuring:* arranging a child's environment to control the stress factors—space, time, language, multiplicity, and level—to the degree that he can handle them and perform successfully *and* enhance his learning.

Since your relationship with your child is probably an almost constant teaching-learning relation, it may be easier for both of you to set up a regular lesson time each day to train him in tasks that do not arise in the ordinary course of the day. Lesson time must, of course, be in the same place, at the same time, in the same basic form each day, so that even if he rebels at first at mother playing "teacher," he will soon look forward to his "lesson." It is important to consider all the stress factors—alternate near-space tasks with mid- and far-space ones, or difficult tasks with simple and pleasant ones; use his better-organized areas to help along his worse-organized ones; and—most important—use a *variety* of training methods, so that neither of you will become bored.

I was lucky enough to have the help of a live-in girl in the evening and of a part-time maid in managing Hannah during her most trying years, until she was nine. If you can't afford such help, and if your husband has neither the spare time nor the inclination to take over for a regular period each day, or if too many other young children in the family will not allow "formal" teaching, this is not your only recourse. There is a lot of "teaching" to be done as you go about your regular household routine, as I shall explain later in this chapter.

Some of you may just be able to get at the lessons each day. I am not that well organized. I found that the only way I could avoid repeating activities too often or neglecting valuable activities too long, while balancing tasks spatially, perceptually, and for degree of difficulty, was to make a weekly schedule. Such a schedule had to be flexible enough to eliminate activities and shorten the period on relatively bad days, and to add activities and make the lesson longer on good days.

When I first started "lessons" with Hannah she was about four and a half. The lessons lasted 15 minutes to a half hour, and included finding and identifying things by touch, movement activities connected with a verbal command, some visual targeting for which she was not ready, and anything else I could find in whatever training books I could scrape up. Even I did not need a schedule for the one or two tasks we could work on at a session.

At six, Hannah's daily training in the methods I had learned at the language clinic[2] and in a few suitable books lasted from 45 minutes to one and a half hours. In June, 1964, when we added Gerald Getman's procedures to our program (see Schedule I), we continued to run about the same time, and the results were even more remarkable. In September, 1965, after our visit to Dr. Ray H. Barsch, we not only increased our lesson time to about two hours a day, but structured everything according to the principles we have just stated and will describe below (see Schedule II). During the following three months, Hannah improved from six months to one and a half years in various developmental areas.

☆ ☆ ☆

What follows is an example of a week's lessons with Hannah when she was eight, and another week of work when she was nine. Details about the games and activities listed in these schedules are given in the text which follows. Also, suggestions for these and other similar activities may be found in Dr. Getman's and Dr. Kephart's books. (See bibliography.)

---

[2]Central Institute for the Deaf, St. Louis, Missouri.

SCHEDULE I *August 1964*

MONDAY

Interlocking plastic bricks

Exercises

Roly Poly

Chalkboard work:

    Tracing lines to complete squares

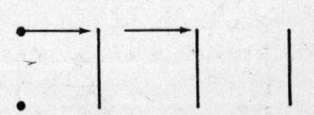

    Drawing patterns

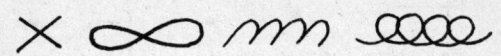

Read *Weekly Reader*

Cut with scissors

    on line

    or between lines

TUESDAY

Snap-together beads

Dance: march to music with strong rhythm

Roly Poly

Desk work: Templates

　　　　　　　Trace a picture using onion-skin paper

Picture story sequence: (Put pictures in proper order)

Punch-out and Stick 'em books

WEDNESDAY

Simple jigsaw puzzle

Races

Roly Poly

Chalkboard work:

    Copy pictures

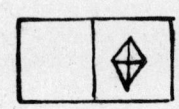

    Draw a man and trace the word "man"
    Trace a circle clockwise, and then counterclockwise
    Clock game

Link letters

Color, cut and paste a picture (barn)

THURSDAY

String beads

Hop

Roly Poly

Desk work:

    Parquetry block designs

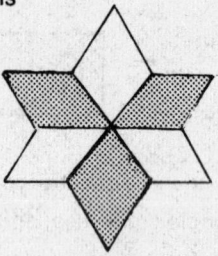

        Copy

        Put blocks on top

        Pegboard pattern

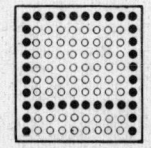

FRIDAY

Copy figures made with
   long sticks

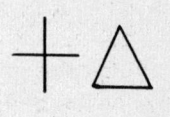

Kraus Weber

Balloon game
   (try to keep balloon in air)

Color, cut out, and paste a simple picture

Chalkboard work:

   Copy design

   Copy a boat scene as I draw it

   Complete a pattern

SATURDAY

Modeling with *Play-Doh*

Stepping stones:
   Walk upon path
   of colored
   cardboard squares

Roly Poly

Desk work:

   Templates
   Memory cards

Complete a pattern

SUNDAY

Pegs

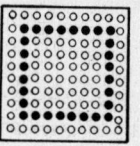

Races

Balloon game

Chalkboard work:

Simple maze (move from
Hans' house to Mike's house—
follow path with pencil)

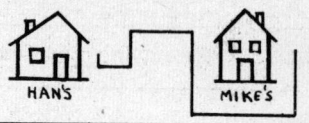

Flash cards

"Follow-the-Dots" book

Coloring book

We had lessons seven days a week—a break only made it harder to get started the next day. One Sunday I left for a dinner party, regretful about having to miss our lesson. My sitter patted Hannah, "My goodness, even a mule gets one day off a week."

Each day we started with some pleasant activity and ended with something pleasant.

SCHEDULE II *September 1965*

MONDAY

Do jigsaw puzzle
   while lying on stomach

Lifts

Playing ball, throwing, catching, and bouncing

Flashlight

Chalkboard work:

   Make patterns with both
   hands at same time

   Trace a word (boy, ball) and copy
   the picture for the word

Link letters

Follow-the-dots

Kraus Weber

TUESDAY

String beads while
  lying on back

Dangle ball

Push-ups

Tilt board

Desk work:

  Play books in which to trace, read, and count

Finger play: *Where Is Thumbkin?*

Wrestling

WEDNESDAY

Lying on stomach, put doll's clothes on doll

Roly Poly

Tongue exercises

Chalkboard work:

    Clock game

    Copy a house scene as I draw it

    Trace numbers

    Write Hannah

Hop

Exercises

Visual memory

THURSDAY

Lying on stomach, copy block design

Lifts

Pitch and catch a ball

Flashlight

Roll

Desk work:

   Trace letters

   Trace words

   Finger play: *Ten Little Indians*

FRIDAY

Lying on back, play with plastic manipulative toy such as *Crazy Ikes*

Wrestling

Finger games

Push-ups

Chalkboard work:

   Patterns with both hands

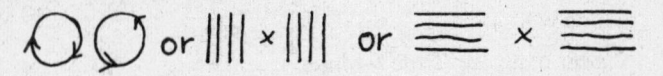

   ◯ ◯ or |||| × |||| or ≡ × ≡

   Copy a water scene as I draw it
   Trace words: boat, moon, sea, canoe

Visual memory

Color, cut, and paste

Balance board

SATURDAY

Lying on stomach, play the *Cootie Game*

Roly Poly

Tongue exercises

Kraus Weber

Desk work:

   Trace words

   Shape game

Wrestling

Finger games

Hop

Exercises

In February, 1966, after she had been out of any school for seven months (because she had outgrown the program she was in for three and a half years and was not accepted anywhere else), she suddenly started a very busy schedule.

8:30-12:00	Perceptually handicapped class
12:15-12:30	Play outside
12:30- 1:00	Lunch
1:00- 1:25	Trampoline, jump rope, play ball, or read
1:30- 2:30	Visit first grade
3:00- 4:00	Tutoring
4:30- 5:30	"Play" with mother: dress dolls, doll house, some sort of blocks, board game, clay, color, punch-out or dot books
5:30- 6:00	Television
6:00- 7:00	Dinner
7:00- 7:30	Dance, play a game, or talk with daddy and Andy
7:30	Bath
8:00	Massage and sleep.

With no more time for our home lessons, we sort of insinuated our teaching into vacant moments. If Hannah was not too tired, we had "races" before the massage, and always now included eye and tongue exercises, finger games, or "lifts" with the "massage." Hannah thrived for a while. But, when both the first-grade class and the perceptually handicapped class fell through for her, she was so let down that we did not go back again to our formal lessons. We continued this general schedule, substituting chores and shopping for the morning class and visits to the park, the zoo, or—on rare occasions—visits to a friend for the afternoon visit to the first-grade class.

TRAINING

Every parent, especially one who is a teacher as well, must deal with the present but plan on a long-term basis. A child with learning disabilities needs more spatial training than an astronaut, more perceptual training than an art critic, and plenty of help to develop the degrees of freedom he needs to operate comfortably.

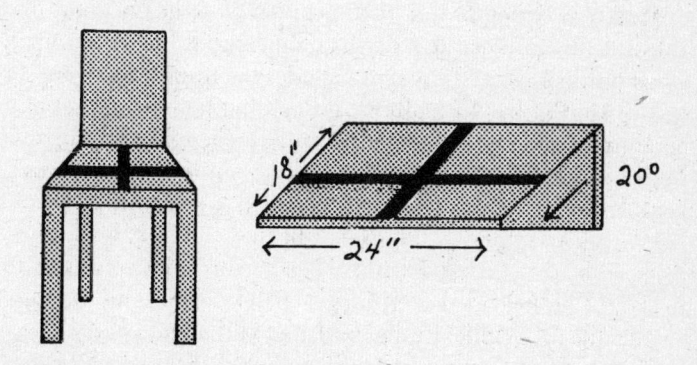

IDEAL WORK SETUP

POSTURAL TRANSPORT ABILITIES Your child's work table and chair should help him develop the best balance or postural alignment he can. His feet should be flat on the floor when he is seated, his back resting comfortably against the back of his chair. The chair seat should fit him, so that his knees do not touch the edge of the seat. The table or desk top should be at the height of his elbows when his upper arms are almost at his side, his arms bent. All visual work which will not roll off should be done on a desk that slants, at a 20° angle, which can be accomplished with a removable desk top. If his chair is so high that his feet miss the floor, he should have a foot rest.

We have mentioned a spotlight or any sufficient contrasting light which does not cast a shadow or a glare, and other means to focus his attention. If his body awareness is very poor, it is helpful to draw a vertical line and a horizontal line on his desk top and chair seat to help him distinguish left, right, top, bottom.

The chalkboard should be green, and large enough for his arms to extend in all directions. Large amber chalk is best, long enough for him to grasp with his whole hand. Wrapping it with tape prevents breakage.

☆ ☆ ☆

Training activities for various aspects of postural transport are:

Muscular strength. Let *him* open and close heavy doors and drawers (within reason; we will not be responsible for hernias). Good outdoor play equipment includes the frame of a swing set or any kind of bar for pulling and holding himself up, set at a height of a few inches above his outstretched fingers; an Irish Mail; ladders for climbing (low enough not to be dangerous); comparatively heavy blocks of polished wood, cut in brick-sized chunks from 4×6 or 6×8 beams, to stack, load, pull, push, unload, and build with; wheelbarrow and/or wagon to push and pull—loaded with toys or blocks or not, he shall use two hands if possible; bushel baskets to fill up and carry.

Good indoor muscular strength activities include rolling and kneading clay, modified push-ups, pushing, pulling, and lifting objects of various weights, physical fitness activities adapted for a younger child, and what we called "wrestling."

Wrestling. Lie down with your child on the floor, feet-to-feet, soles touching. Have him push his legs against yours, both legs together, then alternating legs. Sit up, facing each other. Have him push his arms, palms of hands against palms of your hands, both arms together, then alternate arms. Let him try to keep you from touching your hands to your shoulders as you flex your arm, then have him try to touch his hands to his shoulder as you keep him from doing it. I start anything that needs rhythm by singing a song (dum-de-dum, not words), such as "Volga Boatman" or "Pop Goes the Weasel" for a strong rhythm. As Hannah's skill at the activity and all-around rhythm improved, she got less auditory help. "Weasel" or "Boatman" faded into counting; then, more and more, we "wrestled" without auditory structuring.

Kraus Weber. Other activities to improve muscular functioning are the Kraus Weber exercises. Child lies flat on back, hands behind head, legs outstretched, and tries to pull up into sitting position while you hold his feet. Then, flat on back, he bends his knees and pulls up into sitting position while you hold his feet. Then, flat on back, hands behind head, child raises extended legs ten inches from floor, keeping them straight.

In other exercises, child lies face down and tries to raise head and chest off floor, then legs off floor.

Postural alignment; dynamic balance. The important thing to watch in any physical activity of your child is the *relationship* between his two sides and his two ends, *not* just how well one side or one part works alone. If any body segment is out of line, another one will have to counterbalance it. If any movement is "off-direction," as a foot pointing to the left rather than straight when walking, an opposite movement or action must counterbalance it. So don't worry too much about speed and grace, but concentrate on helping him keep his body and his direction in proper alignment as he performs the following activities.

Jumping and hopping will help orient him *vertically*, while most other physical activities help orient him from side to side and back to front.

A simple balance board can be built using an 18-inch by 24-inch board. Attach a 2-inch by 4-inch board to the middle of the larger board as a fulcrum. The child can learn to balance himself on this contraption.

Walking. Give your child plenty of chances to walk on all possible planes, all possible surfaces, in all possible directions (backward, forward, sideways). What you are aiming at is that his feet be parallel and pointing straight ahead; that his walking be *visually directed.* (Point to something ahead at his eye level.) If he cannot keep his eyes on a distant target, get in front of him, facing him, crouching down so that your face is at his level, moving backward as he goes forward and forward as he goes backward. His movement is to be in a *rhythmic pattern* whatever his speed (his right arm moving forward *with* his left foot, his left arm with his right foot), in a *direct fashion.*

Most children love to play "circus." Set up a board in the yard supported by a brick at each end, so he can pretend to be walking a tightrope. Later, he can play tightrope on curbstones, an easier place for you to walk in front of him with your face at his level.

Jumping. The point here is to remain vertical while thrusting against gravity, whether jumping off something, onto something, in one spot, over something, forward, or backward. His feet should act in unison when jumping rope, jumping over a low object (small pillow or horizontal wastebasket), or making a standing broad jump. His feet should land together in a running broad jump or jumping over a high hurdle (standing wastebasket). An *obstacle course* (a series of jumps of different heights, at different distances apart, different widths, set up indoors or out) can be lots of fun for a group of children or if the family will join in. On a *trampoline,* jumping should be continuous and in one spot, visual target at eye level (a tree, a roof, a bush, your face), feet parallel and moving in unison.

Rolling. Most children love to roll—in the snow, on the beach, down a grassy hill, across the room (where you can use a rug or linoleum edge as a guide to see if he is rolling straight). He should roll in both directions so that both sides of his body get to initiate the thrust, and roll as slowly and rhythmically as possible. There should always be a visual target, which you can stick on the wall inside and find outside, at his head level. He should roll in a straight direction, his head, shoulders, hips, legs, and feet coordinated (the rhythm is: head up and eyes on target, shoulder thrusts, hip thrusts, and body rolls, with legs and feet following).

Races. We called a collection of play movements "races," because they were so hard for Hannah at first that I had to compete with her to hold her interest. My sound effects and pratfalls made it worth the struggle to her. We had a visual target for all our races, and tried to go straight toward the target, whether moving forward or backward.

1. CRAWLING LIKE A BABY. Right hand and left leg thrusting, alternating with left hand and right leg counterthrusting. Body should be level, head up, with eyes on target, direction straight toward target, hands flat on floor with fingers pointing ahead and slightly inward.

2. FROG OR BUNNY HOP. Child squats (sits on heels), thrusts both arms forward as he brings both knees forward in a one-sequence movement, feet hop in unison and body is ready for the next hop. Again, head up, eyes on target, hands flat, parallel, pointing straight ahead.

3. BEAR WALK. One side of body (right arm and leg) moves, then the other (left arm and leg). The idea is to move in a straight line, trunk level and head up, with eyes on target, trunk moving forward and *not* rocking side-to-side. This is a hard one.

4. DUCK WALK, INCH WORM, AND CRAB WALK. Also fun, but not as important as the others. So, if you don't know them already, don't bother. If you do use them, they too should be visually targeted and performed forward *and* backward.

Hopping. We actually included hopping, along with rolling, in our "races."

1. TWO-FOOT HOPPING. Body should be vertical, feet parallel, leaving the floor and coming down in unison. Child should be guided by a visual target to move in a straight line. Hopping in place is much harder.

2. ONE-FOOT HOPPING. To help the body remain vertical, the lifted foot should be close to the body at knee level (storklike). Movement should be guided by a visual target. The aim is for rhythm and equal facility with both feet, either forward or backward, feet pointing straight ahead, body straight.

3. RHYTHM HOPPING. When he gets pretty good at hopping 1-1-1-1, try him at 2-2-2-2, with two feet before one foot.

4. SKIPPING. Which is reciprocal hopping and must come after the other kind.

All these directional and spatial movements will one day emerge in pencil-and-paper movement patterns and, eventually, in thinking ability. If you really watch for it, you may see improvement in hopping and rolling showing up in chalkboard work. As he learns to move himself correctly, he will know right from left and will be able to visualize space and movements within the alloted area. Mastery of these skills will later enable him to comprehend what he reads, to solve problems, to reason. Given a math problem, he will know *where* to begin, *what* process to use (what move to make), and *how* to solve the problem (how to move). He will be able to understand the *kind* of answer required (concentration on the target is the key). Finally, when he knows he has found the *right* answer (having moved to the "right place"), he knows his task is accomplished and he can stop.

Body awareness. If movement practice is going to help your child, training in body awareness must be combined with it. He can only move properly and economically to a certain place if he knows where his arms and legs are and what he must move and how to move it. More than that, he must "remember" movements so that he can make them without having to think about them; in other words, he must be able to "look and do." He can never know "Where I am" (how he relates to people and things around him) until he learns "Who I am."

We must remember that all development proceeds from head to feet, from the middle out. We must aim for equal awareness on both sides of the body, on the back as well as the front, bottom as well as top.

Bathing and Dressing. Both mother and child have to be present for these activities, so use them. Before I was sure she could understand, I started naming every part of Hannah's body as she dressed and as I bathed her—arms, legs, hands, neck, feet, shoulders, etc. Later, when she began to bathe herself, I would say, "Wash your right arm . . . now your hand . . . your left leg . . . knee . . . thigh . . . foot . . . ankle," etc., and she had to find the right part, so that she eventually really knew them.

Massage. A regular bedtime activity that combined a lot more than massage.

1. LOCALIZING. Touch the child in various spots all over his body and have him indicate each time where he was touched. With good body awareness, a light touch will do, but use as much pressure as he needs to feel the touch. Concentrate on his worst areas, although he may be poorly organized tactually all over his body.

2. MASSAGING. Knead, pat, pound, stroke, tickle, spending most of your time on his poorest organized parts. As in Hannah's case, it is often, but not always, the legs and feet. Don't forget the back and the sides, fingers and toes, shoulders and neck. Use a cream or ointment that tingles,

feels cool or warm to the skin. He'll probably love his massage.

3. TOUCH AND LABEL. Then touch his body with a soft brush, sandpaper, ice, a feather—anything for adding and varying sensation. Either keep quiet or name the places you touch, but later let *him* name these spots. When he has learned to distinguish between left and right, he must be able to apply this distinction to "my ankle on my right foot, on the outside . . . my back, on the left . . . my right shoulder," etc. It is hardest for him to move a part or to point to a spot, and *only* that part or spot, which mother has specified.

Lifts. This is a rhythmical movement of various body parts, gross to fine (as, whole arm, from the elbow, from the wrist, finally the fingers), together and in alternation. They can be done standing, as to "Hokey Pokey" or "Loopdeeloo," but are easier lying down where the child does not have to fight gravity at the same time. I initiate all rhythmic activities, as I have said, with boisterous "dum-dee-dums" or some such objectionable sound, then go to counting, then no verbal help, which we will assume from here on. You need not resort to this unless your child, too, depends on audition a great deal.

Have your child raise and lower both legs five or six times, first together, then alone, then alternating. Then have him point his toes, then flex his ankles. Then have him move his unbent arms together, singly, and alternating. Next, have him rest upper arms on floor and move arms from the elbows; then from the wrists. Next have him move his shoulders up and down (a very hard task for Hannah). Everything should be done five or six times, first together, then singly, then alternating. We usually threw in mouth and tongue exercises for a finale, but they will be described in a later section.

Outline Drawings. If you can get hold of large sheets of brown wrapping paper or newsprint, outline your child as he lies on the floor on his back. Then fill in the eyes, nose, and other details. He'll be delighted and probably very surprised at this life-sized outline. Let him match his own body parts to the picture.

Left and Right. By six or seven a child usually has some awareness of left and right, top and bottom, front and back, in and out. If he does not, then he literally does not know what to move or which way to go. Get a girl a dress that has a contrasting line down the front, or mark your child's midline with plastic tape on his clothes. If you sew, you can make him a clown-type outfit, with a side, a sleeve, or a leg in a contrasting pattern or color. If you don't, he might consent to wearing non-matching socks or bedroom slippers when he is at home, and you can tape or press on a contrasting picture of an apple or a cat on one side of his shirt or pants. But, long before he is six or seven, give him plenty of chance to use *both hands* and *either hand*. And let *him* use the hand *he* wants, so he'll learn about both of his hands and feet.

Top and Bottom; Front and Back; In and Out. Make him some cardboard dolls with top and bottom, front and back in different colors. Let him wear a contrasting belt or plastic tape around his waist to divide top and bottom. The midline tape for left and right can also be a guideline for in (toward tape) and out (away from tape) activities.

"Giving Orders." This can be very funny with only two people, a riot if the family will join in. The person who is "it" must get everyone else to do what he tells them—but by describing the action, not naming it. In other words, he cannot say, "Sit down." He must say, "Keep your feet still, make your seat go down. Wait! You move to the right first. Stop!" and on and on. This game is as effective if he is "it" or simply moves what he is told to move.

Roly Poly. Dr. Gerald Getman's invaluable manual *The Physiology of Readiness* describes many excellent, visually-targeted exercises involving the use of all parts of the body in various combinations and degrees of difficulty. We gave the name Roly Poly to Dr. Getman's "Practice in General Coordination." Instead of using X's as visual targets, we used pictures of a nurse and a doctor.

Spatial awareness. Muscular strength, postural alignment, and body awareness—all center in the child himself. Only after he has developed these abilities *in himself*, can he relate to objects and people *outside himself*, projecting what he knows about himself onto the world. This is *spatial awareness*. Objects are up, down, top, bottom, behind, near, right, left, in front of, etc., only in relation to *him*. Use prepositions and show him what they mean—in pictures, with toys and dolls, with each other, and with furniture.

Judging Size Relationships. In or out of the house, have your child find things that are "bigger than you are" and things that are "smaller than you are." Later, let him use a toy, a book, a pencil, or a stick as a reference, instead of himself. He should also find things that are the same size.

Let him arrange his books on a shelf or canned goods in the pantry according to size—smallest to largest or largest to smallest. Remember to use words like tall, short, fat, thin, high, low, wide, narrow, small, large, full, empty, so he can pick up the vocabulary.

Judging Shape Relationships. Let him pick out objects on the basis of shape, disregarding size. "Square" things can be books, papers, tables, chairs, doors, windows. "Round" things can be glasses, tree trunks, light bulbs. Later, he can be more exact. Let him pick out square, round, and triangular objects in his books, magazines, or coloring books.

Judging Distance Relationships. He can do this in the house or out, but it may be easier at first on a walk or in a park. Which is closer? Let him put his arms around a small tree, then look at a tree that looks smaller (but is larger) because it is farther away. Then have him go to that tree and try to put his arms around it, and compare the size of the trees. He will begin to realize that things are farther away when they look smaller, when they take more movement and more time to reach. They are closer when they take less time and less movement to reach. Pretty soon, he may be able to point out things that are closer and farther away in picture books. He will find out during these "experiments" that a desk or a salt shaker looks different from the top than from the bottom, from the right than from the left, but that they are, nevertheless, the same.

Judging Directionality. Help him match his own directions to something else, by matching the colors for his middle, top, bottom, right, left, etc., to those of a chest or a window or a figure on the board. He need not be stained for life, since washable chalk or crayon or colored tape work fine.

Have him match his own body parts to a hexagon, rectangle, square or any form you have drawn on the board, as he faces it. Have him trace simple forms in various directions, or follow a simple maze. Let him practice and feel vertical, horizontal, and depth directions by stacking blocks in these directions.

As he begins to know his own directions, give him a chance to make wider use of his knowledge. Let him tell you which thing or which part of a picture or toy is on the left, top, bottom, etc., when you read a book or magazine, play dominoes, sit in a room, ride in a car, or have a snack. Have him match his own body part to a part of a drawing or illustration—his right arm to the top right, his left leg to the left bottom, etc.

Two great pencil games are tic-tac-toe and the dots in rows that must be connected to form boxes. Hannah and I play a special tic-tac-toe as well as the usual game. Each of us takes turns directing the other as to what to put in which space. For instance, she might say, "Mother, draw a moon in the middle right," and I must do it. I might then say, "Hannah, draw a tree in the bottom left," and she must do that. No pointing allowed. We could end up with:

Jigsaw puzzles and copying simple designs with building blocks, parquetry blocks, or pegboards are good practice in spatial awareness.

Your child may have to learn how to copy block designs in easy stages. First he may have to copy from you as you do a design step by step. Then you do the whole design and he copies it. Then have him copy a design from a picture; and finally, remove the design and have him do it from memory. He may also need verbal directions to help him at first.

Someday, if he is ever to do desk work in school, he will have to learn that "up" on a desk is away from him, "down" is toward him. It will help to let him draw, trace, or copy on paper fastened to the wall, then retrace the same work on the floor or a table or desk, so that he can see for himself that the results are the same even when the movement is different. Only when he really absorbs this directional information will he someday be able to follow such academic instructions as "Find the left side of the page . . . write your name on the top right corner . . . draw a line from the middle to the left of the page." Many "normal" children who have not progressively built up their spatial awareness find themselves "lost" on the piece of paper lying on their desk, run into trouble when directions and tasks get more complex—and no one seems to know why.

Spatial awareness is the basis for reading, writing, arithmetic, and all other academic skills. Last year, I had to tell Hannah, "Start here, go down, stop, turn right, stop, now pick up your pencil," to allow her to write the numeral 4. Now I can say, "Write 4." She "sees" a four, translates it into the appropriate spatial movements, executes the movements with her arm to match what she sees with her eyes (although still crudely), and *voilà* 4! She is on the way to academic success now.

PERCEPTUAL PROCESSING MODALITIES The space in which your child must learn to move is filled with a multitude of varied stimuli. His job is to organize his perceptual systems in such a balanced interdependence that he will be able to integrate these numerous and diverse stimuli, will manage to pay attention to matters of his choice or to tasks dictated by necessity, and will be capable of learning and performing—that's all!

The child with learning problems is unable to accomplish all this by himself. He may need special training in *each* perceptual system, as well as in the *integration of all* systems. Before a child can speak and perform well, he has much to learn. Let us take a look at the training he may need in each ability, in the natural order.

Gustation. The child must learn to discriminate taste, temperature, and texture and then must gain experience in placing his tongue and moving his mouth as and when he wants to, first in imitation of others, and eventually spontaneously.

Eating. The greatest basic training for gustation is eating. A child has made a lot of preparation for talking when he can chew on both sides of his mouth, get and keep food between his teeth while he chews, move his lower jaw in a semicircular pattern for grinding action, blow on his hot soup, and drink through a straw. It has nothing to do with eating, but blowing his nose whenever he wants to is another important accomplishment.

Discrimination. Include in his menu as wide a variety of textures, tastes, and odors as is suitable to his well-being. Let him taste and smell a lot of less nutritious seasonings that you use in cooking: vanilla, Tabasco, curry powder, dry cocoa, etc. Chewing ice is bad for the teeth, so let him lick it, to feel the cold, and try something very warm on his tongue. Have him try lots of new tastes and talk about whether they are bitter, sour, sweet, almost tasteless, strong, or sharp.

Tongue Exercises. Use his favorite dry cereal, placing a piece at a time on various spots around his mouth, pieces he must retrieve with his tongue. If he must lick it to make it stick, make him stick his tongue way out, straight, to do it. Touch spots on his lip and around his mouth with the blunt end of a toothpick, and see if he can touch them with his tongue each time.

It should amuse him to exercise his tongue, as he does his arms and legs.

(1) Have him move his tongue rhythmically from side to side, up and down, in and out (freely, not pressed against his lower lip).

(2) Have him put the tip of his tongue on the roof of his mouth behind his upper teeth, behind his lower teeth, in front of his upper and lower teeth—all inside his mouth.

(3) Hannah invented a fine game, in which I asked her questions and she answered yes or no with her tongue.

(4) Have him point to nearby places and track a moving object with his tongue, as he holds his head still.

Tactuality. We need tactuality all over our bodies (basic for good body awareness), not just in our hands. Give your child a chance to feel all variations of temperature, from quite warm to icy. Try to vary the texture of his clothing, then talk about the way different materials feel in his clothing, in yours, on furniture. Talk about how rough sandpaper or a heavy straw rug are, how soft a rabbit's fur or a cotton ball, how smooth satin or a mirror. Let him compare one kind of feel with another. Let him play with clay, sand, dough, mud, finger paint, or whatever other "feel" you can dream up. Use all the tactual words you can, and ask him to describe objects with as many tactual words as he can think of. Play tactual games with him:

Feelies. Show him an object or a picture of an object and have him find it in a bag or box of objects by touch alone.

Sorting. Give him a bunch of objects and have him put them in piles, according to hardness, wetness, roughness, etc. Let him sort other bunches for relative differences in a single category, as smoothest to roughest, hardest to softest, etc.

Scrap Book. Cut or tear pictures from magazines and group them according to tactual information only: hardness, lightness, roughness, etc.

Kinesthesia. We dealt with basic kinesthetic training under Postural Transport Abilities. Now let us consider it on a higher level, in symbolic, problem-solving and sequencing activities.

Symbolic Activities. Help him learn to jump, hop, stop, run, sit, stand, etc., when he is told the word, without having to imitate the movement. It is fun to copy the movements and activities he sees in his books or that you can draw on the board for him.

Problem-Solving Activities. Start to do something yourself or pretend to have trouble doing something, and ask him, "What shall I do?" You cannot move until he tells you, either by word or gesture. If he tells you wrong, do it wrong. If you are putting crayons back in a box, he must tell you how to pick up a crayon, where to put it, and what to do next. When it is time to close the box, he must let you know how to close it. If someone else in the family seems to be having a problem opening a bottle, moving a chair, or closing a window, ask, "What should she do?"

Sequencing.

1. EXERCISES. These are especially suited for the father to do with the child, especially if the father has had calisthenics in school or in the army. Face the child and have him imitate your movements.

START WITH TWO MOVEMENTS.

BILATERAL MOVEMENTS   *Gradually add more movements. At first use only bilateral movements, both arms doing the same thing at the same time.*

ADVANCE TO RECIPROCAL MOVEMENTS.

ROTATE ARMS EXTENDED AT THE SIDES.

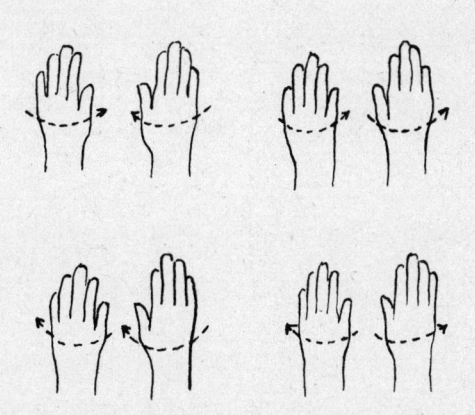

ROTATE ARMS EXTENDED IN FRONT.
SIMPLE ARM MOVEMENTS

Other exercises to include are: hop in place on both feet. Then, when the child has the balance and control, hop on one foot. Put hands on hips and kneel and stand. Clap and sway to rhythm.

As a grand finale, we used to end with the familiar Jumping Jack, the Army's side-straddle hop. This exercise should be performed in balance, working both arms, both legs and the torso together in rhythm.

2. FOLLOW THE LEADER. Have your child imitate a series of walking patterns—first you walk a certain route, then he is to follow the same path—such as around a chair, between two tables, or over a stool. Since it takes some motor planning to get the child to move in the same order and direction, start with a simple pattern and increase the complexity of the patterns in line with his level of readiness.

3. SEQUENCING THINGS. Have him put colors, sizes, shapes, picture stories in order—in *all* directions, to give him practice in the depth, vertical, and horizontal planes:

4. SEQUENTIAL THINKING. This is K at its highest level, visualization, and is the basis for arithmetic, meaningful reading, and orderly expression: (a) *Commands*—Give him instructions to be carried out in order. Start with only two,

at first as simple as "Go to that closet and get your coat," or "Sit down and fold your hands." When he has mastered such elementary commands, gradually increase not only the number but also the complexity of commands step by step. (b) *"What would you do if . . . ?"*—Ask him this often to help him learn to think in sequence and to figure out the end result when given some initial information. For example, ask, "What would you do if you can't find the dog's leash and it's time for him to go for a walk?" Or, "If I forget to put out the list for the milkman, what might happen?" Hannah's favorite phrases when she was eight and nine were "If I do, what might happen?" and "What happened next? . . . and next?" in answer to which I had to list in order the events just past or the events on the agenda for the next day.

Audition. I will risk your boredom by stressing a vital point; that you *must* learn to describe, in words your child can understand, every move he makes, everything he does, everything he tastes, smells, touches, moves, hears and sees. This does not mean yakking away at him all the time, as three words usually do better than thirty. Stay simple, clear, and to the point, but help him structure his world through language.

Language represents (re-presents) previous experiences. A child cannot understand the word for something he has not already experienced. Obviously, then, auditory symbols depend upon the organization of all his other perceptions.

Audition is organized in this order: He must first learn to know where a sound comes from (small babies will turn their heads to the tinkle of a bell), then to identify it, then to match sounds with what they mean, then to understand words, then to speak words, then to use grammar, then to express his own views in words and, finally, to use language so that he can learn other people's concepts of the world and express his own concepts. He may need practice in all these auditory stages.

Localizing Sounds. When you hear a bell, a horn, a bark, or a splash, ask him where it comes from. Blindfold him and let him try to tell or show you where a ring or clap comes from in the room—behind, in front, right, left, up, down—whether it is near or far away. He must learn to relegate background noises to the background one of these days. (Hannah has. I have not.)

Identifying Sounds. When you hear the sound made by a vacuum cleaner, a plane, a slamming door, cutting scissors, chalk on a board, feet running, or a balloon popping and so forth, *tell* him what it is he is hearing. Later, *ask* him what it is he is hearing.

Matching Sounds. If you label everything that you and your child see, hear, and do, he will begin to match the label to what it means. With enough bombardment, he will eventually use the labels himself, spontaneously.

Using Words.

1. SEQUENCING. Under Kinesthesia, we spoke of having him hand you objects or follow directions in the order you give them, starting with two, "Give me a ball and a block" or "Pick up the book and put it on the table." When you are riding in the car or swinging or seesawing in the park, give him nonsense sounds or numbers to repeat, beginning with two, and working up to four or five in a row.

2. PHONICS. Play games with words. Give him a word, be sure he understands it, then have him say a word that rhymes. Or have him match words that start the same way. Have him match your words for the vowel sounds. When you use a word, ask him what rhymes with it, what starts the same, or what has the same sound in the middle, making sure that he understands what you are doing.

3. QUESTIONS AND ANSWERS. Make up a little story or tell him something that has happened and ask him questions about it. Since he has no pictures to help him now, be sure the story is very simple, as simple as, "I went to the store. I

bought some milk and bread." Now you can ask, "Where did I go? . . . What did I buy? . . . Who went to the store?" You can do this several times a day.

Grammar. Hannah, like many other children with learning disorders, had a hard time answering questions about what she had heard or read or what had happened to her, partly because she had "what," "where," "who," "when," "how," and "to do" all mixed up. "Where did you go, Hannah?" . . . "Tuesday." "What is that man doing?" . . . "Policeman."

It helps to stress the key word, and to repeat it. It helps to demonstrate what the right answer is by offering the correct category—if the answer is "zoo," you might say "To the beach?" but never "egg?"—until a child can tell the difference. If your child has this problem, you may be the only one who realizes that he knows the answers, but does not know which answer to give.

If abstract words, pronouns, prepositions, and conjunctions are hard for your child to comprehend, use them. Stress them. Demonstrate and indicate what they mean. But use them. Supply them for him when they are important. He will finally catch on. As his spatial awareness develops, he will begin to handle prepositions.

Young children usually use the present tense exclusively for a while. Hannah's efforts to change tenses sometimes caused exciting reactions, like the day she told us, "Mrs. Jones had a baby," meaning "Mrs. Jones is going to have a baby." Complete mastery of the future tense is still in the future for Hannah.

Expressing Himself. A child who knows so well what he wants to say but cannot say it because of an expressive language problem may chatter pointlessly, repetitively, and inappropriately. He may appear foolish. What he *is* is frustrated. The best and only cure we found for this was "rehearsal."

Hannah first learned to put words together by "reading," feeling, seeing, memorizing, and saying, "What is *this*? This is a _____. What do you see? I see a _____." at Central Institute for the Deaf's outpatient clinic in St. Louis.

The next and biggest step was "I want some _____." If she wanted something and could not say what, she "read" from her "book" until she found the right word. The possibility of losing her was not so dreadful after we drilled her on "My name is Hannah Hart. My daddy's name is Ken Hart. I live on Old Dobbin Circle." In the same way, she learned "May I be excused, please" and changed her violent eruption from the dinner table to a polite leave-taking. We rehearsed her "show and tell" news for school each day. At first, she had to "read" it from her "book," then she could remember it with prompting, and finally initiated her own news.

She was nine when we realized how badly she wanted to converse on the phone, exchange small talk with visitors and service people who came to the house, friends she met on the street. We finally thought of using the same old tricks. We rehearsed general telephone clichés, for both calling and answering, conversation for chance encounters, and what to say to the milkman. Then we concentrated on specifics, beginning with an anticipated visit of some close friends of ours. We drew pictures and wrote phrases on the chalkboard and in her "book"; we made cards with all the phrases on them, which I, then Hannah, had to arrange in order (this is a step only a child who can read well enough can manage); we played the scene with dolls, and then we acted out all the roles ourselves. Incidentally, we briefed our guests.

When the bell rang that night, Hannah flew to the door and ran through her entire routine without a flaw:

> Hello. How are you?
> > I'm fine. How are you?
>
> Just fine, thank you. . . . Come in.
> > Thank you. We will.
>
> I'm glad you came.
> > I'm glad too.
>
> Won't you sit down? I'll go tell Mother and Daddy you're here.
>
> (At leaving time:) Come back and see us again. . . . Goodbye.

We were surprised that it went so well. Hannah was ecstatic. Her delight kept pace with the manners and phone-answering ability that improved now by leaps and bounds.

Dictation is another way a child can be helped to express himself. He can dictate simple stories which you can write down and illustrate on the board, in a booklet, or both. He will love hearing them read back to him, which can be done in two ways: corrected for structure and grammar, which he will recognize; or exactly as he said it, which he can then correct himself. Even more exciting is dictating a letter to Grandma or a friend, with the added pleasure of scribbling or signing his name to it after he hears it read.

Vision. If a child is neither blind nor blindfolded, he will have been using his vision for all the activities he has been doing. This is the only way he has of developing good vision, of course —matching what he sees with all the other information he is getting through his other perceptive systems.

Dr. Gerald Getman's manual *The Physiology of Readiness* contains some excellent and clearly explained visual-training procedures, including target tracking and shifting from near to far for eye-movement skills, specific chalkboard exercises for eye-hand coordination, and a wealth of visual-memory material, so that we will not attempt to describe them here. We will instead talk about activities which contain a major element of play, and which can be supervised as well by an interested baby-sitter as by an exacting mother:

Eye-Teaming. Eye-teaming is the basis for good binocular vision. It is increased by any and every activity you can devise or rearrange which will require the child to apply both his hands in his midline—for example, anything from climbing a rope to pulling a wagon to bringing in a fish with the pole, the latter touching the child's middle.

1. DANGLE BALL. Hang a plastic softball on nylon or cotton string from the ceiling or a tree so that the ball is at the

child's mouth level. Give him a paper-towel tube to grasp overhand, hands just far enough apart for the ball to hit, and tell him to keep hitting the ball. His weight should be on both feet, feet parallel, and he'll have to stay in rhythm to do the job.

When he can hit the ball as many as 15 times in a row without failure, dispense with the tube and have him hit the ball a number of times first with each hand separately, then with the right and the left hand alternating, and finally with both hands overlapping. As soon as his hands have learned to master this routine, lower the ball to 18 inches above the ground and make him learn the same procedure, from start to finish, with his feet.

2. FLASHLIGHT CHASE. Both of you lie on the floor on your backs, each holding a flashlight. The child's light chases mother's light all over the ceiling, in verticals, horizontals, diagonals, circles, and haphazard patterns. He won't find this too hard or boring if you make it the Big Bad Wolf chasing the Little Pigs, a cartoon cat chasing a mouse, a good guy chasing a bad guy, mother chasing a naughty child.

Eye-Hand Coordination. Many tasks such as tracing, coloring, copying, cutting, stringing beads, working with pegs or blocks and with small toys whose pieces must be fitted together, and doing jigsaw puzzles are usually performed as a table or a desk. But these tasks can also be managed while lying on the floor on one's stomach, and some can even be done lying on one's back. Not being flexible, the child may not like this new position for accomplishing his tasks but that is exactly why he needs to practice this skill. Hannah, for one, absolutely hated the change. That's why we started with her favorite activities for very short periods on the floor. Writing, drawing, tracing, copying should all start on the board, before they are moved to a table or desk.

Since eye-hand coordination includes everything from painting and hammering to commercial books of dot-to-dot games, coloring large, widely outlined pictures, and Hannah's favorite punch-out-and-lick-and-stick books, we list only a few of our favorites.

1. COPY CAT. Divide the chalk board in half. Draw a VERY simple picture and have your child copy step by step. Pictures can be timely for the season, a holiday, or a recent experience. Change board sides from session to session, sometimes taking the right side yourself, sometimes the left.

SIMPLE DRAWINGS TO COPY *Divide the chalkboard in half. On one side you draw a simple picture of a house, boat, play yard, or other common scene. The child copies your picture on the other side of the chalkboard, line by line as you do it.*

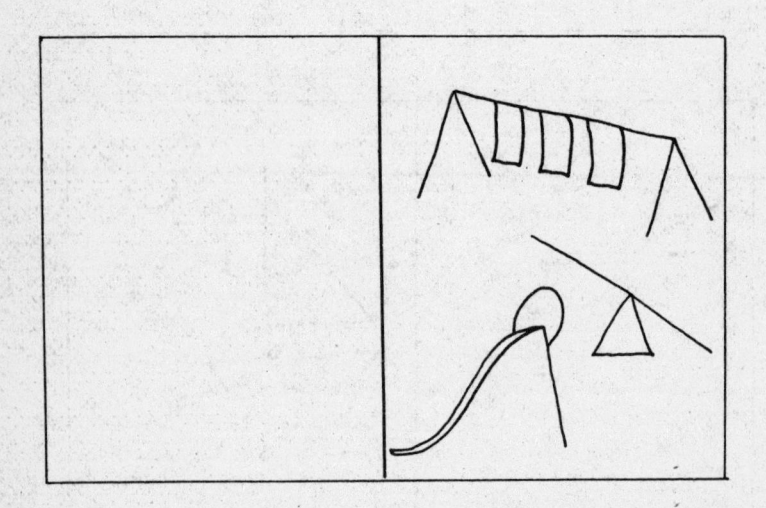

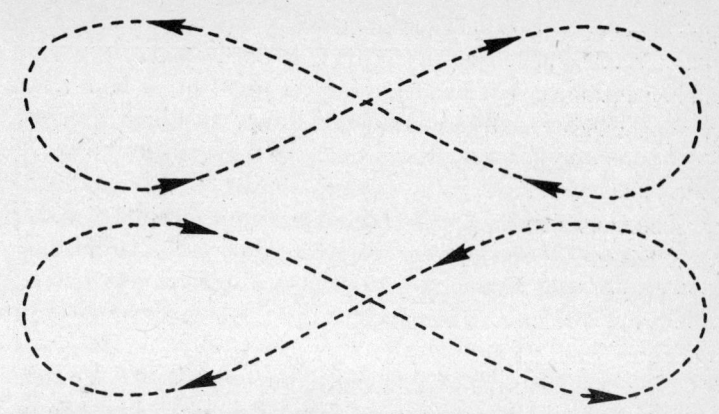

2. LAZY EIGHT.³ Child should trace this figure over and over, continuously, in both directions, with each hand. The figure should be about 24 inches wide and 10 inches high.

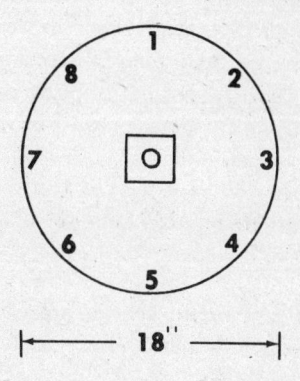

3. CLOCK GAME.⁴ Draw this figure on chalkboard. The child is told to place his right hand on one number and his left hand on another number. Then call out directions, telling him to move both his hands simultaneously to specified numbers. You will call for movements in all directions and all meridians: opposing movements—e.g. left hand on 8, right hand on 2; now bring both to zero; now back to

---

³Newell C. Kephart: *The Slow Learner in the Classroom* (Columbus, Ohio, Charles E. Merrill, 1960).
⁴*Ibid.*

8 and 2—parallel movements—e.g. left hand on 0, right hand on 3; now move left to 7, right to 0;—and cross movements—e.g. left hand on 7, right on 1; bring both to 0. The movements are also graded from outside in, from inside out, horizontally, vertically and diagonally.

4. FINGER PAINTING. On easel or table. Try to get child to make large, bilateral movements. It may be easier to let him paint right on a surface like formica, so he won't be bothered with crumpling paper.

5. TARGETS. Snowball fights and throwing rocks at a big tree or in a puddle are fine target games. Any child can throw at a target; you just regulate the size and distance of the target to give him a sporting chance. He can throw beanbags or big balls at circles drawn on the board if he can move his arm and see at all. He can throw beanbags (or rolled-up socks or dish towels) into a wastebasket or through holes that you cut out of plywood or cardboard in different shapes and which you outline in different colors. He can throw beach balls through hoops and clothespins into buckets. He should, however, throw with both hands, each hand, alternate hands; his target should vary in height from floor to eye level.

6. BALLOONS. Let him try to keep a big round balloon aloft, while you count how many times he taps it. There is no better way to practice moving than in relation to a moving target, while maintaining visual contact and establishing eye-hand combinations.

You may be surprised at the beginning that your child does not move, turn his head, or put his hands out in the right direction to keep up with the balloon. Hannah just stood there, expecting it to come right back to where it left. So you, too, may have to keep reminding him to "move" and "look at it" until pretty soon he'll be better at it than you are—and a lot better at all those things that keeping a balloon aloft requires. When he can tap at it ten times or more, you can play "volleyball" with him, pushing it back and forth to each other through the air.

7. BALL. Pitch-and-catch and bouncing a ball are marvelous eye-hand coordination activities. But if your child is as poorly organized movement-wise as Hannah was, you will have to teach him movement by movement—how to hold a ball at his chest with both hands on the ball's sides, thumbs separate from fingers and nearer chest, fingers spread; how to push the ball out, away from his chest, then let it go toward the other person; how next to put his hands down until the ball is on the way back so they won't get in the way and knock the ball down. Bouncing a ball was so hard for Hannah that one bounce-and-catch, one bounce-and-catch was all that she could do for a long time.

8. SCISSORS. Cutting can be very hard, even opening and closing the scissors, let alone keeping them vertical enough to the paper to make an incision. Once he can do this, make an inch-wide path with a colored marking pen, and tell him to cut on the line. Add corners and curves only after he has mastered cutting a straight line on a narrower path. Hannah could not curve or turn until I numbered the path for her, as I had done with the pencil maze, to get her started. Cutting from 1 to 2 to 3, etc., she knew where to go next.

9. COLOR, CUT, PASTE. If you make the line in the right place on construction paper, a child can cut out parts for a house or a tree by simply cutting one line. Later he can cut out parts of a man, for that takes a round piece. He can color the parts before or after he cuts them, then paste the parts into a picture.

Eye - Foot Coordination. Besides kicking the dangle ball, dodge ball and kicking beanbags from target to target are very good. Before he kicks a rolling ball, let him try kicking a stationary ball. Maze walking, stepping stones (stepping on colored cards placed in a pattern), hopscotch, and many other childhood games are good eye-foot coordination practice.

Visual Form Perception. A child must *experience* shape, size, likenesses, and differences tactually and kinesthetically before he can deal with them visually.

1. MATCHING BY SHAPE. Stacking blocks according to shape, copying block and parquetry designs, copying simple forms with long sticks, tinker toys, straight pretzels, and toothpicks (when he is ready for anything that small) are all good practice.

2. PARTS OF SHAPES. If a child recognizes a triangle as a triangle whichever way it points or whether it is equilateral or not; if he knows that a square has four equal sides and four corners, so that he can make these forms with sticks or toys, he knows the shapes. Perhaps he cannot draw them. Perhaps he cannot name them. But he knows them. Cut squares, triangles, circles, and rectangles into two, three, and four parts, and have him paste them into the outlines of the whole forms on a piece of paper.

3. MATERIALS. There are readiness materials, from workbooks and flash cards to special blocks and learning games, for finding likenesses and differences, matching shapes and directions.

Templates are very useful and can be easily made. Take a sheet of cardboard and cut a shape (a circle, a square or a triangle) out of the middle of the sheet. The child can then insert his finger inside the cut-out area and run it around the shape. Later, the cardboard sheet with the cut-out pattern can be held against the chalk board or a piece of paper. The child can then trace around the inside of the cut out edge with chalk or pencil to produce a shape.

Later the child can trace a shape which you have drawn. At first use a very heavy colored crayon or chalk for drawing the shape. The child can trace around it with his finger before using chalk or crayon himself. Gradually remove the color clue and reduce the width of the line.

4. MEMORY. We have previously referred to the Getman manual which contains an ample supply of visual-memory material. But there are plenty of memory games you can play on your own. Have a child name the objects in a familiar room without looking. Have him look at a group of objects (three to five), close his eyes, then open them and tell which one you have removed. To make the game harder, use more objects, remove more than one, use pictures instead of objects. Hide objects (later pictures and word cards) in obvious hiding places as he watches. Wait awhile, then have him find them as you name them.

5. MORE ADVANCED. When he is ready, let him put link letters together, stamp out words with a child's print set, or type if a typewriter is available. With any of these, he can answer questions, fill in blanks in statements you make, write his name, address, and phone number, provide the words you leave out of stories, put things in sequence (days of the week, months, seasons), make lists of concepts (friends, colors, animals)—copying until he can work from memory. A child can reach this level of visual performance and still not be able to draw anything that anyone could recognize. That is why he needs plenty to keep him busy, even if he cannot write or draw.

PARENTS AS TEACHERS

A mother is always teaching her child. When the child happens to have a learning problem, he just has a lot more to learn and needs a lot more help to learn it. Sometimes Andy would say, "For gosh sakes, Mom, can't you stop teaching all the time and just leave her alone and let her have a good time?" No, I couldn't, because Hannah did not even know how to have a good time until somebody taught her. She could not play with toys. She could not play with people. She could not carry on a conversation that many people would listen to.

You may have to teach your child a lot before he is acceptable to any school. And then you may have to teach him a lot more that he is not going to learn in most schools.

TEACHING YOU HARDLY NOTICE When in the world can you find the time and still do anything else? Well, you may be a very busy mother, with other young children, no help, and countless chores. But remember, there are a number of periods every day when two things are true: your presence is required anyway, and your child is a captive audience (when he is bathing, dressing, eating, riding in the car with you, going to bed, shopping, taking a walk, playing with you, or "helping" with the housework). Just learn to seize your opportunity. You don't have to have two or three hours a day to sit down and play teacher.

- **In the kitchen**. He probably tastes all kinds of things (G), so talk about how they taste, the likes and differences. He'll be smelling (O) soup, soap, garbage, onions, all kinds of marvelous odors. When you are baking, give him his own bit of dough to bake, knead, pull, and squish (T); let him feel the wet dishwater, the soft suds, the dry towel. Whenever you can, let him fetch, carry, move, and "fix" things (K) for you. When you are doing so many different tasks and using utentils of all kinds, it is no trouble to name (A) everything you do and use. Point out (V) to him the eyes in a potato, the way the sun creeps through the window, the color of the food. Let him observe the sequence of preparing a meal, of setting the table, and of clearing away and cleaning up afterward.

- **Laundry**. Show him and tell him where supplies are kept; how you sort by color or by fabric; the sequence of what must be done first, next, and next; how clothes are folded; where they go and who they belong to. Here, too, there are lots of interesting smells and sounds. Explain how the big clothes go to the big members of the family, the smallest to the smallest, and grades in between; how you tell boys' clothes from girls', etc. Stripping the bed to wash the linen is always done in a certain order, as is making it.

- **Cleaning the house.** To learn how to clean, or even to profit from watching you while you do it, the child must begin to notice the various pieces of furniture, to look for the dust, to spot ashtrays that need emptying, and to know where to put things that are out of place. He will soon know that there is a sequence to how you clean the house and each room in it. He will realize that washing windows and sweeping and mopping involve seeing (V) what is clean and what is dirty. In addition, most of these activities require different kinds of movements that are good kinesthetic practice—from the muscular strength of wringing a mop to the bilateral job of pushing a broom.

- **Clearing drawers and closets.** The child must remember where things are kept to get them out, remember where they go to put them back. He will find out something about sorting, matching, the sequence of what must be done next. He'll be faced with problem-solving, having to figure out the best place to put things, and why.

- **Shopping.** Hard as it may be, try to think of him as something more than an added burden that must be held onto all the while. Making shopping trips a learning experience for him may make them more interesting and bearable for you. He can feel the cold of the freezer in a grocery, the heat of the freezer lights. His beginnings in reading may well come with remembering the "look" and the colors of the labels and containers of his favorite foods. He'll need muscular strength for pushing or pulling the cart, lifting things in and out of it. He can find out about big, little, soft, hard, high, low, etc., from the myriad of products and packages. He will eventually realize that everything has a number, its price, which then goes on the cash register, and that it is all added together and must be paid.

In other words, everything you do when he is around, and everything he does in your presence, whether you can steal a few separate hours a day to devote solely to him in addition or not, can be a learning experience. If he is made to notice and experience all the tastes and smells and textures that are constantly coming up (and, by the way, you may find that you too are getting some valuable experience you may never before have had), he is learning a lot.

If he is given a chance and encouraged to move around and explore his world (his house and yard and the neighborhood, when someone can be with him outside) instead of being cooped up in a chair or playpen of some kind, he will be learning more and more how to move himself from here to there. If he is allowed to climb and crawl and creep and worm into all kinds of places and things (as long as the situation is reasonably safe), he will learn about moving himself and about how things look and feel and how far or close they are.

If you tell him what you are doing, what he is doing, what things are, give him names for what he sees, hears, smells, tastes, feels, and moves, he will be learning about language and how it is used. If you point out things he may not see, or interesting sights, pretty or ugly, that he would have missed; if you talk about how things look, how they look alike and different, he will be learning how to "see."

You see, you don't really have to have extra time; just use the time you have the best way you can. The fact is that mothers can teach children lots of things at home that they could never learn in school. There are learning areas that can never come up in school, which a teacher could never properly re-create, even if there was time to spare from the more urgent activities; the kinds of activities that are important to living and learning but that do not fit into a school atmosphere.

TEACHING FOR WHEN YOU HAVE THE TIME Or when an older child in the family has the time. There are a number of everyday activities which combine several postural transport and perceptual-cognitive abilities.

1. **Cards**. Matching cards by their colored backs, or matching numbers of cards, or the pictures on them. Casino (a simple version), Slap Jack, Battle, Concentration, etc. Counting cards, or just picking a few up and straightening them out, getting them in and out of a box.

2. **Setting the table**. "Let's see . . . who will eat?" Put up a finger for each one he mentions, perhaps with your help. "How many fingers is that?" If he counts four, "Now how many forks do we need?" When he can answer "four" for forks, knives, spoons, and napkins, and get the right number of each out, he will know about one-to-one, about counting things, about where things are kept, etc. "Now where does the napkin go . . . the fork?" etc., which requires visual memory. "What did you forget?" More memory for the salt and pepper, catsup, or whatever is regularly used on your table. He can fill the water glasses, place them in their proper places. He will, of course, have to learn just one simple step at a time, go on to the next only after he understands and can do the first one. But this is a great training experience.

3. **Picking up toys**. He can learn to take turns. "You put an animal in the box . . . Now I put an animal in the box . . . ," *or* obey commands, "Pick up the long blue block. Wait. Put it in the yellow basket. Pick up the round red block. Put it in the green box . . . ," *or* a sequence of commands, "Pick up the red block and put it in the green box," *or* the sorting experience of putting away several different categories of toys in their proper containers.

4. **Games**. London Bridge, Steal the Bone, Duck-Duck-Goose, Drop the Handkerchief, and lots of others are all learning games, especially for movement. "May I?" is a fine game (he must remember to say "May I?"; wait his turn; stay in his spot; take little or big, back or side steps, hop on one foot or both, etc.; obey commands). So is Simon Says, Hokey Pokey, Loopdeloo, and many others.

5. **Toy instruments**. He will learn that there are different

sounds when different things are done, that high notes go one way, low notes another. For a toy piano, xylophone, or organ, he must learn to strike only one key with a finger, strike hard enough to make the sound. Later, he can match the colors on the charts (as you point to them) to the colors on the keys, find the right key, and have the joy of hearing himself play a tune.

6. **DEGREES OF FREEDOM**. Most of the above activities help develop bilaterality, rhythm, and motor planning. Here are examples of a few more ordinary activities in each of these three categories:

Bilaterality. Swimming (backstroke, breaststroke, frog kick, flutter kick, crawl); pedal toys; paddling a canoe or rowing a boat; taking things out and putting them away with each, both, and alternate hands; swinging; rope climbing; pulling sled, truck, or pull toy with both hands; pushing wheelbarrow, toy carriage, sweeper, or lawn mower with both hands; dusting with both hands or cleaning windows with both hands in large circles.

Rhythm. Dance to records, piano, radio, to music with a strong beat, especially in family dance session; clap, stomp, nod head, sway, rock back and forth, bend knees, beat tomtom to music; march, clap, or stomp to drum, tambourine, or pan; pound nails, put in pegs, put blocks away to rhythm; bounce, walk, clap to metronome.

Motor planning. Climbing a tree and getting back down; acrobatics on a play set; figuring out for himself how to wash a spot off his hand, or how to rub a smudge off the back of his leg; learning how to open the car door to get in and out, how to hold packages, how to open the front door and get packages into the house, how to open gifts, how to unwrap a package of chewing gum, how to open a letter, how to fold and hang up a towel on a bar—all these activities, ranging from gross to fine movements, involve motor planning.

And we haven't even mentioned puppets, doll houses, toy

animals, trucks and trains, dressing and undressing dolls, tea sets, skating, flying kites, or helping to care for live pets—all of which are marvelous learning experiences in kinesthesia and audition or vision.

TRICKS OF THE TRADE It was not just a question of how much time I could spare and how much I wanted to teach Hannah. She had to be willing and able to learn. Many times I would give her something to do which I was sure she was ready for and nothing would happen except, perhaps, a little rebellion. So I tried to change it or add to it, so that she would *want* to try, and so she would be able to accomplish the task.

You may have noticed that we gave silly names to our kinesthetic activities. I also sang songs for them, usually her choice. When they began to get boring, I made up silly words for "Old MacDonald," "Popeye the Sailor," etc., according to her requests. We did not use an X for our visual targets, but pictures of people, animals, or objects that she liked. The "races" were hard for her, so I "raced" too, and it made it a contest—even a laugh riot when mother fell all over herself or did something wrong.

We did our flashlight chase against the background of an interesting story. In desk and language work, she often played teacher and told me what to do (and, incidentally, was required to learn more language to do this). I cut out the funniest magazine pictures I could find to illustrate prepositions, verbs, left and right, top and bottom. If something funny happened during our lesson, I not only laughed, but called her attention to it if she had missed it. We illustrated "too many" and "not enough," "more" and "less," "bigger" and "smaller" with cartoon characters on the board or in her favorite story books.

Hannah and numbers had little use for each other. She had had a good start (she counted things up to 5 and counted up to 100 when she was five or six; at eight, she knew that 1 and 1 more was 2, 2 and 1 more were 3)—and then nothing! She did not know or care about the difference between a nickel and a quarter, between last Tuesday and week-after-next.

But, when she was nine and a half, Dr. Barsch said that she

must learn about numbers, so we went at them with G, T, K, and A. We numbered stepping stones 1 to 10, and had her yell and whisper the numbers as she walked forward and backward, by twos as well as by ones. We counted frontward, backward, and by twos by writing with colored soap paint on the tile squares around the bathtub. We chose and ate cookies, played blocks, threw balls, sang "Ten Little Indians," seesawed, jumped, and fed the dog frontward, backward, and by twos. In two weeks, Hannah could look at a number on the board and tell what number came before, after, and two away.

We taped the pictures, words, letters or numbers we were working on over the printed labels of some of her board or manipulative games.

If a kinesthetic activity got too easy or too boring, I tried to add to it. An addition can be external: putting an obstacle in a child's path as he tries to continue a good rhythmic pattern while overcoming it; playing pitch and catch as he keeps his jumping rhythm on trampoline or mattress; setting up a maze of varying activities so that he must adapt quickly and still maintain a good pattern.

Internal additions can be language, concepts, audition, or problem-solving. You might give him a noun (rose) on one hop, and have him respond with a suitable color (red) on the next hop. You might give him a noun and ask for an adjective or verb as his answer. As the dangle ball swings away, you might name an article of clothing, a friend, a cartoon character, a piece of furniture, and he must name another as he kicks it. You may find, as I did, that you have a harder time initiating the nouns and adding to lists than he does answering you. I thought Hannah's first six verb responses to my nouns were worth recording: *boys* "cry," *girls* "giggle," *birds* "poo-poo," *fire* "hurts," *rain* "gets wet," and *lamp* "breaks."

YOUR REWARD It does not come in heaven. It comes *here*, all the time. It comes in trickles and it comes in big waves, like Hannah's sudden blossoming at the end of three months of intensive Movigenics training and one week of first-grade visits:

As we walked to school, I tried to pull up her coat collar

against the cold. "Not here," she said quietly, pulling away. "At home, but not here. You touch me at home. At school, I'm big."

I was always pointing out things to her, most of which she never saw in time. Now, in one drive downtown, *she* showed *me* a jet stream in the sky, a man washing a third-story office window, and a distant water tower.

When our temperamental television set went off in the middle of her favorite show, she did not run in whining, stamping, pulling at us or demanding, "Fix" or "Come!" Calmly smiling, she told her daddy, "I have a problem. The television doesn't work. Will you fix it for me please?"

She no longer pestered the dog when she spent the night at her teacher's house, but merely fed him when she was asked and immediately returned to the book she was reading, alone.

It is logical and obvious that since a child exists in space, depends upon all his perceptual abilities to learn, and develops in a progressive manner, he can learn when he is trained spatially and perceptually in a developmental way, building progressively on a solid foundation.

But when it happens—when a child suddenly and quickly accomplishes tasks that "experts" predicted shortly before he could *never* learn—it is no longer logical. It is a miracle!

6

How to Live with Hannah

MANAGEMENT

"I don't see how you cope.... You're wonderful.... I couldn't do it."

The people who think parents of children with learning disorders are wonderful because they cope with their children's problems are almost as aggravating as the pseudo-experts who believe that there is nothing wrong with these children but poor parental discipline.

How do you cope? You cope. If you have buck teeth, diabetes, a "normal" teenager, psoriasis, or a wooden leg, you cope. Everyone has problems. He either copes with them or is crushed by them. There are no medals for coping.

But a child is more than a problem to cope with. He is first of all a person, a member of a family, someone to be loved and cherished and, hopefully, to be taught to live with himself and society.

Meanwhile, what does a mother do with a three-year-old who tears up everything in sight . . . a four-year-old who tries to climb out of a moving car . . . a five-year-old who smears the walls with feces . . . a six-year-old who never sleeps . . . a seven-year-old who vanishes the second mother turns her back to answer the phone or go to the bathroom?

She does the only two things a loving but realistic parent can do: she accepts whatever *cannot* be changed, and she does her best to change whatever *can* be changed.

1. Accept behavior which the child cannot help.

The most obvious and urgent need of the child with learning disorders is to become an acceptable social being. Yet all the rules that worked so beautifully on his brothers and sisters either don't work at all for him, or do so in reverse.

The social behavior described in the books on child development does not grow by itself in a vacuum. It is merely an outgrowth of the same developmental process we have been considering. If a child has learning problems, he is bound to have problems learning social behavior, since his ability to handle space, time, language, multiplicity, and level is the same in a social as in an academic situation. His bilaterality, rhythm, motor planning, and flexibility—his degrees of freedom for fluid, successful movement—all are as underdeveloped for successful social adjustment as they are for academic achievement.

When he is better organized spatially and perceptually, he will not be so dependent on T that he has to tear up, so inflexible that he must keep tearing, so inefficient visually and kinesthetically that he has to "run away" from the yard or out of a moving car, so rhythmically disorganized that he cannot establish sleep and elimination patterns. When he learns to deal with near space, he will be able to play for longer periods and shrug off the interruptions of other children. With more visual and spatial flexibility, he will begin to interact with other people. As he learns how to communicate, he can modify his behavior according to the wishes of others, exchange ideas, and indicate his needs.

The child with learning disabilities is not plain ornery. He is "bad" because he does not know *how* to be "good." Most parents of such children already know this. It would help greatly if teachers, too, recognized this truth. If they did, they would cease blaming the parents for not teaching the children what these youngsters are not yet ready to learn, and it would enable the teachers to use the time now wasted on recriminations for *getting* these children ready.

2. *Try to change his world so that he can learn better behavior.*

ACCEPTANCE Once parents accept the fact that their child has a learning problem, they must then separate the child from the problem. Then they can help him accept his own limitations—without sympathy, without judging him, but with the confident expectation that things will be better.

They must also help him find his place. All of us need to belong somewhere. When Hannah had been out of school for most of a year and was ready to leave for her week's trial at a residential school, her only and repeated question was, "Do those children have brains that forget . . . do not work?" She did not fit where she was, for she was not in school like other children; maybe she would finally find her place.

Real acceptance by the rest of the family is as priceless as it is rare. If I have resented the aunt who cringes at Hannah's visits because she could not behave like other children her age, I have shuddered at the uncle who gives in to every whim out of pity.

ROUTINE A child like Hannah must have a daily routine that he can depend upon, so that he can experience the same events at the same time in the same way, and not be continually upset by change.

A big picture calendar tacked to a wall at his eye level can be the basis for this security, if it is used wisely. First, it is a good idea to make the calendar as the child watches, according to his "directions" as you probe them from him. Pictures are essential if he cannot read, important even if he can, for easy reminders. To weekly and monthly calendars, refer at least once a day. To the daily calendar, refer as often as seems necessary. Pretty soon, if it hangs in a conspicuous place, he will study the calendar on his own every day. But let him X out the previous day only in your presence, so that he will not ruin it and so that you can talk about what has already happened, is over, gone, and what will happen today and tomorrow, and even later.

You can study a long, yearly picture calendar with him to convey to him how long a year is. But most children can absorb little more than the length of one month or so. A monthly calendar will have birthdays, holidays, any trips or excursions, and the most important daily events (one or two) which appear on a weekly calendar. Since illustrations should be on his level, don't worry about your artistic skill, just so you can draw a birthday cake, a car, a Santa, or a child well enough for him to identify it.

The current weekly calendar you see here resembles the weekly calendars of the past but for one aspect: Hannah now needs illustrations only for very special events. Moreover, we now confine strict scheduling to those activities that must take place at a set time, for we have reached the stage where we

WEEKLY CALENDAR

	MONDAY	**TUESDAY**	**WEDNESDAY**
Morning	8:00 Leave for School 8:30 School starts	School	School
Afternoon	2:00 Come home 4:30 Set table 5:00 Cartoons 6:00 Dinner		4:30 Take Andy to piano lesson
Night	8:00 Bath and bed		

are reducing outside organization for her by degrees, to enable her to use her improved powers of organization to further organize herself. But because she still has difficulties with sequencing, we help her in separating weekdays from weekends.

WEEKLY CALENDAR

THURSDAY	FRIDAY	SATURDAY	SUNDAY
School	School	NO School Cartoons	
2:30 Beach	**1:30** My birthday party at School		
		7:00 Andy's party for big boys and girls, here	

From 9½ to 10½, Hannah was so void of outside activities

	MONDAY	**TUESDAY**	**WEDNESDAY**
	WAKE UP; GET DRESSED EAT BREAKFAST WATCH "CAPTAIN" LESSON WITH MOTHER		
OUTDOOR ACTIVITY	Skate	Take Mollie for a walk	Trampoline
MAKE SOMETHING	Cook	Sew	Hammer
LUNCH			
QUIET ACTIVITY	Type	Tape recording	Read
VISIT	Grocery	Laundry	Park
LESSON	Miss J.	Miss H.	Miss J.
OUTDOOR PLAY	Jump rope	Ball	Ad lib
PLAY WITH MOM	Doll house	Animals	Play-do
DINNER			
TALK, DANCE, OR PLAY GAMES WITH DADDY AND ANDY			
BATH			
BEDTIME ACTIVITY	Wrestling and finger games	Lifts and tongue exercises	Races
MASSAGE			

that we used a much more structured, detailed calendar:

THURSDAY	FRIDAY	SATURDAY	SUNDAY
\multicolumn{3}{WAKE UP; GET DRESSED EAT BREAKFAST WATCH "CAPTAIN" LESSON WITH MOTHER}	Ad lib
Skate	Take Mollie for a walk	Trampoline	
Paint	Cut and paste	Ad lib	
	LUNCH		
Puzzle	Type	Tape recording	
Dime Store	Friend	Walk	
Miss H.			
Trampoline	Jump rope	Ball	
Puppets	Dress dolls	Games	
	DINNER		
	TALK, DANCE, OR PLAY GAMES WITH DADDY AND ANDY		
	BATH		
Wrestling and finger games	Lifts and tongue exercises	Races	
	MASSAGE		

Here is a typical daily calendar that worked for most periods between Hannah's seventh and ninth years:

6:45
Wake up
Get dressed

7:30
Eat breakfast

8:00
Watch "Captain"

8:30
Go to school

12:00
Come home,
play with dog

12:30   Eat lunch

DAILY CALENDAR AGE 7 THROUGH 9

1:15
Play outside

2:00
Lesson with Mother

4:00   Watch TV

6:00   Eat dinner

7:00
Take a bath

8:00
Go to bed

Calendars are only part of the problem of routine. Mother must decide in advance not only what she is going to do, but also when, where, and in what order. Once she has done so, she must carry out her plans exactly, verbalizing every activity as she and the child go along. Such individual activities as eating, bathing, and dressing should always be done in the same place, at the same time, and in the same order as far as possible. For a severely disorganized child, you may have to drive to school by the same route every day, squeeze the toothpaste from the same spot and fill his water glass to the same line.

STRUCTURING Structure everything for him. Cut down multiplicity into small units; interpret cause and effect for him; verbalize each situation; praise and reward positives and in most cases ignore negatives; reduce multiplicity in areas which immediately concern him, keeping bare and orderly his room, his eating place, the bathroom he uses, the kitchen when he works or plays there.

RECOGNIZE FATIGUE Fatigue lowers stress tolerance for everyone, and poorly organized children tire quickly and easily. Their tolerance is low at best; when they are tired it is practically non-existent. If such a child needs rest, negative behavior, disorganization, and explosions are a certainty. Hannah took a "rest" during the day until she was nine, and sometimes needed one even when she was older. It is not always easy to tell, but at the first signs of fatigue, let him rest *before* he is *too* tired. And no matter how much you both have looked forward to an important event, postpone it if he is too tired to handle the additional stress.

REMEMBER HIS VARIABILITY Hannah and children like her are different from each other. They also vary greatly from day to day, even hour to hour, in their own ability, stress tolerance, and degree of fatigue. If something that worked fine on Monday turned into a fiasco on Tuesday, I learned not to blame myself. Hannah was not permanently regressing. She was merely behaving like a child with learning disorders.

UNDERSTAND YOURSELF Few parents (or teachers) are so well organized that they are comfortable and competent in all situations. If we can find our own particular learning patterns and stress reactions, we can adapt ourselves in order to function comfortably, to avoid needless frustrations, and to plan appropriately for our children.

As a product of our unique and uneven experiences in organization, space, time, and our own perceptual abilities (GOTKAV), we prefer the activities and situations that fit us best. For instance, if we prefer to talk and listen, we will learn new games, find locations, keep appointments, follow instructions, study for tests or speeches better if we are told; we will enjoy selling more than bookkeeping. If we rely more on what we see, we will learn better from a book, a list, or a note. If we depend heavily on gestures and movement, we learn better by taking things apart, making diagrams, writing notes, underlining what we read.

We have our spatial preferences as well. If we are better oriented in near space, we may like to sew, read, play board games, play musical instruments, do arts and crafts, fixit jobs around the house; to dance, swim, walk, or any of the individual sports; choose office work over other kinds. If our far space is better organized, we will probably choose creative and imaginative occupations over the humdrum workaday world, have an awful time making ourselves write letters or bother with details, enjoy far space recreations as boating, tennis, golf, camping, traveling, and watching major sports. If mid space is our meat, Ping-Pong, archery, and badminton may be our pleasures.

Make a list of ten things you most enjoy doing and ten things you hate most to do. Observe yourself in action—or in inaction, if you are low K (low on movement)—for a week or so. You may be surprised at the things you like, at the way you have to do things to make them work. You may discover for the first time that the things you enjoy or hate most, the way you adjust to new or routine situations, is *not* the way everybody does it, but the way *you* do it because it fits your personal organization.

You have learned to avoid stress, to "structure" the world for yourself. If you cannot talk sensibly in a large group or with a lot of noise, you don't try. If you want to scream at the sound of someone chomping on an apple or scraping a fingernail on a balloon, you try to stop such noises. If you cannot talk or read with TV on, you turn it off, leave the room, or do your reading and talking another time. If you get upset when you have to read for information over a long period of time or when you try to do handwork, you avoid such reading and shun handwork. If you cannot deal visually with large gatherings of people or crowded highways, you avoid them. You do not fail, because you have learned how to "get along."

But sometimes we cannot avoid what bothers us. Some of the activities and procedures that are important for children with learning disorders may interfere with our way of functioning. If we do not recognize the offending procedures and activities so that we can adapt them to ourselves and ourselves to them, we will either have to deny our children part of what they need or try to give it to them and be constantly under stress ourselves. If we do recognize our limitations and preferences, we can adapt, our children will profit, and we will be happy in our management and teaching.

WHAT THE CHILD MUST LEARN

Now that we have him all set up in the proper atmosphere, what is it he has to learn? It boils down to "how to play the game," which means learning the rules and obeying them.

First, he must fit into his family unit, usually three people or more. He must depend on his parents, but start developing independence. He must learn the rules, routine, and regulations of the family. He must learn to dress himself, use the bathroom, feed himself, entertain himself, and participate in family activities—a tall order for any child, an impossible task for a disorganized, disoriented one. And, when he cannot reach the family goals, he must bear the reactions to his failure from parents, brothers, and sisters.

And that is only the beginning! After trying to "play the

game" at home, he is supposed to learn the rules and regulations that hold for church, the store, the doctor's office, the bus, a neighbor's house, school—and obey those. Every new situation calls for more complicated, more integrated spatial, visual, and language abilities. What other children seem to absorb by osmosis, he must be specifically taught. If parents do not spell out the rules *for* him, he just cannot "play the game."

SELF HELP If your child is a messy eater who constantly spills and becomes entangled with fork and spoon; a non-dresser who either runs or turns limp when it is time to put on or take off clothing; and a terror in the bathroom, he is a typical child with a learning disorder. All he needs is a lot of help.

EATING Even eating alone involves visual-motor, gustatory, and near-space abilities that may be beyond him. To avoid a hunger strike, or his stuffing his mouth with a whole sandwich which he will finally have to spit out, you may have to say as I once did for Hannah at lunchtime, waiting, of course, until each command is obeyed before issuing the next one: "Pick up your sandwich . . . no . . . just one piece . . . take a bite . . . put it down . . . chew it . . . chew it good . . . keep on chewing . . . swallow it . . . eat a potato chip . . . now pick up your sandwich . . . take a bite . . . bite hard, all the way through . . . put it down . . . chew it . . . swallow it . . . finish that piece . . . now you may have your milk."

But the foremost problem affecting both the entire family and the child may be sitting through an entire meal. What was supposed to be our daily happy family get-together, soon began to be looked forward to with dread. Hannah constantly got up to play with everyone's silver, sometimes throwing it about. She didn't shrink from seasoning the drinking water with salt and pepper, from squeezing catsup all over the place, from grabbing whatever she could. Sometimes, when she herself had endured more than she could bear, she would climb on the table or get under it, turn over chairs, or pull off the tablecloth. Much of the time she was incapable of eating anything.

As for the rest of us, we had difficulty in digesting our meals. The experts had told us that Hannah must eat with us. But only Dr. Barsch had told us *how* she could eat with us.

Structuring general space. Hannah always sat at the dinner table in the same place for every meal, including snacks, although the rest of us ate breakfast and lunch elsewhere. Her seat faced a blank wall. Nobody sat by her side. Andy first sat across from her, but he objected to having forks thrown at him, so he and I exchanged places.

Structuring immediate space. We used a large dark-colored placemat for her, over the white plastic-coated cloth that served for the rest of us then. Her plate was bread-and-butter size, white, and painted with an inch-wide red cross. Besides her plate, she was given only a fork and a napkin, always in the same place. We had a spotlight put in the ceiling that beamed on her place, in marked contrast to the regular ceiling light that did for the rest of the table.

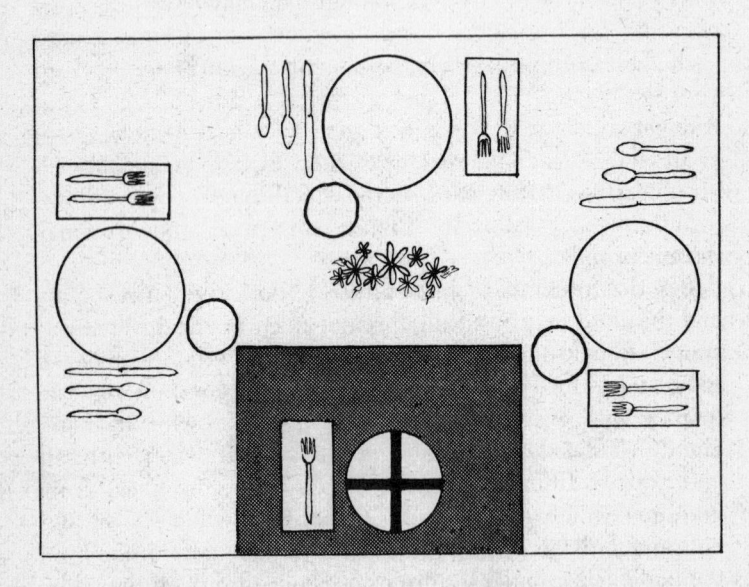

STRUCTURING THE FAMILY DINNER TABLE

Portions. We started serving her one item of food at a time, right in the middle of her plate. When she could handle more, we distributed the various foods neatly into the four sections we had marked off with the red cross, never giving her more than she could eat comfortably.

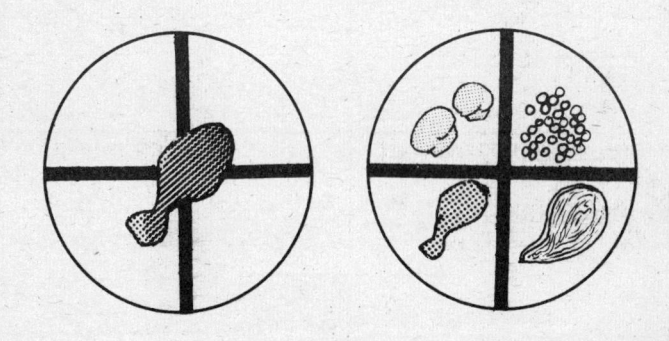

WHERE PORTIONS GO

Her chair had to be high enough for her elbows to be at table level, just as for her lessons, so she needed a foot rest here too. Since her job was to eat, we tried not to discuss anything that was removed in time or distance, which would have distracted her from what she was doing. That was not much of a hardship; we had never before been able to consider carrying on a conversation of any kind. We confined our dinner repartee to what Hannah had done just before coming to the table, what we were doing now, and what Hannah would do when she was finished.

As an additional aid to the business at hand, I made Hannah a little illustrated booklet from very hard slick cardboard pages (cut from spiral-notebook covers), which I covered with transparent plastic:

SIT ON LINE ON CHAIR. PAGE 1	**PUT NAPKIN ON LAP.** PAGE 2
WAIT FOR FOOD. PAGE 3	**PUT FOOD ON MIDDLE OF PLATE.** PAGE 4
PUT ON KETCHUP, PEPPER, SALT. PAGE 5	**PICK UP FORK OR SPOON.** PAGE 6
PUT IT IN YOUR MOUTH. PAGE 7	**TAKE SOME MORE. CLEAN YOUR PLATE.** PAGE 8
WIPE YOUR MOUTH PAGE 9	**"MAY I BE EXCUSED, PLEASE?"** PAGE 10

HANNAH'S TABLE BOOK illustrated on a separate page.   *Each successive step in eating was*

Just as we increased the variety of Hannah's food as she learned to handle more, so we added a salad-sized white plate with a thinner (¾ inch) cross to her utensils and cut an inch off all around her mat after a few months had passed. After another few months, she graduated to a dinner-sized plate with a ½-inch cross and a mat that was hardly bigger than the plate. Before long, the mat was gone, her plate was the same as ours, and we were beginning to enjoy normal dinner conversations. As her tolerance improved, Hannah was expected to display the same manners as Andy.

DRESSING I structured Hannah's space by sitting near her on her bed, my back to the wall, facing her, so that she had both me and the wall for limits. I had her clothes ready and in order before we started. And, if I ever thought of trying to change the sequence for what might be a better one, I put it out of my mind. We started with undershirt; underpants; socks; pants, skirt, or slip; shirt, blouse, or dress; then shoes—and that is the way we kept it. I named all the body parts used and all the items of clothing as we came to them, describing all the movements she was supposed to make when I dressed her and, later, when she dressed herself.

Most clothes just won't stay put, which makes them doubly hard for a Hannah, who does not even know how to move herself the way she wants to. So shoes, with a definite shape, are the easiest place to start "doing it myself." At first, I had to loosen the laces and take them out of the top holes to give her plenty of room, hold the tongue up, and hand each shoe to Hannah facing the right way, right in front of the proper foot. All she had to do was get it on. Later, we got to, "Pick up the shoe . . . Where does it go? . . . Is that the right foot? . . . Pull the laces . . . Find the tongue . . . pull the tongue up . . . hold the shoe with both hands . . . no, turn it around . . . put it on . . . push your foot . . . ," always waiting until she performed one step before telling her what to do next.

Hannah's clothes were always laid out in the order in which they were to be put on: the first garment nearest her, the second next, and so forth. I also laid them out in the position in which they went on: pants with the top facing her and front side up, undershirt with the bottom toward her, front side down, etc.

She could not "see" the difference between front and back, right and left, so I helped her. I marked the backs of shirts, undershirts, blouses, dresses, pants, and socks at the top with colored thread, marking pen, or name labels; marked her right shoe on the bottom with one color, the left shoe with another.

When she was ready to start dressing herself, she had weeks and months and years of my "showing and telling" her where and how her hands, feet, and head went into what. I did not bow out all at once, merely expected her to learn only one part of putting on one item at a time. In handling her undershirt herself, she first learned to get her head in, later added an arm, then both arms, and finally could pull it down herself.

Color clues allowed her to help put her things away—one color tape on her pajama drawer, another color on her sweater drawer, a paper tracing of her shoes taped to the closet floor.

I always looked (not always successfully) for clothes with elastic or self-sticking tape around the waist, in preference to garments with zippers, buttons, or snaps. When she was ready, I searched for *large* buttons and snaps and *smooth* zippers, and for garments that fastened in front (hard to find). She had been struggling for four years to tie her shoes completely alone, and it was still very difficult. But she was embarrassed to have someone else tie them for her, so we bought a loafer instead, as soon as her foot was big enough for that style.

An occupational therapy trick made easy the impossible task of getting her coat on by herself: she laid her coat on a bench, table, couch, or bed, top toward her, front-side-up; put both arms in the armholes upside-down; lifted her arms over her head; and the coat slid into place. Hannah herself thought of using the same trick for cardigan sweaters, pajama tops, and blouses that opened in front.

Gradually we did not need the color clues for putting things away, she could manage simple buttons and snaps, she could sometimes figure out which shoe went on which foot without color markings, she knew what part of her went into which part of her clothing. I gave her less and less verbal support, moved farther and farther away from her as she dressed—from the bed to a chair to a farther chair to the door and, finally, outside the door. Came the happy day when she could come down to say "Good morning" and be sent back up to her room to dress herself and return for breakfast—*alone!*

BATHROOM We have looked at the perils of the relatively simple task of hand-washing. Teaching a child with learning disorders to use the toilet is immeasurably harder. Thanks to the availability of garments with elasticized waists, Hannah was taught to pull her panties up and down with one hand literally tied in front of her. It took her almost eight years to learn such things as not unrolling the toilet paper for fun and to tear it off without unrolling several yards of it; to release the handle, once flushing had started; and to cover herself up properly, without leaving odds and ends of undergarments sticking out, when she had finished. Worst of all was to teach her the unmentionable task of wiping herself, the hardest aspect of mastering use of the toilet from beginning to end.

I verbalized everything. I gave her only one little part of the task to master at a time. I kept everything but soap, towels, face cloths, and her step stool hidden. I tried to confine my teaching to the times when she really needed to use the bathroom so that it all made sense to her—and I still was never quite sure we would live through the trials of the toilet.

Milady's bath is important, recurring, and difficult enough to warrant some detailing. I tried to remember always to make the water comfortably warm, neither too hot nor too cold. Until she was ten, she bathed with a sponge (whose stable shape required no bilaterality). Nothing but sponge and soap, in their special, convenient places, were in sight. She got her bath toys *after* she washed herself.

The hardest part of Hannah's complete bathroom training was to teach her the sequence of the various operations. I had to verbalize each step for her, waiting after each command until she had completed that task before we could start on the next step. We covered every part of her body—face, neck, arms, legs, and torso—in complete detail and practiced the entire drying out process from getting herself dry, to squeezing out and returning to their proper places the sponge and the soap, as well as letting the water out of the basin or tub. At first, Hannah washed only her arms, and I finished up her face and ears and the rest of her body. Gradually, she herself did her legs, then her body, and finally her face, neck, and ears as well.

Toileting, hair-brushing, and tooth-brushing were all a part of the bath-time ritual, so they had to be done in the same order, same place, and same way as well.

It took a few months after Hannah had started to wash and bathe her entire body before I could venture to move from the tub to a nearby seat, directing her from this short distance. In another couple of months I was able to move to a chair at the other end of our small bathroom. Still later, I could merely stand by the door, giving her much less verbal support. Before long, I could confine myself to peeking in every so often. Finally, I managed to leave Hannah almost entirely to herself during her ablutions, without being greeted by a flood. If it sounds as though she improved by leaps and bounds, well, she did—but over a period of some two years.

SOCIAL GRACES A young child relates mostly to his parents. To say that Hannah did not relate positively with other children is an understatement. Any incident not handled at the outset was bound to explode and set off negative learning all around.

Hannah could not move efficiently from here to there, which meant that she could not observe or think sequentially, which meant that she had no way of understanding cause and effect. When she could not even organize her own movement, space, or language, she could not possibly figure out the simplest social interactions without help.

For a long time, Hannah was unable to recognize her responsibility for the undesirable results of her own actions. When she pulled a pony's tail, pushed or hit someone, or tweaked a tempting nose, she was astonished at the resulting screams, cries, whines, kicks, and other negative reactions she elicited. She was also surprised, distressed, or amused, as the case may be, by the response she received for ruffling a visiting child's hair or hugging him. But it never occurred to her to return a well-aimed punch from another child: "He hit me, so I'll hit him," or conversely, "I hit him, that's why he is hitting me back" requires an understanding of cause and effect.

The best way for her to learn cause and effect would have been for her to get back what she dished out. This is not always easy to arrange, especially immediately and without coaching. Other children like her did not know what to do any better than she did. Older children very sweetly reassured me, "That's all right. She can't help it. I don't mind." Whenever I could, I made them repay her in kind. Spontaneous or not, the results of her actions were always explained to her, "Mary pushed you because you pushed Mary. You did not like it. Mary does not like to be pushed either."

Second best for teaching Hannah to learn the relation between cause and effect were the use of illustrated stories and acting out situations—with ourselves and dolls and puppets the principals—to get the point across. Since Hannah is still very dependent on tactuality, especially when she is under the stress of a novel or difficult situation, "bothering" others remains one of her major problems in social intercourse.

One afternoon I poured Hannah and Andy some grape juice. This was before she had much language, so she gestured that she did not want this color juice. "Do you want something to drink, Hannah?" She nodded. "You may have this grape juice." She was very upset. This was not fair. "Are you thirsty?" She indicated that she was. "Do you want the grape juice?" She did not. She still made no connection between being thirsty and accepting the juice. She simply blamed me for denying her something she wanted. I realized that she would never learn how to adapt to such frustrating situations if I let the matter rest there. I tried to be very calm and supporting: "It is all right if you do not want the juice, Hannah. . . . But you won't have anything to drink then, see? And you will be thirsty. Andy and I are drinking the grape juice, and Andy does not like it best either. All right. I will take it away. Andy and I have finished ours anyway."

Since she was still sitting in her chair, I said, "You are thirsty. Your grape juice is still in the glass. You may drink it. If you don't drink the grape juice, you will have nothing to drink. Do you want it? No? Then you may get down and you can go back outside." The next time we had grape juice I asked her only once if she wanted it. She did not, so I took it away, and she did without again. The next time, she drank it. Grape juice became her favorite drink. But the important thing was that she had taken a little step forward toward adaptability.

FAUX PAS When Hannah was trying to be "a big girl" or to do a good deed, she often caused mild havoc instead. She did not know how or why the road to disaster was paved with her good intentions, only that it was.

There was the time I bought Hannah a milk shake at a soda fountain, then turned to greet a friend. Not wanting to disturb us, she carefully picked up the heavy cold metal container to refill her glass herself. She carried off the whole thing beautifully, even to the point of stopping the flow before the glass spilled over. But she had misjudged the height of the counter; she let the container go too soon, and over it went, still half full! She could see the goo oozing toward her over the counter, could hear my shrill admonishments about her pretty new dress, but she had no idea how to get out of the way. When it was too late, she made futile efforts to do something—she knew not what—and overturned her water glass, making a bigger mess.

Cold and sticky, she could not understand why she could not take off her dress and panties in the drug store. She tried to wipe the counter and her dress with some napkins, making things worse. By now she was frantic, confused, and almost beside herself. Seeing how disturbed she was and how completely victimized by circumstances beyond her control, I wanted only to help her. "These things just happen," I said, "to everybody . . . it was nobody's fault."

During our drive home, we talked some more. "I am not angry. You were trying to help. You are a big girl." We thought, and talked some more. "Sometimes, when you try to help, you make a mistake. Your brain forgets to tell your hands what to do. Bill and Sam's brains forget sometimes too. But that's okay, because they can't help it either. Someday your brain will learn to remember. Okay? Would you like to go home and take off that funny chocolate dress?"

At about this time, Hannah's entire class at the school she attended was learning that each of them had problems of one sort or another. This knowledge enabled them to accept the upset feelings of another child with, "He's having a hard time now. I had a hard time yesterday . . . or maybe I will have a hard time tomorrow. His problem may be different from mine, but I am not the only person who has one. That's life." I saw their teacher take a little deaf girl aside when she criticized the way Hannah was cutting out a picture. "Your ears are broken. Okay? . . . Hannah's ears are not broken. But sometimes her brain forgets to tell her hands. So Hannah cuts the picture wrong. She is not bad. Her brain forgets. Okay? . . . Your ears are broken. Her brain forgets. Okay?" The little deaf girl smiled, and went back to pat Hannah.

When Hannah's good intentions go awry, my first reaction (as in the milk-shake incident) is often far from helpful. When she tries to set the table and spills a glass of water in the salad bowl, when she decides to water my plants because she knows I hate to do it and kills half of them, I often sound far more disorganized than she does. By the time I understand her motives and grasp the entire situation, a good deal of damage has been done. And then, mine are by no means the only negative, terrifying reactions our little girl has encountered in her career. I try my best to control my negative feelings, unless they are justified, but I must admit I don't always succeed.

When Hannah was finally ready to relate to another child, initially the only way she could do so was clumsy and direct, by picking on or hitting that child. When she wanted to play with children she did not know, Hannah commanded no socially acceptable methods of commencing an acquaintanceship.

Even at the age of five or six, Hannah was still so highly tactual that she could not stop bothering any child who was near her. She was unable to listen to a story or to participate in a game with another child, because she could not keep her hands off him. Only a rubber band, sticky tape, or a string, something to keep her hands busy, enabled Hannah to stop annoying her playmate and to pay attention to what she herself was supposed to be doing.

But gradually Hannah progressed from aggressive contact to hugging. At this stage, when she had a little visitor whose arrival she had awaited with eagerness, I once again had to structure the situation for her: "We're finished playing with dolls. We shall now put the dolls away. You put your doll here, Alice. Hannah, you put your doll there. Fine. Cover them up. Now you can play ball. Hannah, get the big red ball. Where is it? Is it in a drawer? In a box? ..."

Once I had the children going on dolls or on ball playing, or on any other game they were able to suggest or I had to suggest to them, I made myself invisible and eavesdropped, so that I could miraculously reappear only when needed. I continued to do so until Hannah was eight and a half, an age when she was still very disorganized. But a year later, I was dismissed with, "We play by ourselves. You go to your room." I could now confine myself to suggesting that they might go outside to play this or that game, or to offering a list of indoor activities they might enjoy. Then I felt free to disappear, looking in on them only every 20 or 30 minutes. In any event, still very disorganized or much better organized, Hannah no longer had to touch and pull other children when she could engage with them in concrete, interesting activities.

If Hannah found it hard to understand physical responses to her behavior, imagine how hard it was for her to interpret emotional reactions to her inappropriate conduct. When she seemed old enough to understand the distinction, at about nine, her teacher tackled the meanings of "rude" and "polite." The teacher made one list of all the rude things a child might do and say, and another of the things that are considered polite, and then illustrated these examples of behavior with pictures. These important lessons of what happens to a child when he is rude and when he is polite were boiled down into a small booklet:

RUDE When I am not nice to people, I am RUDE. When I am rude, people will not like me. I will NOT have friends. Rude children say GIMME. SHUT UP. They forget to say PLEASE. THANK YOU. They push, hit, and mess up other people's hair.

POLITE When I am nice to other people, I am POLITE. When I am polite, people will like me. I will have FRIENDS. POLITE *means to say* PLEASE. THANK YOU. EXCUSE ME. I'M SORRY. I will ASK *for help. I will not touch people.*

Once the concepts of "polite" and "rude" had soaked in, Hannah was often able to check impulsive "negative" behavior on her part by being reminded that she was being rude, and that "If you're rude, people will not like you and you will have no friends. If you're polite, people will like you and you'll have friends."

When she was so much better organized at 10½, her chief "rudeness" was foul language, picked up from older children at her residential school. Words came out of her mouth that she could not possibly comprehend and that I had never heard from anyone. But she had obviously gotten a rise out of them, and used them constantly. Talking with her about "rude" and "polite" on her home visits began an immediate cleanup of her language.

HELPING THE LEARNING PROCESS

BE CONSISTENT This is a toughie for an absent-minded mother like me, but it is essential. If sitting on a desk, standing on the couch, or cuddling on the top shelf of the linen closet was not allowed for Hannah—it was not allowed. If she was doing it for a joke, unawares, because she was cranky, or in imitation of another child—it was still not allowed. If I was in a marvelously generous mood, if she had already been corrected so many times that day that I felt like a wicked overseer, if I was up to my elbows in cleaning and stuffing a turkey—it was not allowed. Consistency may be the bugaboo, but it was certainly an effective teacher of a young mind.

What about that daily routine that sounds so great? How do you get daddy off to work, Andy off to school (and you may have three or four more to shoo out of the house in the morning), and Hannah herself ready for class in time if you stick to your routine? Simple. I got up a half-hour earlier—an hour earlier during more difficult periods. When I felt I was headed for exhaustion, I took a nap while Hannah was in school or rested when she did. And there was no law that I had to watch the Late Show at night, or finish a book in one sitting. I did not want to spend my whole family-leisure time putting one child to bed either, so I started at that earlier to get through earlier. Planning helped. But sometimes Hannah was a bit late to school. And let's be honest—a handicapped child is going to steal time from his family. But if that time is spent teaching the child to help himself, he is going to steal progressively less time from those around him.

KNOW WHEN TO CHANGE This is the hardest of all, even for my "normal" child. And no, it does not conflict with consistency. The idea is to keep your training and expectations consistent until your child's development warrants new training procedures and new expectations. I once felt as though I would have to spend the rest of my life kneeling by the tub while Hannah cleaned her ears, and standing behind her ready to leap for the spoon as she put cocoa into her glass of milk. But I didn't. Gradually I moved away, gradually I kept my mouth shut—until she was on her own. The only way she could ever move toward independence was to take the organization upon herself when she was capable enough.

How did I know when she was ready? It's easy to say, "Try her," but I was sort of busy just handling things as they were. I couldn't try her at everything. Oh, I could give her a go at simple movement tasks now and then—opening a car door, riding a bike with training wheels, trying to help make a bed— and I did. But the bigger changes—when she could be allowed a little more freedom outside, when she could try "real" rather than "baby" scissors, when she needed added reassurance of her own worth because she was becoming conscious of her inadequacies—were another matter.

For years she could not follow directions, watch for traffic, tell a friend from a stranger, cut her meat, open a car door, stop tearing up magazines, tie her shoes, behave at a swimming pool, or be trusted one minute out of my sight. Now she can do most of these things, and is learning to do the rest.

How did I know that Hannah finally could tell the difference between stepping off the top of her high sliding board and a low step, between jumping into a fathomless pit and a baby pool ? How could I be sure she knew better than to taste the rat poison, or to run her finger along the edge of a broken windowpane? How could I tell that she understood cause and effect well enough to profit from punishment? It's hard to say. I can't say that I always knew, could be sure. Because I was with her constantly, I did not always have the perspective to evaluate subtle changes in her, almost from hour to hour. It takes an interested outsider, a teacher, a wise friend, or a relative who is not with a child *all* the time to suggest now and then that it is time for a change.

For instance, I knew Hannah's "collapses" were not "temper tantrums," but was not sure she knew what went on, because suddenly she was crying quietly, her sweet and loving self again. When they were over, I ignored them and got her interested in something else. But her teacher realized when Hannah was eight or nine that she was ashamed and embarrassed by these "collapses" and even more disturbed because she had no control over them.

So I had to learn that this could not be passed over as if nothing had happened, any more than the other unpleasantness that her developmental problems caused.[1] "No, Hannah, you are not a bad girl. You are a very big and good girl, and I love you very much. You threw the books because you felt bad. Your head hurt. You could not help it," I said, trying not to rub my bruised shin and standing in front of the large hole her head had made in the plasterboard wall. Only by talking about it could she get rid of her guilt and eventually learn to help prevent the collapses by lying down or telling me if she "felt bad" or her "head hurt." Because allergy pills, peace, and quiet could prevent them. A year earlier, before she was developmentally ready for this kind of explanation, talking about it probably would not have helped.

KEEPING CONTROL When Hannah's brother interrupted what he was doing to attend to something more interesting, he was

---

[1] Too many teachers, confronted by behavior from children with learning disorders that is distasteful and bizarre to them, try to push it out of their own minds and the minds of the children in the class. Beginning psychology students know that unpleasantness is not overcome by repressing it, only by examining it until it is understood.

often having a profitable experience. When Hannah got off the track, she was never going to get back on again unless someone saw to it that she did.

Let's say she was getting dressed in the morning. She might get her pajama top half-way off and start reading aloud from a book that I could not get her to look at the night before. I managed to hold my applause, gently but firmly put the book aside, telling her, "You may read it after you get dressed and have breakfast. Now get your pajama top off." She would remove her pajamas, slip on her panties—and she was over at the chalkboard. What a marvelous opportunity to work on bilaterality! But I resisted the temptation and gently but firmly returned her to her place of business, the bed where she was supposed to be dressing.

She has made what seemed like a hundred side trips in the course of putting on her clothes and completing her bathroom chores. It was up to me to get her back on the straight-and-narrow, and not be led astray myself. It is not only easier to follow the line of least resistance, but natural to become absorbed oneself in the side interest, especially if it is a desirable one in itself. I simply kept reminding myself that staying on the track was the most important thing for Hannah at the time.

We mothers notice early that kids are impossible on the very days we have a headache, are worried, or get too little sleep. Children with learning disorders dramatize this need for parental self-control. When I began teaching Hannah in formal lessons at home, I found out in a hurry that if I lost control of myself (looked angry or upset, raised the pitch of my voice, shouted or threatened) I lost control of Hannah as well. I lost her not only for that moment, but for the rest of the day, sometimes for two or three days.

I made the remarkable discovery that a tranquilizer *I* took improved her behavior immensely. When I learned to look, talk, and be serious and firm without being angry and annoyed, I no longer needed tranquilizers to teach her. When she made a mistake or acted silly, I told myself what I knew was true, that it was because she was under stress and could not help it. As I stopped reprimanding her for mistakes and silliness, she cut down on both.

On the other hand, if I showed I was upset because Hannah would not come out of a neighbor's yard, she was compelled to fight me. And if I joined with her in hand-to-hand combat or tug-of-war, I was sure to be defeated by a little girl who weighed in at about one-third my fighting weight. It was not until I forced myself not to appear anxious, refused to grapple with her, and dared to turn my back and wait that she could let herself be led back to her room as a penalty for "running away."

There is another kind of self-control that allows a parent to listen unshaken and answer honestly and fully comments on sex and matters that distress a child. I never shilly-shallied about the doctor or dentist, and we never had any problems there. But I thought it was better to change the subject or butter-up explanations about the Three Stooges' murderous antics, branding cattle, a little girl she did not like, or any incidents associated with danger, especially burning. These things were constantly coming up in her conversation, frequently appearing in nightmares.

Only when we began talking freely about them, analyzing them from every angle, drawing pictures, making up songs, telling jokes, did she—and we—find out why they bothered her. And then they no longer did. I had tried reassuring myself with the information in books on bringing up children that all children have nightmares, so forget it, but that was a flop. What helped was discovering that all her fears were based on her inability to visualize tactuality. On the one hand, she depended on touch to an unusual degree. On the other, her tactuality was still so poorly organized that, to her, "hurting" and "burning" meant only what she saw and heard of the effects, not a personal awareness or "knowledge" of injury and pain. Consequently, Hannah found it hard to stay away from things and activities that might hurt her.

Once I admitted, "Okay, you don't like Toby. Why?" I found out *why* she did not like a little girl in her class. Then she was able to go on from her new understanding and develop a liking for Toby. Her long preoccupation with sex disappeared just as quickly, as soon as we stopped "misunderstanding" what Hannah said, what she asked, and how she wanted the pictures drawn. At the end of a very "sexy" weekend, the subject was closed.

Apply self-control, or whatever is called for, but don't use a child with learning disorders as a scapegoat. I soon realized that to solve all crimes with "It's Hannah's fault" is hardly cricket, even if she is guilty much of the time. The lamp is broken... the toilet is running over... the gas is turned on... Daddy's watch is gone...does not always have to be "Hannah's fault." Sometimes someone else could have made a mistake.

To recommend self-control does not mean that I always have my emotions in hand, or even that I believe it humanly possible to be objective all the time, in every situation.

When I mentioned Hannah's "running away" and how it was overcome, I did not mean to imply that I coldly observed her misbehavior, then dealt with it. My terror and feeling of helplessness when she was lost or in a precarious situation rarely permitted me to act in a way that might have cut down on the frequency of her disappearances. By the time she was found, I acted hysterically rather than with sternness and wisdom. I might burst into tears of relief when the patrolman brought her home an hour later. I might temper my relief with horror, as at the two men in bathing trunks who calmly conversed at the side of a pool, while Hannah—fully dressed—was floundering in the deep end until I managed to fish her out. I might have to hide unreasonable indignation, as at the hotel cooks who were feeding Hannah cookies during the 25 minutes I had been frantically racing through corridors, shops, elevators, stairways, and storage rooms looking for her (she had vanished from a small drugstore, opening streetside onto an eight-lane thoroughfare in a strange city, and into a block-long hotel under renovation).

The time I delivered Hannah to her residential school, I only pretended calmness and good cheer. The next morning I saw her in the playground through the office window. Sober-faced, she was standing alone, head down, brushing her toe in the dirt (I knew she had not cried her first night before they told me; she seldom cried, and then only when her feelings were hurt).

To me, she looked utterly lost . . . hopeless . . . friendless. I felt the same desolation—for her and for me. I was also violently resentful that I had to leave her in a place where I felt no one knew her, understood her, loved her, or cared what happened to her. Why did *my* little girl have to choose between no school and no friends, or leaving behind everyone whom she loved and counted on?

It was not guilt that I felt, because this school seemed the only possible thing to do. In fact, when I turned from the window, I began to feel nothing. All afternoon, as I sat alone in a motel, I seemed to be watching myself and wondering at my calm. I did not unpack or wash or think of eating, or even smoke a cigarette. I felt no pain, only disinterested pity for my child (as I had long ago felt after a miscarriage). Only when my husband phoned did I break down. The shock was past. I cried the entire night. But, during the next six months, I carefully pushed Hannah to the back of my mind, except when I was writing her daily letter or calling her once a week. Even though I was amazed and thrilled at her social progress, maintaining my attitude of detachment was the only way I could bear the separation.

As for embarrassment, I would find it hard to credit a mother who said she had never experienced it. A child who looks like an eight-year-old and behaves like a five-year-old brat, a child who throws royal tantrums in public over "nothing," a child who seems to be wantonly destructive and the product of shocking mismanagement is going to get plenty of negative reactions from onlookers. I cannot imagine a mother so detached that she will not constantly be suffering embarrassment, often tinged with resentment against the world which does not understand her child. Sometimes the embarrassment is almost solely for the child whom she wants so much to be accepted and to have friends; sometimes it is for herself; often, it is for both.

Gone are the days of wrestling Hannah down in a movie lobby to get her coat on and remove her from the premises, as a six-abreast waiting line stares with a thousand eyes. No longer do we have to chase her around the building while the family is "dining in a restaurant" on a motor trip. But, even today, Hannah may answer the doorbell, look out, and say, "It's you again!" and slam the door in the face of her brother's friend. Even today, she may go alone into the rest room at the swimming pool, but come outside with her suit around her ankles because she cannot pull it up wet.

Sometimes I die a little when she upsets the social apple cart —with obscene language (courtesy of residential school) or "You got a baby?" to a ten-year-old—just because she is trying so hard and acting so logically in the light of what she can observe and understand. Sometimes I cringe when she plunges into the baby pool, in imitation of two bigger girls, but wins scornful looks because *she* has splashed smaller children whom she did not notice. Sometimes I am ready to bite and scratch adults who openly show disgust for the same immature behavior that bothers me. I can tell myself that this woman could not be expected to understand the problems of a child who looks like any other child her size and age, or that that man is so stupid about children that he should be pitied. But it doesn't help. I still get mad at the intolerance of others toward my child. I still become embarrassed for both Hannah and myself. I still feel frustrated by my inability to solve the remaining problems posed by Hannah, even though I know that, at this point, they cannot be solved.

ANTICIPATE AND PLAN I think we have made the point that it is important to have a routine and to stick to it, to decide what you will do with a child and stick with your decision.

It is also better to hide the bottle than to cry over spilled milk. By the time Hannah was four (better I had learned sooner), I knew that we could not begin an excursion if she was not up to it that day. If she was fine when we started, we cut it short if she showed signs of fatigue. We took a favorite toy, book, or drawing utensils to the doctor's or dentist's office and, if the wait was too long, we went for a walk, an elevator ride, or for a soft drink.

I learned that locking up medicines as well as cleaning and painting materials and securing the door to Andy's room were preferable to having to rush to an emergency room for a stomach pumping, to being compelled to redecorate Andy's room, or to being forced to listen to a brother-sister brawl.

I tried to stop an activity that got too much for Hannah *before* she exploded. When her voice rose and her "no's" increased, I tried to rock her or get her to lie down in her darkened room. If she was too "mad" to cooperate, I gave her heavy pillows or a big plastic punching toy to kick and hit or throw. If she was beyond even this, I wrestled her into a warm bath. Often, in her aimless search for release from some terrible tension, she headed for the big outdoors. I learned to fight this, even if it sometimes took another adult to prevent her escape. At best, leaving the house could only postpone the explosion; at worst, make it worse by adding new stresses. In either case, getting her back inside was an awful job, even for two people.

Hannah and I accompanied Andy twice to his dental appointment, to meet the gentle child's dentist, examine his instruments and chair. On her first appointment, he looked at her teeth and gave her a prize. A year later, when he actually cleaned her teeth, she was a model patient.

Instead of completing her skin tests for asthma in two visits, we did it in five, the first time talking with the doctor and meeting the nurses and looking at all the bottles; the next time starting with a few tests on her arms where she could see them instead of on her back. The next time the doctor did nothing, Hannah not feeling up to it. Each visit was followed by a treat. When we learned Hannah would have to have shots for a long time, we used empty syringes without needles to play doctor at home and at school. And, for the first year, her favorite pediatrician, not a nurse, gave her her shots. By then, she could go to the treatment room alone, pull up her sleeve and thank any of the nurses for her injection.

We always rehearsed for shopping trips, parties, attendance at special events, and of course enrollment in a new school. For example, before Hannah's first visit to a circus performance, we started by talking about where we would sit and what we would see and do. Then we read books about circuses, drew pictures of circuses, and discussed clowns, acrobats, tightropes, and the like. Hannah actually managed to remain seated until the intermission at this first visit to a circus—quite a record for her.

Each time she was about to enter a new school, we arranged in advance to learn the teachers' names and to visit the school rooms, to see where Hannah would sit and what the place was like. We talked about how many children there would be, what they would be like, how old they were, and how they and she would behave. We rehearsed and planned what Hannah might do and say in various circumstances.

We prepared Hannah with equal thoroughness for her week at a camp for the perceptually handicapped. The camp itself had done a fine job of planning, providing a detailed schedule and almost one counselor per child. Thus, each child could be carefully supervised and still enjoy a rich camping experience. Intending to write to her daily and aware that some of the campers could scrawl letters, I tried out an idea she has since used in writing to her grandparents and friends and in keeping us informed while away at school. To enable her to "write letters" too, I prepared a few stamped, self-addressed postcards for her to complete and sign:

Dear Mother, Daddy, and Andy:

(PLEASE CHECK THE RIGHT WORDS)
I am having a very _____ _____ _____ time.
                silly   good   sad

My tent mate is _____ _____ _____.
              nice   funny   tall.

Today I went _____ _____ _____.
          for a ride   on a hike   swimming

(WRITE NAME HERE) ☐☐☐☐☐☐

Sometimes planning is not enough. When Hannah was never given any work and could not use the black satchel she "had to have" for the first grade; when she waited starry-eyed for a week, dressed-up each afternoon in leotards and ballet slippers, for the dancing lessons arranged for her class, and then was the only one not permitted to return after the first lesson; when every class she was in, from three to ten, for which she always came through beyond our expectations, was suddenly closed to her for some reason she could not understand—she knew what she had lost, knew that she had failed, no matter how we "explained." Planning is necessary, but even planning is not a panacea.

REMEMBER YOUR PURPOSE Your purpose is to help your child acquire acceptable social behavior. Showing him who's boss—waiting until he picks a flower so you can spank his hand—won't do it. And neither will the way that works with "normal" children—moving him to something else, while telling him that flowers are to look at and smell, and are too pretty to hurt. Until he finds out about flowers, he has got to touch and pull and tear—so let him.

I grew awful-looking annuals in a spot in our yard that Hannah was allowed to examine as she would. I removed her from other people's flowers and shrubbery, reminding her of her own flowers. As soon as she could handle pint-sized garden tools without mortal danger to herself and others, I gave her her own "garden." She dug it, planted, sprinkled, and weeded it herself (with a little help from me, but usually when she was not around). Very little came up, but she had a great time digging and chopping the dirt, wallowing in mud, tearing up green stuff by the handful, and—I hope—enjoying the few flowers that managed to survive before she sent them to their eternal rest.

Came the summer when she was nine and a half, and she protected her flowers, trampled on them only by mistake, and never purposely tore them up. From then on, she endangered no one's garden, carefully holding her hands behind her back so that she would not forget and touch as she leaned over to smell the flowers.

Forbidding and foreseeing messes in all cases was impossible. I cut down on messes throughout the house by giving her as many chances as I could to mix and mash, squish and pound, with supervision. It was important to judge her mood before offering finger paints, flour and water, hammer and nails. It was equally important to stop such activities before the painting spread to the couch, the hammering to the piano. I would suggest different ways to play with the clay and sand, that she might leave hammering wide-head nails for screwing large eyes into holes we made in scrap wood. When she was painting with big brushes on her easel, I made a point of being around when she was getting tired so that she would not pour the rest of the cup of paint on the paper, of watching to see when she wanted to quit so I could accompany her to the bathroom to wash out the brushes.

The commercial sewing cards for children confused her. She did not know from which side to go in and through which hole to go, so we fastened scraps of porous cloth over huge campaign buttons with rubber bands, and I made marking-pen dots for her darning needle to go through. When she felt like kicking, I tried to interest her in punching bags and bolsters. If she seemed inclined to throw a bottle of shoe polish, I gave her beanbags, balls, and stuffed toys to throw.

I tried to make playing alone outside more interesting—so she would not need to "run away," and also for the fun of it—with trucks, bendable rubber dolls, cooking utensils, which I suggested how to use for sand or mud; with big building blocks and boards to stack and walk on; with oversized homemade mallets and large rubber balls to hit through giant clothes-hanger croquet wickets; with huge cardboard boxes to play house and tumble in. All these things were learning experiences, kept her busy, and provided a release for tensions that might otherwise result in antisocial behavior.

If my purpose was Hannah's satisfactory performance rather than getting rid of a lamp I did not like, I would not yell "Don't throw that ball there! You'll break the lamp," but "Let's throw the ball over this way. This is better." Which, of course, was only another phase of positive over negative approach.

Under close supervision, Hannah helped with the cleaning, in the kitchen, caring for the dog, and handling the mail. The same principles of learning, stress factors, and degrees of freedom had to be considered in teaching her these things as were utilized for teaching her anything else. It was another way of helping her develop her organization as well as giving her an important feeling of self-worth. I found it took a lot less time to show her and help her clean a window or dust a table than to do it myself, constantly interrupting my own work to see what she had gotten into on her own.

All children, even those with learning disorders, must be made to realize that social behavior is expected of them. But do not expect more of your child than is appropriate for him. That is, if that is all he is capable of, appreciate him when he acts on the level of a two-and-a-half-year-old, even though he is seven. There is no profit in getting upset or feeling discouraged because a child won't share, clean up well, play nicely, or make his bed if he is not yet well enough organized to do it.

Hannah still often laughs at the amusing sounds and positions resulting from minor accidents, because she does not know they hurt. She rumples up people's hair, hugs too tight, kisses too promiscuously, because she cannot help touching quite often. She whispers loudly at a lunch counter, "That man got no hair," or "Her dress is dirty," because she cannot whisper too well softly, and does not understand that what she says may be insulting. As she organizes space and all her modalities, she grows more and more socially graceful. Reminding her of social blunders is necessary; punishing her for them would be ridiculous and unfair.

I do not mean I can let her go haywire. On the contrary, until recently, she had to be held tightly in check. If she abused a child, Hannah was removed. I tried to get a child whom she hit, grabbed, or pushed to retaliate, but this is very hard, so removal was usually the only way. If Hannah ran away, she was confined to her room. If she refused a meal, she was given nothing to eat until the next meal (even though we both went to bed in tears). If she made a mess, she cleaned it up—unless cleaning up was more fun than making it. If she refused to put on her dress, she missed her party. If she would not tie her shoes, she went to school with laces dragging. But I tried not to appear angry as she "suffered the consequences," often showed her that I was sympathetic when the consequences were severe. I did my best to help her *understand what was happening*, that this was the *result* of her misdeeds. The whole thing was pointless unless she saw *cause and effect*, not mere arbitrary brutality.

Rewards beat punishment every time. Dr. Barsch had told us that reinforcing good behavior was the way, but I could not believe that he actually meant to ignore bad behavior. Yet I tried it, and it worked.

Hannah had begun kicking and hitting her best friend George as soon as he got in the car, partly because he would not share the book or toy he was taking to school. Reasoning, threatening, explaining, and punishing made no impression on either of them. Their teacher suggested the positive approach, so I tried it. I had to work fast, rewarding Hannah with a piece of chewing gum for not kicking or hitting George if she held off for two or three minutes; giving George his gum as soon as he shared. The next day, I waited till we were half-way to school to reward them both. In the week that followed they forgot only a few times. After that, I just gave them gum now and then because "you are both very good children," but there was no more problem with hitting or sharing.

Another little "positive" trick from their teacher helped here —using the magic words "remember" and "forget." Before George got in the car, we would talk about what Hannah had to remember not to do. If she seemed ready to backslide, I would remind her what she had to remember. If she did err, it was "you forgot" rather than " you were bad again." This works for "normal" children and adults as well as for Hannahs. To say, "You didn't put your pajamas away. Go and do it" is a reprimand and a challenge to refuse because a child has been accused. "Oh, you forgot to put away your pajamas" is a reminder of something he meant to do all the time, and he will be grateful. It's sure-fire.

Hannah's worst trick that season was giving the thermostat a whirl whenever she passed it, our temperature sometimes varying from 30° to 90°. *Nothing* seemed to work here. She simply could not help turning the thermostat whenever she noticed it. But when I dared to ignore her slips and caught her in a hurry, before she could twist the knob, to praise her for being such a big girl and leaving the thermostat alone, we were dumbfounded to end this thermostat-turning episode in a few days.

You must remember your purpose if the world seems against you. At the dinner table, at home and out, at a swimming pool or on a visit, I was criticized by everyone from my son to friends and strangers for spoiling Hannah, giving her all my attention, making her the center of the stage. Why? Because the conversation centered on her, was principally directed to her. It seemed to others, quite naturally, that I had no eyes nor words for anyone else when she was around. But when Hannah was out or at the table or in any other stressful situation, she needed all the verbal support and structuring I could give her. My choice was letting her explode—which would have been rather more unprofitable all the way around—or facing the disapproval of people who could not be expected to comprehend why my centering of my attention upon her was vital. Sometimes it is hard, and often you can learn from others. But, when you know you are right, stick to your guns!

FORGIVE MISTAKES Your child's *and* your own. Don't merely ignore negative behavior; praise and expect good behavior. When a child must suffer the consequences of an act, forget it when it is over. As soon as he understands why things turned out as they did, you've done your job. More explaining, discussing, warning is not only pointless but apt to spoil the whole lesson. Being a natural nag, I have a hard time doing this.

My own mistakes are worse, and harder to forgive. But I keep reminding myself that parents too are human. If I yell, slap, talk too much, fail to anticipate a calamity, put off handling a situation too long, am too severe, over-react to a piece of mischief that I overlooked the day before, punish behavior that I later realize was well-intentioned and accidental, I try to remember that I am human. I know that feeling guilty only compounds the mistake. Hannah's security and my intelligent management depend upon my confidence that I generally know what is right and how to achieve it. I know that a firm, stable attitude is far better than a wishy-washy striving for perfection.

7

How Hannah Can Learn to Live with Herself

BUILDING A SELF-CONCEPT

"Near year, *I'm* going ride the school bus."

"I going walk to Northside (shopping center a mile from her house) today, *by myself.*"

"Andy and I go to the circus tonight. *Not* you and Daddy... no. Just me and Andy."

"Tim left his ball. I take it to him"—Hannah's explanation when I found her almost at the highway entrance to our subdivision with Tim's ball. Tim lived three miles from us.

We began to get the message that Hannah, at nine, wanted to go places by herself, without her ever-present mother.

A little boy in her school longed as desperately for a pair of cowboy boots as she yearned for independence, but it would be a long time before he could exchange his high-top white shoes, which fit his long-legged braces, for the beautiful cowboy boots. Hannah's desire to ride the school bus was also another way of expressing what most of the children in her special school felt, "Why can't I go to my brother's school?"

Well, Bobby could not have his boots. Hannah could not go on solo excursions. None of them was ready for a "real" school.

So what do parents do? Pretend the situations do not exist? Provide ridiculous rationalizations? Or tell their beloved child, already burdened with extra problems, that he cannot do what other children can, and why this is true? Gradually, as he is ready, they tell him—because they must.

WHY THE CHILD MUST BE TOLD

Why must they tell him? We have just been talking about parents learning to view themselves objectively in order to help both themselves and their children, in order to accept the days when everything goes wrong. If *we* have frustrations and disappointments, what about our children with learning problems? If *we* must understand to accept, our children must understand to survive. They need survival "equipment," and the ultimate equipment for any child (or adult) is his *self-concept*. A child who knows who he is, what he is doing, and why he is doing it will survive frustration and disappointment (plus comments outside his home) with much less emotional stress. To learn this, he must start developing positive, objective attitudes about himself early in life, with the help of the nearest available teachers, his parents. We give this help, unawares, to our other children. If we are to succeed in teaching Hannah and children like her "who they are," we must approach this task consciously.

Parents in this enlightened age know that all children must get the facts regarding sex, to avoid confusions and misconceptions. Experts have stressed the importance of telling a child the facts in a way he can understand, as he indicates a need to know, for sex is an integral part of his life. Should we expect him to be *less* curious about an all-inclusive aspect of himself, a handicap that influences all of his behavior and the whole world's reaction to him? If sex information is important, how much more important are these facts: why he cannot ride a two-wheeled bike, why he does exercises that other children do not have to do, why he goes to a different school.

In Hannah's case, we hoped to help her understand why certain of her plans were unrealistic at this time without squelching her desire for independence. We were relieved as we began talking about the reasons for her "ever-present mother," because a weight lifted off her once she realized, "Ah, there are reasons. Mother doesn't just pick on me and never on my brother. There is a reason for hitting that ball twenty times a day, for crawling around like a baby. There is a reason for me to go to my school, instead of the one near my house, the same reason that Joe and Mark and Judy go to my school."

WHEN, WHAT, AND HOW WE TOLD HANNAH

Once you have grasped both the need and the logic of telling your child about his limitations, you are still faced with the problems of *when* to tell him, *what* to tell him, and *how* to tell him.

This is not an easy task. In Hannah's case, we had to translate complex information into *her* language—a language that reflected the learning problems of a nine-year-old. We found out that we needed just the right time and the right place for our talks: not at the dinner table, not in front of the TV set, not even during our "lessons" (although these filled in gaps). Knowing that Hannah's poor visual organization handicapped her in distinguishing among mad, sad, and sober faces, we soon realized that when she did not ask for guidance in certain confusing situations, she was usually hoping that someone or other would clue her in anyway. We were often not aware when Hannah was unsure of our love or suspected our disappointment in her. We did not always do or say the right thing the first time. But we learned, as we helped her learn. Perhaps what we learned together will help you help your child to understand himself better, with as little worry (or "wary" as Hannah would say) as possible.

WHEN In the beginning I was never sure that *this* was the *time* to offer Hannah new information about herself. So I put out "feelers." If she reacted favorably, I went on. If she ignored or rejected what I offered, I dropped it. Sometimes it was hard for me to stop when *I* was ready, only to find that she was not, but I knew I must. I knew from previous experience that if Hannah was not ready to receive, I was wasting my time and hers. I was not exactly "flying blind." There were various "signs" that Hannah wanted and needed information and understanding.

1. She might become unusually upset from frustration. For instance, the effort to tie her own shoes alone did not usually bring her to tears. When it did, I tried to offer sympathetic but factual reassurance, "I know you're mad because you cannot tie your shoes. But maybe it will be easier after a while. Remember? Sometimes Joe has trouble tying his shoes because his hands haven't learned that yet. He'll

learn how and so will you. That's why we do the exercises so your hands will learn. Andy doesn't know his new piece on the piano well yet either, and that makes him mad sometimes, but afterwhile his hands will know too." Sometimes she would want to hear more and more about this kind of thing. Sometimes, if she ignored me, I simply stopped.

2. Another "sign" was Hannah's hypothetical "You know what I am going to do?" And she would always wait until someone said, "No, Hannah, what are you going to do?" "I'm goin' ride Andy's bike to school." Andy had a large English bike. Hannah could not yet ride her small bike with training wheels. And she had not the vaguest notion of the direction she would have to go to reach school. These were the facts, but they did not concern her now. My usual answer would be, "Yes, sometime you will probably ride Andy's bike, when you learn how." If Hannah kept it up, she would get a fuller, more realistic explanation.

3. Joe, Hannah's special school friend, indicated his need for reassurance and explanations with bravado, with a "Guess what!" tossed into a conversational lull, "Guess what! David reads *Blank* book, and he said I read baby books cause I'm dumb. Isn't that silly?" He was obviously not sure this was silly. When his teacher told Joe that David once read "baby books" too, and talked about how David learns and how Joe learns, that neither way was right or wrong, Joe showed his relief in uproarious laughter. When he was provided with a rejoinder for David at their next encounter, he was even happier.

4. Joe's bravado was comparatively easy to analyze. Hannah's "no reaction" reaction was an avoidance technique that could easily fool others. If she tried to join a group of children who ignored her, she looked very sober but acted as if it had not happened. When she made an airplane by nailing three pieces of wood together and painting them, she got that "frozen" look on her face when we praised her for her accomplishment. She seemed to be saying, "I know it's awful, and you're pretending, but what can I expect?"

It was hard to toe the line between reinforcing and teaching by praise while modifying our judgments to fit her own evaluations and her pride.

5. One day, at the height of the allergy season, Hannah had had a series of catastrophic reactions, episodes of crying, biting, and kicking. By the time I finally got her up to bed, her head had left an impression in the dining room wall. Empathy with Hannah's wretched mood, concern for her physical safety, and utter exhaustion with trying to handle both had me extremely upset. When I called her teacher for moral support, she came over to the rescue.

The first thing Hannah said to her teacher was, "Mother is mad at you. You are a baby." When questioned further, it seemed that mother was mad because "some baby" had made a hole in the wall. There was no question now that she knew she, Hannah, had been responsible, and that she likewise knew that she had had little or no control over what had happened. It was quite a lot to *know* about herself. I had usually returned to the ordinary routine as quickly as possible after such episodes, hoping that Hannah would thus realize that all was well. But, apparently, now she needed something more. This time, and after later episodes, we talked it out. Going over what had happened, and assuring her that I was not "mad" but sympathetic to her "condition" at the time and her grave concern following it, left Hannah beaming with relief. *Then* she was ready to resume her usual routine. To a child who is highly developed auditorially, but poorly developed kinesthetically and visually, actions do *not* always speak louder than words.

SELF-UNDERSTANDING As Hannah had to develop muscular strength, dynamic balance, and spatial awareness as a *foundation* for movement, she had also to develop a positive foundation for self-understanding, consisting of two parts.

1. **Acceptance of negative or atypical behavior**—in other children and in herself. At home, my first step was learning

not to yell every time a lamp went over, a glass was broken, or some other unforeseeable and unintentional disaster occurred. At school, interpretation of events was a natural part of any activity: "You didn't know the table was too far away when you put the glass down. That's why it spilled. It was an accident. You did not mean to drop it," or "We're not going to laugh at Joe's picture (a mass of scribbles) because that is what he knows how to do and that's fine. When you were two you didn't know how to walk, and now everyone knows. After awhile, Joe will know how to make a different picture."

After a few uneasy starts, I learned to practice such interpretation myself. The atmosphere which Hannah's teacher and I tried to maintain was "It's all right. All of us have times when things don't work out." Her "I have trouble" was true for all of us, not merely for Hannah alone. This was everyday building of part of her foundation for learning a positive self-concept.

2. **Basic physiology**. As she learned the names of body parts, she learned their functions. First, she learned about the external body parts; about each of the senses and about the limbs—all the modalities that we had been working so hard to improve. Then Hannah and her classmates learned internal anatomy as well—where were their hearts, brains, stomachs, lungs, and what did they do? Why were they important? Their teacher drew pictures on the chalkboard and on paper, and had a flannelboard set made so that the children could manipulate the heart, lungs, stomach, intestines, brain, bones, muscles, and skin, and begin to visualize their proper places inside themselves.

LEARNING THE PARTS OF THE HUMAN BODY On a blackboard, make simple outlines of the human body and of the body parts. Then make these parts in flannel or of other materials so that the children can move the parts around on a flannelboard.

203

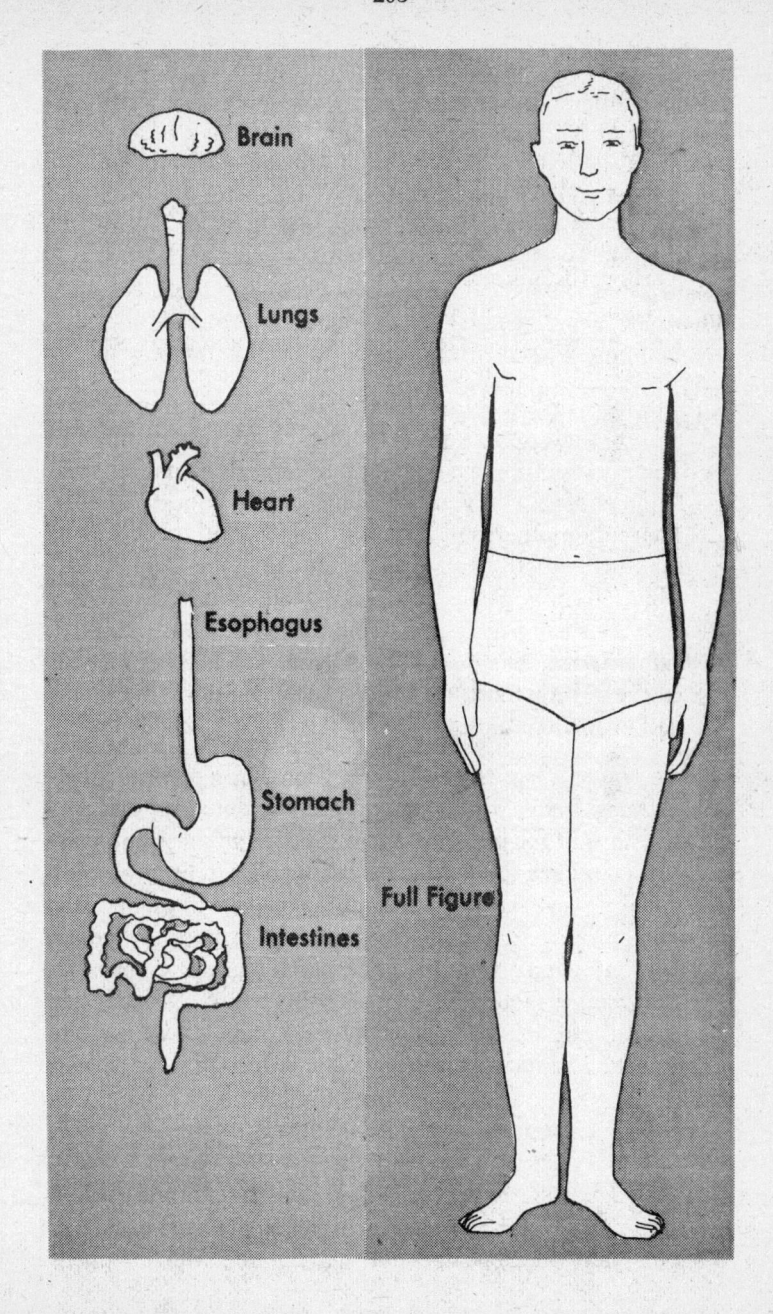

At home, we drew more pictures, took books from the library, borrowed her brother's encyclopedia, and talked about digestion, breathing, etc., whenever she brought it up. It was hard enough to shift my language to Hannah's level. To explain such matters as digestion in her terms was a real challenge. An excellent example of how to handle this comes from the mother of a little boy with severe learning disabilities.

Tommy violently resisted change of any kind, particularly one which affected him directly. When he discovered a loose baby tooth and learned that it was going to come out, his world was threatened. His mother had exhausted herself and every approach she could dream up, but Tommy's tooth was *not* going to come out, no matter what happened to every other child in the world. Finally, Tommy's mother had a brainstorm. She pretended to be the "little tooth" and Tommy became the "big tooth," which literally pushed the "little tooth" out. After several days of such play-acting, Tommy's objections subsided. When the moment actually arrived, Tommy came to his mother, "little tooth" in hand, jubilant that the "big tooth" had been victorious.

Once Hannah had the two foundations—acceptance of herself ("I know I have trouble saying what I want to say and people have to wait for me. That's how it is."), and basic anatomy and physiology ("I know I have a brain and it 'tells' my mouth how to talk")—we had only to combine the two to produce the third dimension ("Sometimes my brain forgets to tell my mouth, so I can't say what I want to."). She had a reason for her problems, a reason as factual as "eyes are to see with." Not only had she learned that her "bad" behavior did not matter as much to others as she had thought, she knew better how to accept it herself.

When physiology lessons had advanced to learning ("My brain sends a message to my legs and says 'Move legs.' . . . My eyes send a message to my brain 'I see something,' and my brain says, 'It's a tree.'"), it was an easy progression to the next step. What happens when one does not "see" the tree? What happens when the arm "gets a different message?" Hannah ate all this up, not only because she was delighted with the idea of her brain telling the rest of her body what to do ("Brain says 'Hi there, arm'"), but mostly she seemed so relieved that somebody else recognized her difficulties.

PROBLEMS IN COORDINATING DIFFERENT ABILITIES Here the brain gets a true picture of the table's position through the child's eyes (Vision). However, the brain has trouble telling the child's arm where to put the glass (Kinesthesia).

LANGUAGE PROBLEMS The auditory mechanism receives the message and sends it to the brain. In order for the child to make the correct response, the brain must interpret the verbal symbols correctly, associate meaning to the verbal message and produce a verbal response in turn. Sometimes the brain cannot integrate all these functions and communication breaks down.

DISTRACTION *The child sees that the ball is behind the tree and goes to get it. On the way, she is distracted by the bird, and she forgets about the tree. If the child remembers the tree again in time, she will walk around it. If she doesn't, she will bump into it.*

Four-year-old Billy, with severe cerebral palsy, was dictating a letter to Santa at Hannah's school. After he had listed all the toys he wanted, his teacher reminded him to tell Santa about himself. She was stunned when, instead of "I've been a good boy," he said, "Tell Santa I have cerebral palsy." Questioning indicated that he did not know what cerebral palsy meant, except that it had to do with him alone and it was not a good thing to have. Perhaps Hannah too had absorbed misinformation and needed explanations without being able always to formulate specific questions.

Often we would review Hannah's accomplishments, because we felt she needed to be proud of what she could do. We made lists of things she did not know how to do when she was five, that were easy for her now, at nine. We made lists of things she wanted to do now but could not, and assigned a future age when she could probably do each of them—*probably*, since they included matters like driving a car, marriage, having babies, as well as riding a bike or a bus alone.

Since she had so much to wait for, for so long, we would think of some new responsibility or act of independence and offer it as a badge of "being a big girl," a recognition of her having arrived at a higher level of independence. Her intense interest in this fascinating "growing up" process assured us that we had "hit it." All children her age are fascinated, but Hannah needed the same kind of specialized "instruction" about growing up as she needed to learn everything else.

Hannah and Joe had always been "special" friends, very aware and sympathetic of each other's problems. Both had difficulty remaining in one place; each could do something the other could not. Joe was very verbal, yet patient with Hannah's language problems; he understood numbers better than Hannah. Hannah outdid Joe in phonics and reading. But they seemed to understand that they had much in common and took comfort from each other, beyond what any adult could give them.

After learning about brains, learning, and something of their own problems, they would remind each other, "Tell your brain to help you sit still." One evening, they were being taken to a restaurant together, and spent the drive there preparing for the pleasant "ordeal" ahead, "Brain, help me not to run, and to sit still." By the time they arrived at the restaurant, they were "ready." They had to stand in line to wait to be seated. They sat at a table in the middle of the room, ordered independently, and ate everything. Their joy at the end of the meal was more pride in their accomplishments than the treat of eating out.

When she was about the same age, nine or ten, it dawned on us that Hannah was personifying her difficult learning areas by associating them with Moe (of Three Stooges fame). She had been badly frightened by an episode she had inadvertently seen on television, and had been bringing up Moe and all the terrible things he did for years. We assumed this was a perseverative thing and tried to discourage it. When she was young she was probably not associating herself with Moe, but, as her self-awareness grew, she used Moe as the scapegoat.

She became very interested in motors, was both fascinated and frightened by them. Asking about the motor of a car she would keep saying, "What might happen if Moe puts his head in?" or "Moe might touch it." This was accompanied by much laughter, but we began to wonder if she was really saying funny things about Moe. When we also talked about Moe in the same terms, not indicating that we were talking about her, the laughing stopped. Serious discussion followed. We agreed that maybe Moe would want to touch the motor when it was running. Maybe he would forget not to touch, even though he knew it was dangerous. But we assured her that Moe *would* remember, and that Mother and Daddy would help him remember, so that he would not get hurt.

Even after a few days of such discussions, we were not sure that we were all talking about the same thing. Then one afternoon, on the way to the bathroom, Hannah was talking to Moe, "Are you going touch the motor? If you do, what might happen?" giggle, giggle "Awwww, Moe, I'm not going to listen to you anymore!" This was the beginning of the end of Moe.

This was only one of many incidents which we were not sure of at the time, but could see clearly in retrospect. But even when we were not sure what some of the signs and situations meant, we tried to stay alert. We were not trying to play "psychologist," only to help Hannah learn some things and not to learn others.

This kind of teaching was a lot harder than helping her to recognize an airplane outside. An airplane is concrete, objective, easy to recognize. You talk about an airplane when it is there; you associate it with things she knows; you help her discriminate it from other things she knows so that she does not get misconceptions. Helping her attain an adequate self-concept is not concrete or objective, yet she had to learn it in much the same way—at the time a situation occurred, associating feelings with past experience, discriminating accurate information, building up realistic future associations. So teach we did, as best we could.

How has our teaching worked? Hannah asks about new children she meets, "Does she have a problem?" She asks not indiscriminately, but as though she were simply seeking information. She is more relieved when the answer is "yes" as it has been when she entered her last two schools. If the answer is "no," she shows appropriate apprehension, indicates a need to know what she should do and what will be expected of her. She has never tried to avoid this kind of situation; her drive toward independence and the acquisition of *her* social goals is too strong.

She still wants to walk to school by herself, but she is resigned to the fact that this will have to wait awhile. She tells us what she can and cannot do by herself. If she needs help to zip her dress, tie her shoe, or anything else, she asks for it—not to avoid trying, but to get the job done. Many times, though, she does not ask, as if she were saying, "Okay, let's try it again . . . and again . . . and again."

She resents any help in writing (one of her hardest tasks) that seems "phony"—as someone holding her hand and then praising her for what she did. Her own evaluations are more important to her now than our evaluations, and we are as pleased as she is that she is exercising this independent judgment. More often than not her judgments about herself are based on reality —disgust when her efforts produce mediocrity, happiness when her perseverance pays off.

Have we been successful? Hannah knows that many children can do more things and are more independent than she. But she also knows that she is accepted as part of the family, regardless of what she knows, what grade she is in, or how well she plays ball—or we think and hope she does. This kind of learning never stops. But we think we know more now about helping Hannah over future "rough times." We hope that Hannah's experiences will help other parents to recognize this important learning area.

8

Where Is Hannah Going?

Where is Hannah *now?* In a world that is not quite ready for her.

Scientists are trying hard to find out what caused her initial problem and how it can be prevented in the future. But they got a late start and have a long way to go.

Relatives and friends do not even know what to call her, much less how to accept her. They certainly do not know what she needs.

Society still laughs at her, fears her, places her outside the pale, because it does not understand her. Unlike other minority groups, hers is not discriminated against as a group, or as part of a family. She is an individual facing the disapproval and misunderstanding alone. Society must discover how many children like her there are, and how much they need help, before it can provide enough classes in enough places throughout the country.

Professionals classify children like Hannah as mentally retarded, emotionally disturbed, culturally deprived, or physically handicapped, and recommend for them accordingly. Until they know the difference, they will continue blaming parents, predicting disaster, and placing children in the wrong classrooms.

Teachers—too many of them—have been coerced into filling a vacant position in special education, and are scared to death of a handicapped child. Too many good-hearted, well-meaning, pity-filled teachers could not handle even a model child, for they cannot stop touching, talking, insisting on perfect performances, which are impossible. Too many eager, gifted teachers, who want only to understand and help their children, stumble along in the dark, leading their stumbling pupils, teaching them not what they need to know, but the same old Three R's in the same old way because this is all they have been taught themselves. All such teachers, guided by planned academic curricula which they conscientiously mean to follow, let the emotional and behavioral problems fall where they may.

This rigid system means that even the teachers filling posts in special education don't think of gathering the children closely around them to structure each child's near space for him when he must listen and observe as one of the group. It means the teachers are unaware that a child can *learn* to stay in his seat and attend to the business at hand with the proper support and help from the teacher, that he is not "just that way" but "that way" for a number of good reasons. It means that they dare not steal the time from academic work to teach a young child and the rest of the class *why* he or she has behaved in an unacceptable way, *how* he can learn to improve his behavior, and how they *all* can sympathize and understand each other's imperfections. Until special education teachers are taught to evaluate and to teach *a child* rather than to teach special techniques for particular classifications of children, proper class placement alone will not provide satisfactory results.

Movigenically, the world is at a very disorganized, low developmental level in regard to children with learning disorders. Actually, the world is still at a T (tactual) level, with everyone feeling his way around. It is just beginning to move (kinesthetic level). Auditorially, the world has hardly made a start with regard to this problem. The time will have to come when everyone involved in this situation will talk about it and will listen to each other, will try to understand each other's symbols as the only means of true communication. Visually, the world is at an infant stage in this field, not even recognizing children with learning disorders when it sees them; while the aim must be to visualize what can be done and the best way to do it.

How can we *get* the world ready for Hannah so that it will be a lot easier to get the Hannahs ready for the world?

More scientists must study the causes and prevention of learning disorders from every possible angle, to speed up the work.

More diagnosticians (pediatricians, neurologists, psychologists, psychiatrists, educators) must recognize Hannah's problem for what it is, and familiarize themselves with where she can go and what she can do to get help. Only when they are convinced that the problem involves a continually growing, enormous number of children will it capture their interest.

Teachers must learn to evaluate, teach, and manage children with learning disabilities and to help their parents do the same in the home situation. To do these things effectively, parents and teachers must learn to evaluate themselves. For their own personalities and personal ways of dealing with the world determine how they structure their classrooms or homes, how they manage behavior problems, and what activities they emphasize.

It is not easy to live with a child who has learning disorders. But then, what worthwhile endeavor is easy?

Mothers may have to forgo golf and bridge games, club work and paid employment. Fathers may lose the peace and relaxation at the end of a hectic business day that they want and deserve. Brothers and sisters may get as much of their parents' time as other children, but never so much as their one brother's or sister's share. The whole household may be in a perpetual state of anxiety and uproar, often striking out at each other as well as at the offending child.

Family occasions may be spoiled or canceled because one member is not up to it. Holiday celebrations may be missed because a parent must take one child to a long-awaited appointment out of town. A parent might get so exasperated as to snap out the idiot question, as I have, "What is the matter with you?" One day Hannah will answer, "I have a learning problem—what's your excuse?"

In the broad light of day, parents must overlook—when they cannot overcome—childish snickers and adult stares directed at the child they love, a child who is doing his best. In the loneliness of night, parents are bound to wonder if their child will ever play with the kids on the block, ride a bus alone, go to a slumber party, have sweethearts, find a job, marry and have children, live securely when his parents are no longer around.

Again and again, parents must cater to the rude and to the ignorant as the price of getting and keeping as much help as they can for their child. They must listen respectfully to experts who say there is no hope for Mary when they know Mary has ability; watch silently while teachers mishandle Harvey because there is no one better around to teach Harvey; agree pleasantly with advisers who announce that Marty's real trouble has been his parents.

If there is no help close enough, parents may move to another town. Or they have to give up the child who needs them as much as they need him, but who needs the help and companionship of other children more—if they are lucky that is, because many schools which specialize in children with learning disorders specialize in children with not-too-severe learning disorders. Parents may have to stand by and watch their child sealed up in homes and classes for the trainable retarded or the severely emotionally disturbed, not because such classes and homes know what to do with him, but because no place else will take him.

And yet the sum of *all* these negatives does not equal *one* of the hundreds of positives that are always happening:

... When Hannah put two words together ... learned to lace her shoes ... to sit still for five minutes ... to stop when she was finished squeezing catsup bottles or squeezing and kissing cousins ... knew how to greet a guest ... noticed a cloud or a car by herself ... recognized a stranger from a friend ... realized what next week meant ... did or said or knew a little more each day than she had the day before ... made people laugh, by mistake ("Hannah, give Johnny your address, and give Mike your address." "Give them my dresses?" she asked in shocked surprise, "then I won't have any anymore.") or purposely (Mother: "I've got a sore thumb." Hannah: "From yelling at me?"—Mother: "Would you like to taste my grapefruit?" Hannah: "I can't. My tooth ache. My nose ache. My brain ache. 'Sides, I'm 'lergic to grapefruit.") ... had former camp counselors and student teachers dropping by because "She's got so much on the ball. I just wanted to see how she's getting along." ... finally heard an expert say something that did not make me fighting mad, such as, "See that skinny little runt over there, Hannah—she looks like she doesn't have sense enough to come in out of the rain, doesn't she? Well, that's the kind of child *I* like to teach, that I hope you student teachers get plenty of. She tries. She learns." . . . heard the expert we respected most in the world rate Hannah higher than even I had dared dream . . . saw her accepted by a school *because* she had a problem.

The biggest positive of all is when Hannah is happy or when she is pleased because she has accomplished something.

Where is Hannah going? I cannot say. I am too involved to judge. But I believe a letter from someone who has never guessed wrong about Hannah or any other child she has taught, a letter written after a weekend visit with Hannah at the end of her first month in residential school, a letter about a little girl who had been diagnosed as hopeless, extremely mentally deficient, severely emotionally disturbed from eleven months to nine and a half years (when Dr. Barsch evaluated her high-normal capabilities), may say it for me. Beverly Jones wrote:

> Hannah's present state of organization, which is remarkable, is the payoff of ten years' hard work, not the result of one month in a residential school. It is like putting all the ingredients for a cake in a pan and then baking it. The ingredients need the *opportunity* to work; the oven does not make the cake! What Hannah is getting at this school is a chance to "bake" her ingredients, all carefully developed by both of you, Dr. Barsch, Norma [her colleague], me and Dr. Wolff. The school is providing the *place*.
>
> This new organization, which is just emerging, could not have happened as well at home because there were fewer unknowns to struggle against. One cannot learn to balance a surfboard on the sand; only in the water. Hannah was too sure of all of us and our reactions. She could walk through your house, around your furniture and yard without having to make any *new* accommodations. Now there are many new people, of all ages, treating her more like a "normal" kid and Hannah is having to "read" and adapt to these situations.
>
> A few examples may graphically describe this emerging Hannah, quite a contrast from a few months ago. Saturday, we went shopping. As Kenny described, she walked near us, not once wandering away. I'd ask her if she knew where she was going, and, about 50% of the time, she did! We went in a

big toy store. She did not touch a thing. She walked very fast and became a bit excited, but maintained the control! Back at the motel, she was in the pool for over an hour. Marvelous! A girl of about eleven was standing near us, so I told Hannah to ask her to help her (Hannah) dive for a rock. "I can't," she said. "She's a stranger!" I convinced her it would be okay, and then I floated away. Hannah did, the girl did, and they played from ten to 15 minutes. Then Hannah wondered where *I* was! (Miracle of miracles!) I went back to where Hannah was and the girl left. I casually asked the usual "hovering" question, "Did you ask her her name?" "Yeah, it's Mary," was the normal, nonchalant reply!

The timing of this new experience seems to be the most fortunate of all. Without Dr. Barsch's Movigenic training, Dr. Wolff could not have moved as fast with Hannah. Without Dr. Wolff's training, Hannah would be "lost" now. But she certainly is not! Without the loose environment she has at school she would not have this kind of organizing task precisely when she needs it. I think the goal should be to know when she has organized consistently. Then the situation should be changed, so that she can begin to catch up academically, because she can! I've never been so confident about Hannah. The school is giving her the chance, but Hannah is organizing *herself!*

There's much, much more. But we wanted you to know that "everything is comin' up roses" because we are absolutely convinced, as never before, that Hannah is going to make it.

9
Hannah at Eleven
by BEVERLY JONES

Where is Hannah today? Ask Hannah—at last *she* knows! She knows she is a young lady; she knows her strengths and problems; she knows when the adults around her *don't know*, or don't remember, and begin to treat her like a "hyperactive, brain-injured" child. Organically, Hannah is undoubtedly still brain-injured; behaviorally, she is not!

Chronologically Hannah is 11½. Her interests are those of a preadolescent: she's becoming a bit vain about her hair and clothes; she is eager to develop relationships with girl friends; she is very conscious about "grown-ups" getting married and having babies. At her best Hannah functions like a 9- to 11-year-old; at her worst she is socially clumsy.

In six months Hannah's learning organization has moved from AKVT (audition-kinesthesia-vision-tactuality) to AVKT and, in some situations, to VAKT (ideal). That's quite a jump from the ATKV organization of one year ago. Hannah has become reliable, although it is still difficult for parents and teachers to rely on this. She now "looks before she leaps." Her "leaping" is not as good as it should be; but, oh, so much better than ever before. When crossing the street she now *knows* when a car is coming and she *moves*, whereas she would have become "frozen" before. Since she doesn't always move fast enough, she cannot yet cross streets alone. When using the stove she *reads* the burner labels *before* she turns one on; she reads all the titles of film-strip containers, then takes *only* the one she has chosen. Gone are the hand-holding days, the stage-whispered directions, the hand brushing the wall. Hannah knows where she is going, and she can be relied upon to get there.

ACADEMIC PROGRESS

Academically, Hannah is still behind. Her motto has become, "I'll do it by myself or not at all." Reading is what she does best by herself, and read she does. Her level of reading has progressed from second grade to fourth grade this past year. The quality of her reading is excellent in books with standard-sized type. She does not skip words, rarely loses her place, and can unlock new words better than most children her age. Most important, she understands and remembers what she reads. Silent reading is just emerging. Certainly there are children who are in classes appropriate for their chronological ages who do not read as well. They began to read at age six; Hannah began at nine.

According to the director of the small, excellent private school which she now attends:

> *Hannah works independently within a group for a normal span of time (as reading lab, spelling, math), but she still cannot work in a group without feeling very self-conscious and drawing attention to herself.*
>
> *Given a particular assignment, she can, and does, work independently for as much as 30 or 45 minutes, until the assignment is completed to her satisfaction. She must still have a specific job to do, and no lapse of time for waiting between academic tasks.*
>
> *Her attention span for group activity with normal children has increased tremendously in five months —from two minutes to a half-hour—but as a spectator only. She does not yet participate in group discussions. However, she does participate, happily, in group singing.*
>
> *Hannah's greatest improvement, I feel, has been in her ability to move, work, and play alone within the confines of space and activity limitations. In other words, the fences set by discipline contain great choice within their areas. Hannah usually responds wisely and cheerfully. When she occasionally suffers the consequences of disobedience, she meets the demands of "the fences" the next time.*

Since social studies and science are so closely linked with reading ability, Hannah does fairly well in these subjects. Unfortunately, she has gaps in her past experience much like a culturally deprived child. Consequently, reading about banks, the post office, or other community institutions does not have for her the meaning that such reading has for other children of like reading ability. She is ready only now to absorb direct experiences in the community. She has the ability to conceptualize aids in her learning of scientific principles, but her movement deficiencies and meager previous experiences prohibit her from truly understanding the physical principles of machines and motors at a level commensurate with her reading ability. The "peaks and valleys" profile still exists.

Arithmetic and writing, far below her age level, could be improving faster; but, typically Hannah, she has not yet seen the value of them: therefore, she is not interested in learning them. She does not see the "why" of numbers in her life. She chooses not to put forth the effort needed to learn to write, although she now has the basic skills necessary to learn. When she wanted desperately to write and draw, she couldn't; now that she can, she doesn't want to because the product of her mighty efforts is so far below her expectations.

Independence is the byword now. She does not want *help* to learn; she's too busy doing those things which she can do without help. For so many years there were so few things she could do independently, it is understandable that she is enjoying her new skills. Hannah is a "learner," and an independent "learner" at that. Her academic progress is now up to her, with only guidance necessary from parents and teachers.

SOCIAL PROGRESS

Socially, Hannah is maturing faster than parents and teachers can assimilate. The will is there; the finesse is not. Hannah could be compared with someone from another culture who has yet to learn the finer social mores and folkways of our culture. She is aware of social rules and etiquette, but is unsure of the appropriate behavior. She is almost asocial.

In recognition of her tremendous need for independence, she was recently helped to make out a short shopping list (for a dinner she was to cook), taken to a large local supermarket, given a briefing on the "layout," and "set free." The apprehension and hope her out-of-sight supervisors felt can only be imagined. Hannah was supremely confident; and her confidence was well-founded. Much to everyone's surprise and delight she "passed the test." Not only did she not bump anyone with her cart, she located all eight items on her list. She found her way from aisle to aisle by reading the subject headings and numbers overhead. She knew when she needed help and when she did not; she knew when she was finished (with not a single extra item in her basket), and pushed her cart to the checkout counter with the announcement, "Well, here I *am*," to no one in particular. As she struggled with the bag of groceries when leaving the supermarket, she commented, with a slight smile, "Thank you very much. . . . By myself!" As always, Hannah had known before anyone else that she was ready for this kind of responsibility.

Her success in the supermarket can be duplicated in other situations if the situations can be anticipated and she can be given a brief "rehearsal." Otherwise, she makes a valiant effort. With a few pointers prior to the event she can order what she wants in a restaurant, handling the verbal give-and-take with the waitress; without the rehearsal she is apt to ask, "Are you married?" and answer, "I dunno," when asked what she would like.

The difference between strangers and friends is now clear, but the relative differences in behavior with total strangers, service people, and casual friends of the family escape her. She recently became very upset with two little girls, complete strangers to her, to whom she said, warmly, "Hi, there!" They ignored her, and she tried again and again, each time a little more insistently. They finally looked up and said, "We don't know you!" She was stunned; but a few more such experiences and she will have taken a social step forward.

Hannah is very much the "young lady," a concept that was artificially created for her so that she could sort out the differences in behavior expected from "children," "young ladies," and "women." A vital part of becoming a "young lady" is the approaching of puberty. She has known for some time the anatomical and physical changes related to puberty; but she was unable to sort out, chronologically, "having a 'period,'" "getting married," and "having a baby." The distinctions between "you're not a baby," "you're too young for that," "you're not old enough," "starting to grow up," and "grown-up" were very fuzzy until someone gave her a visual representation of each of these stages and assigned an age to it. As she began to assimilate these new distinctions, she was better able to monitor her own behavior. If she is acting rather "silly," only a comment about the behavior appropriate to a "young lady" is needed. Once Hannah understands the reasons for and the results of a situation, she immediately begins to perform appropriately. "Don't do that because I say so" is the least effective means of reaching her.

Watching Hannah today is like watching a miracle. What made this "miracle" happen? For over two years Hannah has not had any formal "special education"; yet, in many ways, she has made the most spectacular strides during this time. How did it, and is it, happening?

Two years ago Hannah was establishing basic movement and visual skills with Dr. Barsch's program. The skills would have been of little use to her unless she had an opportunity to "test" them, refine them, augment them. This opportunity she has had, first in a residential school where she was free to experiment in *her* way, not according to some external criteria. Second, she has had an opportunity to learn about conforming to group behavior in a modified "normal" school situation; again, with the freedom to experiment, develop, and advance at her level, in her own time. This would only have been possible in a relatively unstructured atmosphere, where external controls were at a minimum, expectations for exercising internal controls at a maximum. If she had been expected to conform to rigid methods of teaching, to meet established criteria, she might well have succeeded; but she would not have been able to exceed expectations as she has.

Hannah *has* continued to have "training." She has it 100 percent of the time: she wears training lenses. Dr. Bruce Wolff's prescription for lenses is determined by how much support her visual system needs in order to maintain binocularity, to sustain at near tasks, to develop freedom of movement. She has had and will continue to have the prescription changed as she changes. Without the lenses she might have learned; with the lenses she learns more quickly and with less effort.

At this time Hannah doesn't really have a problem; she is teaching herself and rapidly closing the gaps in her development. Her greatest difficulty is, and will be, with the adults who guide her in her development. It is difficult for them to forget that she no longer needs supervision, that she will not "wander off," that she can find her way, that "foggy days" and extreme reactions are things of the recent past. It is hard for us to remember, even though she continually reminds us, that much of her present behavior is "normal," that she can stop herself appropriately and doesn't need external guidance or interference.

It is even more difficult to recognize that expectations for performance and behavior must be three or more years ahead of what they were just six months ago. Without these expectations and goals, Hannah will persist in reminding those who err —with behavior that matches the lowered expectations; the only times she behaves like a "brain-injured" child is when she is expected to. It is as if she is saying, "O.K., you don't trust me to go outside alone, then I'll act accordingly." When she is trusted, she performs as any other child her age might. Perhaps Hannah has known this for a long time, and we adults are only now discovering it. Is this not a lesson adults might learn regarding most children?

Where is Hannah? She's Here, functioning in a stimulating academic situation not specifically designed for "brain-injured" children, gaining ever-increasing independence within her family and, most importantly, in her community. Hannah Jill Hart—11½, "brain-injured," "learning-disordered"—is becoming the self-sufficient, intelligent, responsible, empathetic, humorous young lady it was predicted she would never become. The successes that her parents were warned not to hope for are now a fact.

We pray that this will be so for all the other Hannahs!

Appendix

A. An Early History of Hannah

AGE	DEVELOPMENT	EVENT
BEFORE 11 MONTHS	Very quiet baby; held head up and sat alone late	Pediatrician: usual physical checkup
11 MONTHS	Sitting alone and moving on floor; not crawling	Hospitalized for illness; another pediatrician consulted
20 MONTHS	Attempted to stand, fell; no speech	Ophthalmologist: left eye turned in
2 YEARS	Walking unsteadily; fell a lot; used right hand consistently	Neurologist: EEG performed
2 YEARS, 3 MONTHS	Unsteady gait; a little more active than peers; no speech; language comprehension questionable	Orthopedist: help sought to improve gait
		Social worker: Crippled Children's Nursery School for guidance in training Hannah
2 YEARS, 6 MONTHS	Becoming more active; no speech; not sure of comprehension	Speech Clinic at local university
		Audiology Clinic at local university
2 YEARS, 7 MONTHS	Very active; a few words, including "shut up"	Nursery for physically handicapped children
2 YEARS, 9 MONTHS	Increasing single-word vocabulary; began extensive climbing in the house	Neurologist-orthopedist: out of state
	Began to develop social awareness and "empathy"	

RESULT	OBSERVATIONS AND COMMENTS
"Fine healthy baby"	Too quiet and placid an infant; a feeling "something is not quite right"
"Cerebral palsy" (C.P.); wait until she's two before seeking treatment	Mother felt the illness made diagnosis of C.P. questionable, but accepted that "something was wrong"
Prescription of lenses; Hannah stood alone the next day and walked in 10 days	Parents convinced the glasses were the major factor for improvement and minimized C.P.
Diagnosis: "extensive brain damage . . . no hope"	Believed "brain damage," but resentful about "no hope" and the sympathy offered to parents instead of to Hannah
Prescription of corrective shoes	No noticeable changes; mother felt she was "doing something"
Recommended Hannah attend the nursery school in six months	
Hannah rejected for therapy because she didn't talk	Negative experience for Hannah and mother
Hearing test and attempted psychological evaluation	Satisfied that hearing was normal and opportunity to find what help she needed
No positive experiences; no other child was ambulatory	Parents withdrew Hannah after a few weeks
Diagnosed Hannah as "brain-injured"; called tantrums "convulsive equivalent"; major problem: speech; no specific treatment	Parents grateful for background information about Hannah's problems; disappointed with lack of treatment plan

AGE	DEVELOPMENT	EVENT
3 YEARS, 3 MONTHS	"Tantrums" had begun	Speech therapy begun at Audiology Clinic
	Looked at books; pointed to pictures named; single words in speech; hyperactive	Return to first neurologist for sleep EEG
	Used single words; not really communicating with words; more socially aware	Began nursery school for normal children
4 YEARS	Good receptive vocabulary; single-word usage; initiated "looking at books"; began to show sense of humor	Return to out-of-state orthopedist-neurologist
4 YEARS, 9 MONTHS	Learned to lace high shoes; still single-word speech; more active outside; frequent "foggy" days	Began another nursery school for normal children
5 YEARS, 9 MONTHS	Very hyperactive and more socially adept at "entertaining," manipulating; started "dumping phase"; still single-word speech	Language evaluation at nationally known school for aphasic children
	Beginning word combinations as result of special methods; only eye-hand task was pegs-in-board	Psychological test requirement for attending private special education class
6 YEARS	Good receptive vocabulary, (normal limits); eager to learn; severe visual-motor and language problems	Speech-language evaluation: as requirement for special education class
6 YEARS, 3 MONTHS	Using "role" switching—"you Hannah; me mother"; couldn't stand on one foot; could do only simplest jigsaw puzzles	Mother and Hannah returned to school to prepare for home training aimed at developing phrases and sentences and improving comprehension

RESULT	OBSERVATIONS AND COMMENTS
Continued once a week for 3 years	No appreciable improvement; no specific guidance for mother; Hannah enjoyed it
Extreme reactions to sedation; EEG results unchanged	Parents feared drug dosage had been fatal
Rejected after two weeks because of behavior and saying "shut up"	Increasing frustration for parents because no specific therapy available
Recommended binding Hannah's left arm as treatment for language problem; arm was bound to her body for 18 months	Mother satisfied that something specific was done; father disliked form of treatment
Remained 1 year only with teacher, supported by speech therapist	Parents felt it was an opportunity for social experiences with children, but knew it was not helping her
No specific diagnosis; interested to know if she could learn language with special techniques	Parents felt this was first concrete help designed for Hannah's problem
"Trainable mentally retarded"; not recommended for class for "brain-injured" children	Mother felt it unfair to predict Hannah's eventual attainments when no opportunity to learn available
"Expressive aphasia," open prognosis; recommended for class on trial	Mother felt Hannah was being given opportunity to learn, was not condemned for not having learned
Immediate results in expressive language and "reading" letter symbols	Parents gratified that Hannah learned so quickly and showed interest

AGE	DEVELOPMENT	EVENT
6 YEARS, 4 MONTHS	"Foggy" days and "tantrums" still occur	Mother began daily language training
	Language steadily increasing, along wth hyperactivity, sense of humor	Hannah entered special class for 4 children, on trial; teacher inexperienced and not trained in special education
7 YEARS	Beginning to use word combinations and sentences spontaneously; began "running away"	Neurologist: school suggested; possible control of hyperactivity with medication
7 YEARS, 8 MONTHS	Still running away and active; medication discontinued	Reentered special education class with trained, experienced teacher; remained for 3 years
8 YEARS, 3 MONTHS	Use of sentences became common; visual-motor skills at infant level; except for grammar, language more in normal range; perseverative circles when copying; 5-year-old-level jigsaw puzzles	Dr. Barsch met Hannah informally ("That's a bright litle girl with severe visual problems")
8 YEARS, 6 MONTHS	Still runs away; expressive language steadily improving, as are motor skills; can match pictures and words independently, copy a single circle, draw a man at 3½-year-old level	Visited Dr. Gerald Getman in Minnesota, specialist in child visual development
		Took psychological test for consideration in public school special education class ("too old" for private class of 3-year-olds)
9 YEARS	Fewer "foggy" days; ran away less often; sustained better at "near"; read single words if print was large; did simple pegboard designs	Public school turned Hannah down on basis of psychological test scores
9 YEARS, 6 MONTHS	Read large type at first-grade level; had trouble with prepositions and questions	First time at summer residential camp for "perceptually handicapped children"

RESULT	OBSERVATIONS AND COMMENTS
Hannah used word combinations only in formal lesson structure	
Hannah very hyperactive, disruptive to group; almost expelled	Mother felt this was first placement that would meet Hannah's needs
Hannah reacted negatively to commonly used medications; had more and more severe behavior "episodes"	Extremely difficult peroid owing to drug reactions
Beginning of rapid advancement, particularly in language	Parents' education in the "why and how" of Hannah began
Dr. Barsch recommended special optometrist	Considerable encouragement that Hannah was "headed in the right direction," at last
Getman prescribed bifocals and recommended a home motor-training program	Running away decreases with bifocals; more and more "intact" days
Scored "trainable mentally retarded" on test, but psychologist guessed, from her behavior, that she "probably has normal potential"	First psychologist to credit Hannah's behavior rather than judge her merely on test performance
Parents began applying to residential schools	No school; Hannah felt sad watching kids go to nearby school, asked, "When can I go school . . . why I big enough?"
Enjoyed camp and behaved much better than anyone expected	Language and independence improved from this experience

AGE	DEVELOPMENT	EVENT
9 YEARS, 7 MONTHS	Pasted simple shapes but could not cut them out; could stand or hop on one foot, but poorly	West to Wisconsin for Barsch's evaluation to determine if her "high potential" was real
9 YEARS, 8 MONTHS	Read at second-grade level; became depressed about "no school" to go to; simple rhythm developed; "tantrums" now controlled by allergy medicine	Barsch's home program with mom and twice-weekly tutoring by B. Jones and N. Harris for language and reading
10 YEARS, 1 MONTH	Running away stopped; reading and language continued to improve; learned to use typewriter; could draw a man at 5-year-old level	Hannah visited first-grade class each afternoon for 5 weeks
10 YEARS, 2 MONTHS	Could copy simple pegboard and block designs; knew right from left on self and others	Visited Dr. Bruce Wolff, optometrist, who helped her establish better movement and longer near-space attention span
10 YEARS, 3 MONTHS	Hannah stopped trying to learn; except for grammar, her language was within normal limits; visual-motor skills at 4- to 5-year-old level	Local public school tried Hannah in class for "minimally brain-injured" children with untrained teacher
10 YEARS, 4 MONTHS	Basic skills still improving, but Hannah depressed and negative	Went to Philadelphia for psychological evaluation to prepare for trial in residential school for "brain-injured" children
10 YEARS, 5 MONTHS	Visual-motor skills at 5- to 6-year-old level; "foggy" days very rare	Trial as day student in Florida residential school for "brain injured"; Hannah and her mother lived in motel for a week
10 YEARS, 6 MONTHS	Read above second-grade level; could write her name and type; good expressive language; still "wandered"	Went to a residential school for emotionally disturbed children 1000 miles from home

RESULT	OBSERVATIONS AND COMMENTS
Barsch: "Bright; above-average potential . . . but very handicapped in movement and spatial function"	Barsch outlined a home program as an alternative to residential school (which might raise her "lows" but lower her "highs")
In 3 months Hannah showed 2 to 3 years' improvement—in movement and visual skills	Again, parents' faith in Hannah validated
She was thrilled, though apprehensive; pregnant teacher left and new teacher, without warning, "uninvited" her	Once again, no school and Hannah and her mother were extremely upset
Hannah started using minus lenses for near tasks, plus bifocals for other tasks; fantastic improvement!	Hannah began to lose interest in home training; expressed need for more independence
In 3 months Hannah's behavior regressed 3 years	Family realized Hannah must have a good class out of the home
Hannah gave wrong answers on purpose . . . for fun?	Experienced evaluator realized her capabilities anyway and accepted her for trial
Hannah rejected because she cannot sit as still or talk as well as the other children	Hannah, after again trying her hardest, doing her best, failed again
This school took Hannah because she had a problem; in the 6 months she attended, she matured about 2 years	School's progam was unstructured, nonacademic, but Hannah "blossomed" under minimum supervision

AGE	DEVELOPMENT	EVENT
11 YEARS	Foggy periods rare; no tantrums; greatly improved social maturity; much calmer, needed much less supervision	Hannah returned to live at home (in the state where her family moved to be near her school); began attending a small private school for children with academic problems
11 YEARS, 6 MONTHS	No foggy periods; no tantrums; read on fourth-grade level; began to print legibly; typed; still found writing, arithmetic, and verb tenses "hard"; no supervision above that necessary for normal 11-year-old	Attended summer camp in home state for 2 weeks; returned to private school in Florida for another year

RESULT	OBSERVATIONS AND COMMENTS
Hannah was happier than she had been in a long time, eager to do her "school work" independently	This is the closest Hannah has come to functioning in a normal classroom situation
Hannah was far more reliable; could shop independently in a supermarket, began to cook; had many interests of a 9- to 11-year-old girl	Hannah progressed beyond the hopes of parents and teachers; liked her private school, though not socially accepted, even by the children who liked her a lot

B. Resources for Parents and Teachers

Most of the private and government agencies listed here answer inquiries; refer requests to other information sources and appropriate organizations; provide brochures, pamphlets, bibliographies, or fact sheets, and send the organization's newsletter *free of charge.*

PRIVATE

Adventures in Movement for the Handicapped
945 Danbury Road
Dayton, Ohio 45420
PHONE: (513) 294-4611

Aid to Adoption of Special Kids
3530 Grand Avenue
Suite 202
Oakland, California 94610
PHONE: (415) 451-1748

Alexander Graham Bell Association for the Deaf
3417 Volta Place
Washington, D.C. 20007

Allergy Foundation of America
801 Second Avenue
New York, New York 10017

American Alliance for Health, Physical Education, Recreation and Dance
Information and Research Utilization Center
1201 16th Street, N.W.
Washington, D.C. 20036

American Association for the Education of the Severely/Profoundly Handicapped
P.O. Box 15287
Seattle, Washington 98115

American Association on Mental Deficiency
5201 Connecticut Avenue, N.W.
Washington, D.C. 20015

American Diabetes Association
600 Fifth Avenue
New York, New York 10020

American Foundation for the
Blind, Inc.
15 W. 16th Street
New York, New York 10011

American National Red Cross
Program of Swimming for the
Handicapped
17th & D Streets, N.W.
Washington, D.C. 20006

American Occupational
Therapy Association
6000 Executive Boulevard
Rockville, Maryland 20852

American Physical Therapy
Association
1156 15th Street, N.W.
Washington, D.C. 20005

American Printing House for
the Blind
1839 Frankfort Avenue
Louisville, Kentucky 40206

American Speech and
Hearing Association
9030 Old Georgetown Road
Washington, D.C. 20014

Arthritis Foundation
475 Riverside Drive
New York, New York 10027

Association for Children
with Learning Disabilities
5225 Grace Street
Pittsburgh, Pennsylvania 15236

Association for Education
of the Visually Handicapped
919 Walnut Street
Fourth Floor
Philadelphia, Pennsylvania
19107

Boy Scouts of America*
Scouting for the
  Handicapped Division
U.S. Route 1 & 130
North Brunswick, New Jersey
08902

Camp Fire Girls, Inc.*
1740 Broadway
New York, New York 10019

Council for Exceptional
Children
1920 Association Drive
Reston, Virginia 22091

Cystic Fibrosis Foundation
3379 Peachtree Road, N.E.
Atlanta, Georgia 30326

Dental Guidance Council for
Cerebral Palsy
122 E. 23rd Street
New York, New York 10010

Downs Syndrome Congress
20438 Renfrew Road
Detroit, Michigan 48221

---

* Organizations that have special programs for handicapped children and youth, and furnish information for leaders and parents.

Epilepsy Foundation of America
1828 L Street, N.W.
Washington, D.C. 20036

4-H Youth Extension Service°
U.S. Department of
  Agriculture
Washington, D.C. 20250

**Gesell Institute of
Child Development**
310 Prospect Street
New Haven, Connecticut 06511

Girl Scouts of the U.S.A.°
Scouting for Handicapped
  Girls Program
830 Third Avenue
New York, New York 10022

Human Growth Foundation
Maryland Academy of Science
  Building
601 Light Street
Baltimore, Maryland 21230

**International Association of
Parents of the Deaf**
814 Thayer Avenue
Silver Spring, Maryland 20910

John Tracy Clinic
(deafness/hearing
impairments, deaf-blind)
806 W. Adams Boulevard
Los Angeles, California 90007

Juvenile Diabetes Foundation
23 E. 26th Street
New York, New York 10010

Leukemia Society of America
211 E. 43rd Street
New York, New York 10017

Little People of America
P.O. Box 126
Owatonna, Minnesota 55060

**Mental Disability Legal
Resource Center**
Commission on the Mentally
  Disabled
American Bar Association
1800 M Street N.W.
Washington, D.C. 20036

**Muscular Dystrophy
Association, Inc.**
810 Seventh Avenue
New York, New York 10019

**National Association
of the Deaf**
814 Thayer Avenue
Silver Spring, Maryland 20910

**National Association for
Mental Health, Inc.**
1800 N. Kent Street
Arlington, Virginia 22209

**National Association of the
Physically Handicapped**
76 Elm Street
London, Ohio 43140

**National Association for
Retarded Citizens**
2709 Avenue E East
Arlington, Texas 76011

° Organizations that have special programs for handicapped children and youth, and furnish information for leaders and parents.

National Association for
Visually Handicapped
305 E. 24th Street, 17-C
New York, New York 10010

National Center for a Barrier-
Free Environment
8401 Connecticut Avenue
#402
Washington, D.C. 20015

National Center for Law and
the Deaf
Gallaudet College
Florida Avenue & Seventh
  Street, N.E.
Washington, D.C. 20002

National Center for Law and
the Handicapped
1235 N. Eddy Street
South Bend, Indiana 46617

National Easter Seal Society
for Crippled Children and
Adults
2023 W. Ogden Avenue
Chicago, Illinois 60612

National Epilepsy League
6 N. Michigan Avenue
Chicago, Illinois 60602

National Foundation of
Dentistry for the Handicapped
1121 Broadway, Suite 5
Boulder, Colorado 80302

National Hemophilia
Foundation
25 W. 39th Street
New York, New York 10018

National Society for
Autistic Children
306 31st Street
Huntington, West Virginia
            25702

North American Riding for the
Handicapped Association, Inc.
P.O. Box 100
Ashburn, Virginia 22011

Orton Society
(dyslexia)
8415 Bellona Lane
Towson, Maryland 21204

Scoliosis Research Society
Orange County Medical
  Center
101 S. Manchester
Orange, California 91768

Sex Information and
Education Council of the U.S.
(SIECUS)
137-155 N. Franklin Street
Hempstead, New York 11550

Spina Bifida Association of
America
209 Shiloh Drive
Madison, Wisconsin 53705

United Cerebral Palsy
Associations, Inc.
66 E. 34th Street
New York, New York 10016

Western Law Center for the
Handicapped
849 South Broadway, Suite 206
Los Angeles, California 90014

GOVERNMENT

Architectural and Transportation Barriers Compliance Board
Room 1004, Switzer Building
Washington, D.C. 20201

Bureau of Education for the Handicapped
Office of Education
Department of Health, Education, and Welfare
400 Maryland Avenue, S.W.
Washington, D.C. 20202

Clearinghouse on the Handicapped*
Office for Handicapped Individuals
Department of Health, Education, and Welfare
338-D South Portal Building
200 Independence Avenue, S.W.
Washington, D.C. 20201
PHONE: (202) 245-1961

Crippled Children's Services
Office of Maternal and Child Health
Bureau of Community Health Services
Health Services Administration
Department of Health, Education, and Welfare
5600 Fishers Lane
Room 7-15 Parklawn Building
Rockville, Maryland 20852

Developmental Disabilities Office
Office of Human Development
Department of Health, Education, and Welfare
Room 3070 Switzer Building
Washington, D.C. 20201

Library of Congress
Division for the Blind and Physically Handicapped
Taylor Street Annex
1291 Taylor Street
Washington, D.C. 20542

Office for Civil Rights
Director, David S. Tatel
330 Independence Avenue, S.W.
Washington, D.C. 20201

* This is the single best source for information about the handicapped.

OTHER

Closer Look, Inc.
(on educational and other programs and resources for handicapped children)
P.O. Box 1492
Washington, D.C. 20013
PHONE: (202) 833-4160

The Exceptional Parent
P.O. Box 4944
Manchester, New Hampshire 03108
A practical magazine for parents of children with disabilities.

C. Selected Bibliography

Arnheim, Rudolf. *Visual Thinking*. Berkeley, Cal.: University of California Press, 1969.

Barsch, Ray H. *A Perceptual-Motor Curriculum*. Vols. I, II. Seattle: Special Child Publications, 1967, 1969.

Bender, Lauretta. *Psychological Disorders in Children*. Springfield, Ill.: Charles C Thomas, 1957.

Birch, Herbert G. *Brain Damage in Children: Readings*. Baltimore: Williams & Wilkins, 1964.

Gesell, Arnold, Bullis, G. E., and Getman, G. N. *Vision: Its Development in Infant and Child*. New York: Hafner Press, 1949.

Getman, G.N., Kane, Elmer R., Halgren, Marvin R., and McKee, Gordon W. *Developing Learning Readiness*. St. Louis: Webster Division, McGraw-Hill, 1968.

Harmon, Darrell Boyd. *Notes on a Dynamic Theory of Vision*. Austin, Tex.: published by the author, 1958.

Kephart, N. C. *The Slow Learner in the Classroom*. Columbus, Ohio: Charles E. Merrill Co., 1960.

Kirk, Samuel A. *Behavioral Research on Exceptional Children: Readings*. Washington, D.C.: Council for Exceptional Children, NEA, 1963.

McGinnis, Mildred A. *Aphasic Children*. Washington, D.C.: Volta Bureau, 1963.

Strauss, Alfred A., and Lehtinen, Laura E. *Psychopathology and Education of the Brain-Injured Child*. Vol. I. New York: Grune & Stratton, 1947.

Index

Abstract concepts, 44
Abstraction, 35
Abstract thinking, 39, 44, 50
Academic progress, 219–21
Academic skills, 126
Activities: bedtime, 160; far space, 77; getting lost in, 93; individual, 164; kinesthetic, 152; limitations, 220; maze of, 152; mid space, 77; motor planning, 150; movement, 99; muscular, 20; muscular strength, 116–17; near space, 92; outdoor, 160; physical fitness, 117; postural alignment in, 117; problem-solving, 129; quiet, 160; rhythm in, 117; sequencing, 129–33; symbolic, 129; to develop bilaterality, 150; to develop rhythm, 150; verbalizing of, 160
Adaptability, 176
Allergic reactions, 56
Anorexia, 70
Anti-barbituate reactions, 70
Anticonvulsive medication, 56
Anxiety, 60, 61, 65
Anxious behavior, 61
Aphasia, 13, 36, 37, 67n; developmental, 13; expressive, 36, 37; receptive, 36–37
Aphasic children, 68n, 70; clinic for, 70; receptive language training, 68n
Audiologist, 67n
Audiology clinic, 70
Audiometers, 67n
Audition, 21, 21n, 22, 24, 28, 35, 36, 57, 72, 73, 74, 75, 79, 80, 90, 95–96, 133–37, 146, 151, 152; added to visual-kinesthetic task, 95–96; added to K activity, 152; analysis of, 79; evaluation of, 75; learning experiences, 151; organization of, 133; training in, 133–37
Auditory system, 28, 35–36

Balance, 40, 65. *See also* Dynamic balance
Balance board, 112, 118
Ball games, 108, 143, 160, 161, 191; bouncing, 108, 143; catching, 143; kicking, 143; pitching, 143; throwing, 108
Balloon game, 105, 107, 142
Barbiturates, 60n, 70, 70n; effect on hyperactivity, 60n
Barsch, Dr. Ray H., 1–3, 17n, 46n, 72, 86, 91n, 100, 151, 168, 193, 217, 218, 223; approach to evaluating children, 72; evaluation by, 86
Bathing, 121, 146, 164, 173, 174
Bathroom training, 173–74
Behavior: acceptable, 190; acceptance of, 201; anxious, 61; appropriate, 221; atypical, 201; disturbances, 15; good, 193, 194; group, 223; involuntary, 155; learning through imitation, 85; negative, 164, 194, 201; problems, 13, 214, 215; proper, 85; reinforcement of, 193; social, 156, 190, 192; warps in, 26; with people, 42

"Behavioral Syndromes of Central Nervous System Impairment," 15n
Bender-Gestalt Test, 84
Bilaterality, 51–52, 76, 150, 156, 183; activities to develop, 150; in movement, 52; underdeveloped, 76
Bilateral motor system, 40
Bilateral vision, 40
Binocularity, 224
Binocular vision, 40, 41, 137
Birch, Jack, 15
Blocks, 95, 104, 114, 116, 125, 126, 138, 191; building, 126, 191; building with, 116; copying designs with, 104, 126; heavy, 116; parquetry, 104, 126; sorting of, 95; stacking, 116, 125
Body awareness, 30, 31, 116, 121–23, 128; basis for, 128; training in, 121–23
Brain, 36, 51, 68n, 206; control by one side of, 51; dominant side of, 51; inability to organize auditory stimuli, 36; interpretation of visual symbols, 206; reciprocal relationship of both sides, 51; unusual displacement of, 68n
Brain-damaged child, 13. *See also* Brain-injured child
Brain-injured child, 13, 15, 18, 25, 85, 89, 224; schools for, 85
Brain injury, 15, 69n
"Brain wave" patterns, 68n

Calendars, 94, 126, 157, 158–59, 160–61, 162–63; use in structuring time, 94, 126
Catastrophic reaction, 54, 55, 56, 61, 201
Central Institute for the Deaf, 100n, 135

Central nervous system, 13, 227
Cerebral dysfunction, 13
Cerebral palsy, 13, 15, 37, 67, 67n, 208
Cerebral palsy school, 69
Chalkboard work, 101, 103, 105, 107, 108, 110, 112
Chewing, 27, 78, 90, 127; inefficiency in, 27
Chicken pox, 226
Children with learning disorders, 17, 18, 19, 26, 27, 44, 51, 60, 61, 62, 65, 68n, 70–71, 78, 82, 83, 84, 85, 93, 94, 114, 115, 145, 155, 164, 166, 182n, 183, 185, 214, 215, 216; behavior, 182n; comprehension of time, 94; degrees of freedom, 115; description of, 17–19; disease, 68n; distractibility, 18; expression, 18; hyperactivity, 18; IQ classification, 85; malformation in, 68n; organization in, 26; perceptual level, 44; perceptual training, 115; perseveration, 18; psychological testing, 83, 93; rate of development, 18; schools, 70–71, 216; spatial training, 114; testing of intelligence, 82; visual problems, 68n
Claustrophobia, 69n
Climbing, 148, 150
Colors, 22, 34, 112, 132; arrangement by, 34; putting in order, 132
Coloring, 91, 105, 107, 114, 138; book, 107; simple picture, 105
Comprehension: auditory, 84; in reading, 98, 120; in speech skills, 38; of gestures, 43; of signs, 43; of symbols, 38; of time, 94; testing of, 84
Concentration (game), 149

Control, 51, 60, 99, 182, 183; by one side of brain, 51; kinesthetic, 60; of stress factors, 99
Coordination, 20, 71, 137, 138–144, 205; eye-foot, 143–44; eye-hand, 137, 138–43; normal, 20; of different abilities, 205
Copying, 23, 33, 84, 103, 104, 105, 108, 110, 112, 126, 138, 139–40, 144
Counting, 109, 149, 152
Crawling, 22, 29, 33, 79, 110, 148
Cutting, 59–60, 101, 105, 112, 143, 160

Dancing, 17, 102, 150, 160, 161
Deaf, teachers of, 68n
Deafness, 36, 37, 68n
Deformities, 25
Designs, 83, 104, 105, 126, 144
Desk work, 91, 102, 104, 106, 109, 111, 113, 151
Destructiveness, 19
Development, 17–19, 20, 21–23, 24, 26, 33, 35, 53, 82, 115, 150, 201; bilaterality, 150; continuous, 19–20; degrees of freedom, 115; earliest, 20; equal opportunities, 82; ideal, 24; inadequate, 26; intellectual, 17–19; kinesthetic organization, 35; movement, 33; normal, 19–21; organization, 53; out-of-phase, 21–23, 26; retarded rate, 18; visual, 201
Developmental problems, 36, 182; causing poor speech, 36
Developmental retardation, 18
Diagnosis: of brain injury, 69n; of hearing loss, 67n; of hearing problems, 68n; of speech problems, 68n
Diagnosticians, 214

Discovering, Evaluating, Programming for the Neurologically Handicapped Child, 14n
Doll, Edgar A., 15
Doll house, 114, 150, 160
Doll play, 114, 151, 161
Drawing, 33, 79, 84, 91, 101, 103, 122, 126, 139
Dynamic balance, 30, 40, 117, 201; optimum, 40

Eating, 27, 127, 146, 164, 167–171; as basic training in gustation, 127; problems, 167–68; training in, 167–71
"Education of the Brain-Injured," 15n
Education, special. *See* Special education
EEG, 68, 68n, 69n, 70; abnormal, 69n; in diagnosis of brain injury, 69n. *See also* Electroencephalogram.
Eichorn, John R., 15n
Electroencephalogram, 55, 56, 88n
Emotional problems, 36, 214
Emotionally disturbed child, 213
Endocrine glands, 65
Environment, 24, 91–114; arrangement of, 99; interaction with, 24
Environmental deprivation, 25
Exceptional child, 13
Exceptional Child: A Book of Readings, 15n
Exercises, 101, 110, 113, 114, 117, 123, 129–32, 160, 161; bilateral movement, 130; eye, 114; Kraus Weber, 117; movement, 129; reciprocal movement, 130; tongue, 110, 113, 114, 127–28, 160, 161; visually targeted, 123

Expression, 18, 79, 84, 132, 135–137; analysis of, 79; basis for, 132; dictation as aid to, 137; "rehearsal" in, 135–36; testing of, 84; training in, 135–37

Expressive aphasia, 36, 37

Expressive language, 71, 79, 80, 98, 135; evaluation of, 80; level, 98; Mirrors learning organization, 79; problem, 135

Eye-hand coordination, 137, 138–43

Eyes, 51, 52, 68n, 78, 79, 80, 90; diseases of, 68n

Eye-teaming, 137

Family, acceptance by, 157, 166

Far space, 23, 24, 47, 64, 76, 77, 99, 165; activities, 77; organization, 76; tasks, 99

"Far-space child," 77

Fine hand movement, 35

Finger games, 33, 112, 113, 114, 160, 161

Flash cards, 107, 144

Flexibility, 21, 33, 51, 52, 57–59, 99, 156; failure in, 57; in schedule, 99; muscular, 33; spatial, 156; visual, 52

Frostig Test of Visual Perception, 84

Games, 128, 145, 149, 152, 160, 161; learning, 149; manipulative, 152; tactual, 128; visual memory, 145

Gesell, Arnold, 14n

Getman, Dr. Gerald, 32n, 100, 123, 137, 145

Gravitational orientation, 25

Group behavior, 223

Gustation, 27, 50, 78, 127–28; analysis of, 78; discrimination in, 127; training in, 22, 127–28

Gustatory senses, 24

Handicapped children, 25, 90n, 213; organizations for, 90n, 237; society's attitude toward, 213

Hands, 20, 35, 108, 112; fine movement with, 35; making pattern with both at same time, 108, 112; use of, 20

Hannah see Hart, Hannah Jill

Harmon, Darrell Boyd, 26n

Harris, Norma, 10

Hart, Hannah Jill: academic progress, 219–21; arithmetic level, 98; audition, 72; behavior with people, 42; calendar, 158–59, 160–61; cerebral palsy school, 69; clinic for aphasic children, 70; drive to learn, 86; EEG, 68n–69n, 70; eating problems, 167–68; evaluation, 72–74; evaluation by Dr. Barsch, 86; expressive problem, 73; expressive language level, 98; grasp of concepts, 98; IQ test, 70; I.T.P.A., 84; language, 39–40; learning organization, 74, 77; lessons, 99–100; lesson schedules, 101–107, 108–13; movement skills, 73, 74; need for independence, 221; numbers, 151; nursery school, 69n; organization of space for, 91–92; reading comprehension, 98; reading level, 220; school experiences, 87–88; school for children with learning disorders, 70–71; social progress, 221–24; speech therapy, 69; table book, 170; tests, 81, 84–87; vision, 72–73; visual skills, 73, 74; WISC, 84

Hart, Jane, 1, 9–11

Hart, Ken, 1

Hearing loss, 67n. *See also* Audition
Hopping, 17, 79, 104, 110, 113, 117, 120, 132
Hyperactive child, 29, 92, 229; directing movements of, 92
Hyperactivity, 18, 28, 29, 60n; basis of, 28; effect of amphetamines on, 60n; effect of barbiturates on, 60n

Illinois Test for Psycholinguistic Abilities (I.T.P.A.), 83–84
Imitation, 20, 78, 79, 85; in learning correct speech, 85; learning proper behavior through, 85; of sound, 20, 79; of tongue movements, 78
Independence, 161, 181, 210, 221; developing, 166; need for, 221
Independent survival, 21, 24, 25, 49–50
Infinite space, 24
Insomnia, 70
Intellectual development, 17, 18–19
Intelligence, 82, 83
Intelligence quotient. *See* IQ.
Intestines, 202
IQ, 67, 70, 82, 84, 85, 86, 87; classification, 85; test, 70

Jigsaw puzzle, 95, 97, 103, 108, 126, 138; do while lying on stomach, 108
Jones, Beverly, 5–7, 219–24
Jumping, 117, 118, 152
Jump rope, 114, 118, 160, 161

Kephart, Dr. Newell C., 100, 141n
Kinesthesia, 21, 22, 24, 28, 29–35, 38, 43, 50, 73, 74, 75, 79, 80, 90, 92, 96, 97, 129–33, 134, 151, 156, 165, 205; analysis of, 79; learning experiences, 151; training in, 129–33
Kinesthetic control, 60
Kinesthetic development, 201
Kinesthetic problems, 93
Kraus Weber exercises, 105, 108, 113, 117

Language, 20, 36, 37, 38, 39, 40, 43, 60, 64, 71, 79, 80, 83, 85, 95, 99, 133, 135, 148, 152, 156; added to kinesthetic activity, 152; adjusting to child's comprehension, 95; complexity, 60, 64; development of, 38–39; evaluation, 80; expressive, 71, 79, 80, 135; intricacies of, 85; learning about, 148; problems, 38, 68n, 206; receptive, 71, 80; significance, 39; structuring of, 95; structuring through, 95, 133; understanding of, 37, 79; use to represent past experiences, 83
Language comprehension test, 83
Learning disabilities, 14, 26, 44, 61, 68n, 82, 83, 85, 93, 114, 115, 215. *See also* Learning disorders.
Learning disorders, 13, 14, 17, 18, 19, 25–65, 68n, 70–71, 78, 84, 85, 93, 94, 164, 166, 182n, 183, 185, 214, 215, 216. *See also* Learning disabilities.
Learning equipment, 82
Learning games, 149
Lessons, 93, 99–100, 101–107, 108–13, 160; length of, 93, 99; schedule, 101–107, 108–13
Lip movements, 78
Localization, 20, 28, 37, 79, 121, 133–34; of odors, 28; of pressures, 28; of sound, 20, 37, 133–34; of touch, 79

Magary, James F., 15n
Malformation, 36, 68n
Manipulation, 35, 95
Manipulative games, 152
Marching, 102, 150
Massage, 114, 121–22, 160, 161
Matching, 134, 144, 147, 149
Mathematics, 35, 120
Maturational sequence, 50
Maze, 107, 125, 143, 152; of varying activities, 152; simple, 107, 125; walking, 143
Memory cards, 106
Memory test, 83
Memory, visual, 97, 110, 112, 137, 145; games, 145; task, 97
Mentally retarded children, 14, 82, 88, 89, 213
Mid space, 23, 24, 46–47, 64, 76, 77, 99; activities, 77; organization, 76; tasks, 99
Mood swings, 53, 54
Motor pattern organization, 36, 37
Motor planning, 51, 59–60, 150, 156; activities to develop, 150
Movement: abnormal, 68n; adapting to situation, 33; arm, 131; automatic, 59; backward, 23; bilateral, 52, 130, 142; choosing proper, 59; constant, 60; diagonal, 142; directing, 92; directional, 120; downward, 23; efficient, 51, 59; exercises, 129, 130; fine, 33, 35; forward, 23; foundation for, 201; freedom of, 49, 224; full, 29; gross, 33; hands, 35, 141, 142; horizontal, 142; inefficient, 59; in task performance, 78; leading with eye, 80; low level, 33; meaningful, 92; opposing, 141; organization, 29, 76, 117; parallel, 142; play, 119; reciprocal, 130; "remembering," 121; rhythmic pattern, 118, 122; simple, 131; spatial, 120; structuring of, 92; symbols for, 43; teaching through task, 96; testing, 68n; tongue, 27, 78; upward, 23; vertical, 117, 142; wasteful, 59; within allotted area, 120
Movigenic theory, 15, 86
Movigenic training, 87
Multiplicity, 60, 62–63, 64, 96–97, 99, 156, 164; breaking down of, 96–97; handling of, 63; of words, 64
Muscular strength, 29, 116, 117, 123, 147, 201

Near space, 23, 24, 46, 49, 57, 64, 73, 75, 76, 77, 91, 92, 99, 156, 165, 214; activities, 92; evaluation of, 75; maintenance of, 57; organization, 75, 76–77, 91; perceptions operating in, 77; structuring, 76–77, 214; tasks, 73, 99; too much reliance on, 77
Neurological impairment, 14
Neurological testing of young children, 68n
Neurologically impaired child, 13, 18, 89
Neurologist, 14, 67, 68, 68n, 214
Neuromuscular impairment, 15
Neuromuscular disease, 67n
Neurophrenia, 13, 15
Nose, 20, 28, 78, 127; blowing, 78, 127; examination of objects by, 28; sensations in, 20
Notes on a Dynamic Theory of Vision, 26n
Numbers, 35, 79, 110, 149, 151; manipulation of, 35; matching, 149; remembering series, 79; tracing, 110

Olfaction, 20, 27–28, 50, 78, 146; analysis of, 78; senses, 24
Ophthalmologist, 68n
Optometric Extension Program, 32n, 68n
Optometrist, 68n, 80
Organizations for handicapped children, 90n, 237
Orientation, 23, 25, 46–49, 117, 118; back-to-front, 118; gravitational, 25; objects in space, 23; side-to-side, 118; spatial, 25, 46–49; time, 25; vertical, 117
Orthopedist, 67n
Otolaryngologist, 67n
Outdoor play, 116, 160

Pain, 30, 79, 80, 184; insensitivity to, 30, 80; knowledge of, 184; recognition of source, 79
Painting, 142, 191
Parents, 145–61, 197; as teachers, 145–61
Passamanick, 14
Patterns: completing, 105, 106; copying, 23; drawing, 101; making with both hands, 108, 112; movement, 75, 118, 120; pegboard, 104; pencil-and-paper, 120; recognizable, 35; rhythmic, 118, 152; sleep, 156
Peabody Picture Vocabulary Test, 84
Pediatricians, 14, 214
Pegs and pegboard, 22, 104, 107, 126, 138
Perception, 35, 77, 144; forms, 144; near space, 77; training, 144; visual, 35, 144; written words, 35
Perceptual abilities, 65, 75–76, 77, 153, 165; deficiency in, 77; involved in task, 75–76

Perceptual processing modalities, 126–45
Perceptual training, 115, 126–45, 153
Perceptually handicapped child, 13, 18, 89
Performance: analysis of, 80; inability to sustain, 18; movement in, 78; successful, 99; task, 77, 78, 79; tests, 83; time factor in, 93
Phonics, 134
Physical fitness activities, 117
Physically handicapped child, 213
Physiology, 202, 204
Physiology of Readiness, 123, 137
Pictures: acting out, 90; coloring, 105; copying, 103, 108, 139–40; getting meaning through eyes, 90; matching, 149; naming things in, 90; putting in order, 102; recognition of similarities and differences in, 79; tracing, 102
Playing outdoors, 116, 160
Play movements, 119
Pneumoencephalogram, 68n
Postural alignment, 117, 123
Postural transport abilities, 116, 148
"Practice in General Coordination," 123
Problem-solving, 43–44, 83, 120, 129, 147, 152; abilities, 83; activities, 129; adding to kinesthetic activity, 152
"Proposal for Classification of the Terminology Used to Describe Brain Injured Children," 15n
Psychiatrists, 214
Psychologists, 14, 82, 214
Psychological testing, 81–87, 93
Psychoneurological learning disorder, 13

Puberty, 223
Puppets, 151, 161

Quiet activity, 160

Races, 103, 107, 114, 119–20, 151, 160, 161
Reading, 22, 33, 34, 35, 98, 120, 126, 132, 147, 160, 220; basis for, 132; beginnings in, 147; comprehension, 98, 120; level, 98, 220; proficiency, 34; visual confusion in, 35
Recognition: of directionality, 84; of forms, 18; of shapes, 84; of sound, 76; of source of pain, 79; of textural differences, 28; of visual differences, 79; of visual similarities, 79
Response: appropriate, 79; choosing, 57; delay in, 61; effect of time stress on, 61; meaningful, 37; motor pattern organization, 37; reinforcement of, 96; speed of, 57; time for, 93; to odors, 27; to sound, 67n; to speech symbols, 37; verbal, 61, 206
Retardation: developmental, 18; intellectual, 17–18; overall, 15; social development, 17, 18–19
Rhythm, 35, 51, 52–57, 93, 102, 117, 120, 132, 150, 152, 156; activities to develop, 150; clapping to, 132; exceptionally slow, 93; hopping, 120; in activities, 117; internal, 53; jumping, 152; marching to, 102; pattern, 152; pounding nails to, 150; swaying to, 132
Roly Poly, 101, 102, 103, 104, 106, 110, 113, 123
Rules, 166, 167, 221; learning, 166; obeying, 166; social, 221

St. Louis, 135
Schools, 69, 69n, 70–71, 85, 87–88, 90, 158, 159, 216; cerebral palsy, 69; for brain-injured children, 85; for children with learning disorders, 70–71, 216; for severely emotionally disturbed children, 216; for trainable retarded children, 216; nursery, 69n; residential, 90
Self-concept, 197–209, 210
Self-control, 183, 184, 185
Self-help, 97, 167
Self-understanding, 201, 204
Self-worth, 192
Sequencing, 78, 129–33, 144, 159; abilities, 78; activities, 129–33
Sequential thinking, 123–33
Shapes, 20, 22, 34, 35, 84, 132, 144–45; arrangement by, 34; copying, 84; experiencing, 144; mastery of, 35; matching by, 144; parts of, 144; putting in order, 132; recognition of, 84; tracing, 144–45
Signal Corps, 96
Size relationships, 34, 124, 132, 144; arrangement by, 34; experiencing, 144; putting in order, 132
Sleep patterns, 156
Slow Learner in the Classroom, 141n
Social behavior, 156, 174–76, 190, 192
Social development, 17, 18–19
Social stress, 65
Society for Crippled Children, 89
Sorting, 95, 128, 147, 149; blocks, 95; experience, 149; through touch, 128
Sound: association with idea, 37; association with printed sym-

bols, 35; domination by, 21; hearing differences in, 79; hearing likenesses in, 79; identification of, 20, 37, 79, 134; imitation of, 20, 79; interpretation of, 37; lack of, 22; learning about, 150; localization of, 20, 37, 79, 133–34; matching, 134; recognition of, 76; remembering series of, 79; response to, 67n

Space: activities, 77, 92; auditory, 96; delimination of, 91; direct experience in, 38; evaluation of, 75; far, 23, 24, 47, 64, 76, 77, 99; general, 168; immediate, 168; infinite, 24; limitations, 220; mastery of, 35; mid, 23, 24, 46–47, 64, 76, 77, 99; near, 23, 24, 46, 49, 57, 64, 73, 75, 76–77, 92, 99, 156, 165, 214; organization of, 75, 76–77, 91–92, 96; orientation, 25; past, 24; remote, 23; stimuli in, 126, 127; structuring, 76–77, 91–92, 161, 168, 214; tasks, 73, 96, 99; teaching through task, 96; visualization of, 120

Spatial awareness, 31, 123–45, 201; training in, 123–45

Spatially disorganized child, 49

Spatially naive child, 9

Spatial organization, 23–24, 25, 47, 48–49, 84, 156; testing, 84

Special education, 89, 213, 214

Special educators, 14

Speech, 20, 27, 36, 37–38, 51, 80; adequate, 27; articulation, 20; efficiency of, 51; evaluation of, 80; motor patterns which produce, 36; unintelligible, 27

Speech pathologist, 68n, 80

Speech problems, 37, 38, 68; causes of, 37; diagnosis of, 68n; treatment of, 68n

Speech therapy, 68n, 79

Stanford-Binet scale, 87n

Stanford-Binet Test, 83

Stevens, Godfrey, 15

Stimuli: auditory, 36; conflicting, 47; in space, 126, 127; integration of, 63; organization of, 63; perceptual, 47

Strauss, Dr. Alfred A., 15

Strauss syndrome, 15

Strength, muscular *see* Muscular strength

Stress, 25–26, 27, 60, 61, 65, 77, 92, 164, 166, 188; adding, 188; avoiding, 166; effect on organization, 61; effect on response, 61; overcoming efficiently, 65; perceptual, 65; spatial area preference under, 77; social, 65; time, 61; tolerance of, 164; too much, 92

Stress factors, 17n, 60–65, 91, 98, 99, 192; control of, 99; in tasks, 61; reduction of, 91; time, 61–62, 98

Strother, Charles R., 14n

Structuring: auditory, 95, 117; family dinner table, 168; language, 95; movement, 92; space, 76–77, 91–92, 161, 168; task, 95, 96–97; through language, 133; time, 92–95, 126

Sulfonamides, 231

Swallowing, 27, 78

Symbols: association with sound, 35; auditory, 133; comprehension difficulty, 38; groups of, 39; interpretation by brain, 206; movement, 43; printed, 35; recognition of, 43; use of, 43; verbal, 36, 206

Syphilis, 226

Tactual games, 144
Tactuality, 21, 22, 28–29, 50, 73, 78, 80, 128, 175, 184; analysis of, 78; basis for good body awareness, 128; organization, 28; primary learning method, 80; training in, 128; visualization, 184
Tactual words, 75, 128
Targets: kicking beanbags to, 143; moving, 142; throwing at, 95, 142; variation in, 142; visual, 118, 120, 151
Tasks: academic, 220; accomplishment of, 120; achievable, 81; adding audition to, 95–96; AK, 75; analysis of, 75–76, 77–78, 83; auditory clues for, 95; auditory-visual, 84; balancing, 99; becoming familiar with, 95; beginning of, 77; bilateral, 97, 147; body parts in, 75–76; breaking down into parts, 96; completion of, 73, 78; copying, 84; degree of difficulty, 99; degrees of freedom in, 61; demands of, 61; experience needed in, 76; far space, 99; goal of, 95; gustatory, 27; household, 97; kinesthetic-visual, 76; learning, 26; lining up for, 30; mid-space, 99; movement in, 78; near space, 73, 99; parts in, 75; perceptual abilities involved, 75–76; perceptually balanced, 99; spatial areas involved, 78; spatial help in, 98; spatially balanced, 99; spatial relation to, 46; self-help, 97; sequence of abilities in, 78; stress factors in, 61; structuring, 95, 96–97; time factor in, 93; two-handed, 79; verbal help in, 98; vision in, 78; visual-kinesthetic, 83, 95–96; visual-kinesthetic-tactual, 95; visual memory, 97
Ten Little Indians, 111
Testing, 67–90; abnormal movement, 68n; association, 84; auditory, 84; comprehension, 84; expression, 84; hearing ability, 67; intelligence, 82; neurological, 68n; picture interpretation, 84; psychological, 81–87, 93; principles of, 82–83; receptive vocabulary skills, 84; reflexes, 68n; sensation, 68n; spatial organization, 84; timed, 93; visual abilities, 84
Tests, 82, 83, 84–87, 93; arithmetic, 83; block designs, 83; following directions on, 83; intelligence, 82, 83; memory, 83; psychological, 83, 93; understanding directions on, 83; verbal, 83; vocabulary, 83
Thinking, 39, 43, 44, 132–33; abstract, 39, 44; conceptual, 44; concrete, 44; sequential, 132–33; training in, 132–33
Time, 19, 21, 25, 34, 49, 61–62, 92–95, 98, 99, 126, 156, 165; comprehension of, 94; frame of reference for understanding, 49; factor in performance, 93; in task, 93; orientation, 25; stress factor, 61–62, 98; structuring, 92–95, 126
Tracing, 91, 101, 102, 103, 108, 109, 110, 111, 112, 113, 125, 126, 138, 144–45; circle, 103; in play books, 109; letters, 111; numbers, 110; on paper fastened to wall, 126; picture, 102; shapes, 144–45; simple forms, 125; to complete squares, 101; word, 103, 108, 111, 112, 113

United Cerebral Palsy, 89
United Community Fund, 89

Vision, 20–21, 21n, 22, 24, 40–43, 51, 68n, 71, 72–73, 78, 79, 80, 90, 96, 137–45, 146, 147, 151, 205; analysis of, 79; bilateral, 40; binocular, 40, 41, 137; childhood, 80; convergence in, 51; developmental, 68n; imperfect, 51; in task performance, 78; learning experiences, 151; learning through, 22; training in, 137–145

Visualization, 43, 49, 50, 65, 120, 132, 184; of future, 49; of past, 49; of space, 120; of tactuality, 184

Visual memory, 110, 112, 145

Visual skills, 25, 73, 74, 223

Walking, 21, 29, 32–33, 106, 118, 132, 143, 150, 161; backwards, 33; on path of colored cardboard squares, 106; patterns, 132; through maze, 143; to metronome, 150; visually directed, 118

Wechsler Intelligence Scale for Children 83, 84

Weekly Reader, 101

Wolff, Dr. Bruce, 217, 218, 223

Words, 18, 22, 28, 35, 37–38, 39, 64, 75, 79, 111, 112, 128, 134, 135; ability to rhyme, 79; abstract, 135; accurate imitation of, 79; articulation of, 37–38; comprehension of, 43; essential, 39; hearing differences in, 79; hearing likenesses in, 79; multiplicity of, 64; perception of, 35; pronunciation of, 38; remembering series of, 79; repetition of, 18; sequencing of, 134; tactual, 75, 128; talking in, 79; taste, 28; tracing, 111, 112; unfamiliar, 64; using, 134–35; visual, 75

Wrestling, 109, 112, 117, 160, 161

Writing, 22, 29, 33, 79, 110, 126, 138

A selection of books published by Penguin is listed on the following pages.

For a complete list of books available from Penguin in the United States, write to Dept. DG, Penguin Books, 299 Murray Hill Parkway, East Rutherford, New Jersey 07073.

For a complete list of books available from Penguin in Canada, write to Penguin Books Canada Limited, 2801 John Street, Markham, Ontario L3R 1B4.

If you live in the British Isles, write to Dept. EP, Penguin Books Ltd, Harmondsworth, Middlesex.

YOUR CHILD IS A PERSON
A Psychological Approach to Parenthood without Guilt

Stella Chess, M.D., Alexander Thomas, M.D., Herbert G. Birch, M.D., Ph.D.

Mothers, nurses, and pediatricians are well aware that infants begin to express themselves as individuals from the time of birth. In recent years, however, many psychiatrists and psychologists appear to have lost sight of this fact. Instead, they have tended to emphasize the influence of the child's early environment and of his parents (particularly the mother) when discussing the origin of the human personality. To counteract this prevalent one-sided view, the authors of this book present an alternative approach to child care based on the findings of a long-term research project, from which they postulate that the developing personality is shaped by the constant interplay of temperament *and* environment. They have not tried to write a manual of child care, but rather have tried to share with parents some principles of interrelationship important to psychological developments that derive from current knowledge about children and parents.

PUT YOUR MOTHER ON THE CEILING
Children's Imagination Games

Richard de Mille

The theory of imagination is growing rapidly today. Fantasy has been vindicated from charges that it is useless or neurotic and has been recognized as an indispensable resource for normal living. "Richard de Mille's innovative contribution provides children with exercises designed to prolong and preserve their penchant for taking liberties with reality, or to help them recapture this facility if they have lost it in the process of growing up and becoming social persons"—J. P. Guilford, Department of Psychology, University of Southern California.

THE GREAT SCHOOL LEGEND
A Revisionist Interpretation of American Public Education

Colin Greer

In this important challenge to the standard histories of American education, Colin Greer provides a useful historical framework of past and current thought on, and interpretation of, the "true" role of public education in America. He destroys the long-standing myth that public education will successfully integrate all immigrants, poor people, and minority groups into American society and will enable them to achieve the Great American Dream. Our schools, Greer writes, were designed instead to fail, not integrate, these groups of people, and furthermore, "the great school legend" is largely responsible for today's schools' resistance to badly needed change. Greer does not have *the* solutions to the problems, merely suggestions; however, his book appears at a most opportune time, when public education has come under intense study and criticism and when various alternatives to public schooling are being discussed, experimented with, and rejected more and more by those who believe that public schooling can and should be made to work.

CHILDREN ARE THE REVOLUTION
Day Care in Cuba

Marvin Leiner

Today's Cuba founds its hopes on its children. More than fifty thousand young Cubans, from forty-five days to six years old, attend day-care centers that in prerevolutionary times did not even exist. Marvin Leiner, an American educator who lived in Cuba and sent his children to Cuban schools, gives us a firsthand report on the new system, which offers a vast program of play and learning plus medical care and nutritious meals—all with the purpose of creating the new Cuban citizen, "an amalgam of consciousness, conscience, conscientiousness, and commitment."

THE FIRST SEX
Elizabeth Gould Davis

Are women superior to men? This unique book aims to give woman her rightful place in history while repudiating what the author calls "2000 years of propaganda." Drawing on science, mythology, archaeology, and history, Elizabeth Gould Davis comes up with some eye-opening facts: Ancient civilizations such as the Sumerian were matriarchal societies where women ruled and men were servants. . . . The collapse of these matriarchal societies signaled the brutalization of humanity and the increasing suppression of women. . . . Women were the first in the discovery of arts and sciences, first in the march toward civilization, and still first, according to biologists, in physical efficiency. That women are "the first sex" is, in fact, this book's inescapable conclusion.

THE COUPLE
Edited by Marie Corbin

What is it like to be husband or wife in a society very different from one's own? *The Couple* is written by social scientists with widely differing backgrounds and interests. In it the authors explore what it means to be "a couple," married or not, heterosexual or not. Focusing on Britain, the United States, Sweden, Italy, and Japan, they point up the different approaches and rituals that characterize these societies' varying attitudes to marriage, to the sexual and social behavior of a couple, and to separation and divorce.

WOMAN'S BODY, WOMAN'S RIGHT
Birth Control in America

Linda Gordon

Here is a definitive history of the American woman's long struggle for the right to prevent or terminate pregnancy. Tracing the story through Theodore Roosevelt's attack on "race suicide," Margaret Sanger's pioneering crusade, the opposition of religious groups and male supremacists, and the flowering of today's women's movement, Linda Gordon shows that birth control has always been a matter of social and political acceptability rather than of medicine and technology.

SEVEN WOMEN
Portraits from the American Radical Tradition

Judith Nies

These seven extraordinary women—Sarah Moore Grimke, former slaveholder; Harriet Tubman, escaped slave; Elizabeth Cady Stanton, women's rights advocate; Mother Jones, "the Joan of Arc of the coal fields"; Charlotte Perkins Gilman, reformer; Anna Louise Strong, journalist who covered the revolutions in China and Russia; and Dorothy Day, cofounder of the *Catholic Worker*—stand out in a long tradition of American radicals who saw the madness of oppressive institutions. Sustained by a rare courage, a minority within a minority, they brought about far-reaching changes.

CORDUROY

Don Freeman

"A winning, completely childlike picture book in which a stuffed bear waiting hopefully in a toy department finds a home with a little black girl who wants Corduroy so much that, when her mother refuses to buy him, she comes back the next day with her own money"—*Booklist*.

MAKE WAY FOR DUCKLINGS

Robert McCloskey

Mr. and Mrs. Mallard grew tired of looking for the perfect spot to raise their family. Stopping off for a rest in the city, they were delighted to find it had everything they wanted. Although there were no dangerous foxes or turtles, there were still surprises in store for the Mallards and their newly hatched ducklings. This endearing childhood classic is a winner of the Caldecott Award.

MEG AND MOG

Helen Nicoll and Jan Pieńkowski

Meg, the witch, and Mog, her cat, go off to a wild Halloween party with all the other witches. They cast a spell that goes off with a *bang!*

SOME SWELL PUP
Or Are You Sure You Want a Dog?

Story by Maurice Sendak and Matthew Margolis
Pictures by Maurice Sendak

Caldecott Award–winner Maurice Sendak turns to a comic-strip format for this rambunctious encounter with an untrained puppy. After their puppy's dismissal from the West Pointer Academy, a boy and girl learn the hard way that a pup is best trained with patience, love, and kindness.

CARRIE'S WAR
Nina Bawden

Bombs were falling on London. Carrie and Nick were wartime evacuees billeted in Wales with old Mr. Evans, who was a bit of an ogre, and his timid mouse of a sister. Their friend Albert was luckier, living in Druid's Bottom with Hepzibah Green and the strange Mister Johnny, and Carrie and Nick were happy to visit him there, until Carrie did a terrible thing, the worst thing she ever did in her life. . . .

TARKA THE OTTER
Henry Williamson

This classic tale of an otter's life and death has now been made into a major animated film, with screenplay by Gerald Durrell and David Cobham and narrated by Peter Ustinov. It is a story as true as long observation and keen insight could make it. It lets you live with Tarka and see at his level (which is much closer to the ground than our eye level). It will be strange if, after reading it, you do not look with new understanding at quiet country places where birds and beasts live such dangerous lives.

KING ARTHUR AND HIS KNIGHTS OF THE ROUND TABLE
Roger Lancelyn Green

"*Whoso pulleth out this sword from this stone and anvil is the true-born king of all Britain.*" Arthur had drawn the sword from the stone, proving himself king. Now the darkness that had enfolded Britain fades, and the wizard Merlin presides over the wondrous cycle of Arthurian legend: the gift of Excalibur from the Lady of the Lake . . . the formation of the Round Table . . . the magic of Morgana le Fay . . . the love of Launcelot and Guinevere . . . the quest for the Holy Grail . . . and, at last, the journey to the mist-hidden isle of Avalon, where Arthur still sleeps in a secret cave, awaiting the day of his return.

THE EVERY OTHER DAY EXERCISE BOOK
The Easy-Does-It Program for Better Bodies
Fern Lebo

There *is* an easy way to a better body, even if your busy schedule doesn't permit daily exercise. You don't have to join expensive clubs, patronize fashionable "body boutiques," or purchase costly equipment in order to slim down or shape up —and you certainly don't have to pull any muscles, slip any discs, or sprain any ankles. Appalled by the number of injuries resulting from television exercise shows and from ill-advised treatments at slimming salons and "health havens," Fern Lebo helps you choose from 120 *sensible* exercises for every part of the body: stomach, back, breast/chest, arms, thighs, buttocks, back of legs, and waist. There are also breathing and warming-up exercises, a sixteen-minute maintenance workout, pre- and post-natal exercises, and a step-by-step program for the first three months after a heart attack. Much more than just another exercise manual, *The Every Other Day Exercise Book* is for men and women who want to look and feel their healthy best— and stay that way.

GYMNASTICS FOR GIRLS
Dr. Frank Ryan

Women's gymnastics has come into its own as one of the great sports of our time. It is also a breathtakingly beautiful and exciting sport, in which each competitor must demonstrate her skills in four unique and demanding categories: floor exercise, balance beam, uneven parallel bars, and the vault. In these pages Dr. Frank Ryan tells you all you need to know about the fundamentals of gymnastics, individual tumbling and dance skills, control and precision, the split-second timing of work on the uneven parallel bars, the techniques of aggressive performance on the vault, and much more. The author also offers invaluable advice on the development of combinations that will enable the gymnast to devise her own routines. Illustrated with dozens of step-by-step photographs, this is the most comprehensive guide available for today's young student —and tomorrow's champion.